PRAISE FOR LET THE HEALING BEGIN

Kindra's book is amazing.
I literally couldn't put it down.
It's so raw, real, and honest.
I guarantee that you won't be disappointed.
But I do have a warning.
You're going to get emotional.
You're going to get angry.
But you're also going to learn about a subject that many of us know nothing about.

Frank Somerville
Five-time Emmy award-winning anchor at KTVU in the Bay Area

I was captivated from the start! I literally could not put it down. I read "Let the Healing Begin" in a weekend. I was drawn into the character's lives by the vivid words and details that the author used. I felt the pain, the heartbreak, and the joy of Charli, Kindra, and all the other people in the book. "Let the Healing Begin" is a reminder to be kind and loving to people because you truly never know what others are going through.

Beth Caseu

For her first publication, Ms.Lidge presents a vibrant literary tapestry -- shot through with love, pain, joy, sorrow, and ultimately, healing. She deftly weaves the heaviness of tragedy and survivorship with the lightness brought by found family. As Ms.Lidge ties Kindra and young Charli closer, we realize that the threads connecting humanity may yet begin to stitch closed even the oldest of wounds.

A fantastic, well-paced story that will draw in even the most reluctant of readers. While a content-warning may be appropriate for grade-school readers, everyone else should approach with an open heart, willing spirit, and someone to hold.

Saige L. Pilgrim

Accessible yet profound, luminous yet human, Lidge's two narratives and protagonists work together seamlessly to craft a gut-wrenching true story about how love perseveres through the unthinkable. Without discussing divinity, this book is ablaze with the divine. Without knowing it, the world has been waiting for this story.

Brailey Vine

It's been a long time since I finished a book in one sitting as Kindra's story unfolds and she begins her friendship with Charli her pain ends and so does Charli's. Kindra reveals her pain, anger, fear and nightmares while Charli was afraid to speak of hers and somehow together they found solace. Kindra is courageous and compassionate, as she reveals her story and reaching out for help she finds herself being a comforter.

Donna F. Cole

LET THE HEALING BEGIN

WHEN THE LAW FAILS AND LOVE PREVAILS

Inspired by true events

Printed in the United States.

E-Book (Kindle) 979-8-9900759-0-0

Paperback (P.O.D.) 979-8-9900759-5-5

Table of Contents

"Marvelous, just Marvelous."

—Papa Bear

Dear Reader,

Before you go any further, I want you to know this book contains sexual assault, sexual assault of a child, self-harm, suicidal ideation, and attempts. If any of this may trigger you into a bad place, I encourage you to put this book down and perhaps return when you are up for it.

You have nothing to prove, and you don't have to attend every fight you are invited to. If a television show, movie, book, or anything has the potential to trigger you into a bad place, it's OK to walk away from it until you are ready (if you are ever ready). It doesn't make you weak, or a victim, or any of that. It confirms you are your own advocate and practice self-care. I commend you for that.

Sincerely,
A Fellow Survivor

Foreword

It's very difficult for me to tell you about Kindra. It's not because there isn't a lot to say; rather, it's like trying to describe to someone the intense awe discovered in watching a sunset or the intricacies found in a remarkable painting. Some things you just have to experience for yourself before they make sense, which is why it's so ironic that it is through this particular narrative that she is first introduced to the literary world. "Let the Healing Begin" offers its readers a glimpse behind curtains that even those of us who have known its author for years didn't know about. In fact, I'd say that this book allows the world to peer behind a veil that is unfortunately understood to be one of the most common experiences of women worldwide yet remains one of the least explored and understood spaces amongst those of us who claim to love and support them, yet I digress.

As long as I've known Kindra, she's been this bastion of wit, empathy, and charisma. That, for better or worse, made her stick out like a sore thumb everywhere that she went. It's as if God fused Lilo and Jean Grey to create this remarkable amalgamation of child-like enthusiasm and humor that also serves as a guardian to some cosmic well of kindness, mercy, and strength. She carries a flame that people are often inexplicably drawn toward. I've watched otherwise very callous people soften themselves around her. I've seen her capture people in photos and as if for the first time in their lives, see people see themselves as special. These, amongst so many others, are reasons that although I understand, not every moment in life is good, it pains me in ways that I cannot express to know that one of the women represented in the upcoming pages is my friend. However, I'd be amiss to not immediately recognize that though she is one of the countless souls unfortunate enough to have the burden and trauma of sexual assault cast upon their shoulders, hers is a spirit so immensely saturated in God's essence that she was able to wrestle through this darkness and encase this horror into an artifact that will act as a beacon of light for years to come. She was able to transform her life into one rooted in power and turn her tragedy into a vivid declaration of fortitude that screams with all the authority of heaven itself, "I am still here…we are still here…"

"Let the Healing Begin" is a book that hurts, though somehow, in an immensely good way. It's an opportunity for women who may be coping with, or helping others cope with, similar circumstances to connect, to see themselves reflected and to be represented, but it's also a window through which men can see what happens when we shun our responsibilities as protectors, as guardians, and as leaders in our communities. We must hold ourselves and each other accountable for being in control of our thoughts, actions, and the tendencies that can arise when we are at our worst. No matter who or where you are, this story isn't far from you. This only question is whether we can summon the courage to see and the heart to change.

—Brandon "Stitch" Sims

Acknowledgments

First, I want to acknowledge myself. I really don't do that often enough. You go, girl! I'm so proud of you!

This book was truly a labor of love. The late nights and early mornings of writing. The self-imposed deadlines were sometimes met, but most often not. The letdowns, discouragement, and defeat that all led to the ultimate victory of two small and powerful words, "The End," were worth it.

I wrote this book in honor of a young girl who learned too soon how cruel the world can be and learned too late how wonderful love can be. I wrote this for every foster child, every survivor, and every hurt person because pain recognizes pain. I wrote this book as a scream for those who haven't found their voices yet and a guide for family and friends of survivors who don't know what to do and don't understand what is going on, so they do nothing, which causes more hurt.

First off, I want to thank Casey, aka Curly Beaver. When my life went through such turmoil that I'd put the book so far on the back burner, it barely existed to me anymore; you came through. You sat at work one day and read the book cover to cover, and at the end of the day, you came to me with tears in your eyes. You hugged me and reminded me that this story needed to be told. Thank you for helping me find my way back.

Next, my editor, Melissa Drake. It wasn't until the book was almost wrapped up that I realized I truly needed to acknowledge you. A good editor makes all the difference. They force you to look at things differently, they challenge what you think you know, and they will even break the rules (long walks on the beach and Chipotle lol) if that's what it takes to keep you going. There is something almost magical and mystical in a true relationship between an author and an editor, and Melissa you are a magician, an enchantress, and a mentor all rolled into one. Thank you for getting me across the finish line.

To "Uncle Ralph" in accepting me to your class at The Hurston/Wright Writers Retreat, you helped solidify my confidence that can only come from someone who has already been there. If I considered myself Kobe Bryant, you were Michael Jordan, and your confidence and belief in me deemed me worthy--if only in my own mind.

To Dwayne, sometimes you got on my nerves so badly, but you always had my best interest at heart and always pushed me on. Even if I was grumbling while doing it. (Which I usually was). Thanks for believing in me D-weezy.

I want to thank my reading team. These people read my book five pages at a time as it poured out of me. Their critiques, words of encouragement, laughter, and tears as the story unfolded were such a motivation to keep writing. Stitch, Tonya, Angela, Brailey, and Lindsey. I thank you guys so much.

Stitch, you walked the journey of this story with me in real-time without fully being aware of all that was going on, but you never let go of my hand. Thank you for always being my Jiminy Cricket (my conscience). Beyond this book, I would not be who I am without your role in my life. Thank you, and I love you. The world is waiting for you now.

And lastly, Jarvis...Iron Man is my favorite superhero. What I love about him is that when he became a superhero, he had to save himself before he could save anyone else, and that always resonated with me. Alas, Iron Man wasn't as great as he was without Jarvis. I was blessed to have my own Jarvis, who pushed, encouraged, argued, called, texted, bought gifts, gave pep talks, and more--all in the name of helping me get this book finished. I honestly don't know if I would have finished without you, J. Thank you for always seeing me, even in times when I didn't see myself. I appreciate your help getting me through the occasional breakdown and asking the hard questions that sometimes challenged my whole existence. This book is for you, too.

Introduction

The words in this book may hurt to read. They may hurt to reflect upon. They may hurt to talk about. But ultimately, I believe they will help many begin or continue their healing journey.

There is no way to summarize pain. No format attractively packages real trauma. Luckily for us, broken crayons still color. Often, we can't understand how much the world weighs until we walk in another person's shoes. With this book, you'll understand just how much a new pair of shoes or a different perspective can mean.

1 in 6.

1 in 6 bares scars from the gnashing of teeth, touched by the insatiable hunger of someone's shadow.

1 in 6 has no option to walk away.

1 in 6 of us is never allowed to forget.

I am 1 in 6.

She was 1 in 6.

This true story is not told purely from my courage or strength. Rather, this story is told in reverence for one of the most beautiful people I ever met. This story is meant to spite the shadows that still attempt to plague my soul. This story is shared because God insisted to my heart that it be given to the world.

SECTION 1: FLASHBACKS

Kindra

Tim was a little too delighted that I actually knew what I was doing, but he was paying me well for this consultation, so I ignored the aroma of cheap cologne, vodka, and cigarettes he'd filled the room with.

"Damn girl! You know your stuff when it comes to music," he said and scooted so close to me on his mother's couch that our shoulders were now touching.

"Music and writing is my passion," I replied with a smile. I looked down at the pad of paper, trying to think of how else we could rearrange this mess of lyrics into a passable song. I crossed out two lines on the page.

"These are overkill," I said without looking up. I felt an arm go around my shoulder. I froze. Warning bells started to go off in my head, but I quieted them, thinking, "Come on, Kindra girl--you've worked with him on music for weeks; you're good. Just tell him it's not like that."

I took a deep breath, still looking at the pad. Man, was this going to be awkward.

"Tim," I started. But when I looked into his eyes, something had changed, gone cold in him. I knew I was in danger. Before I could react, he threw his 6'2" frame on me, pushing me back on the couch. I tried to scream, but his forearm came down like a bar across my neck; my vision went black around the edges for a second, and I couldn't breathe. He shifted his weight on top of me, and his arm on my neck let up a little, allowing me to draw in breath.

That horrid mixture of alcohol, smoke, and cologne burned

my nose as I fought to inhale. I felt one of his hands go to the waist of my sweatpants, grab, and yank downwards. Fear hit me like a ton of bricks when I realized his plan. I began to move, attempting to get him off of me.

Why was he so heavy? When I attempted to shift, he countered, shifting himself and putting his arm more firmly on my neck. White lights started popping in my eyes. I squirmed and fought--trying to move him, trying to breathe. I felt his whole body shift upward, placing the brunt of his weight on my upper body. His hand went to my waist again, but this time, so did his foot, using his hand and boot to work my sweat pants and panties down to my knees. Tears began to slip from my eyes, and then pain like a searing hot knife cut through me.

I heard a raspy voice crying, “Stop! You’re hurting me, please stop.”

Wait--it was my voice. Pain again ripped through me. I sat up and screamed, “NO! PLEASE STOP!”

My breath was coming in ragged sobs, and my face was wet with tears. I clenched the sheets tightly…sheets. My bed. I frantically scanned the room. Lamp resting on a table in the corner, television turned down low, showing middle-of-the-night infomercials. I scanned the room again, making sure I was alone and safe. I wiped the tears from my eyes and tried to slow my breathing.

“It was just another nightmare,” I told myself again. “You’re safe now. He can’t hurt you here; you’re safe now.”

I lay back down, knowing that I would not be able to fall asleep again tonight. Tears streamed down my cheeks onto my pillow. “Please take it away,” I prayed. “Just take it away.”

Charli

I knew my foster father's nightly routine. We all did. "Please don't pick me, please don't pick me. If I stand really still, I can be invisible. I'm always invisible. Please..."

"Charli!" His booming voice interrupted my thoughts. "Bring me and Jeremy some beers down to the shed."

My heart sank all the way down to my shoes. The three other foster kids I shared a room with looked sad for me but glad it wasn't them tonight. I hadn't been in this home long, but it was one of the worst.

I slowly walked to the fridge and gathered four bottles into my arms, the cold penetrating the thin cloth of my Bazooka Joe t-shirt. I wondered how many orphan kids before me had worn this shirt.

The screen door slammed behind me as I walked to the end of the porch. There were four stairs down to the dirt road and 67 steps to the shed. Some country song blared out of a half-open door. I began walking, counting my steps. There was a hole starting to form in the big toe of my converse shoes. I wondered how long before I could get another pair that fit. 65...66...67. I stopped at the door, took a deep breath, and walked in.

The shed smelled like dust and oil. Mack, my foster father, worked under the hood of some old-looking car, while Jeremy, Mack's biological son, sat on a couch flipping through a magazine. He looked up at me when I walked in, stared at me for a few seconds, then looked back down at the magazine.

"Umm, Mack," I stumbled over my words. "I umm...I

brought your beer," I said while looking at the hole in my shoe.

"Charli," Mack barked at me. "How many times do I have to tell you to call me Dad?" I kept looking down. "Sorry...Dad," I said, hardly above a whisper.

"Put the beer on the table and go sit by your brother," Mack said from underneath the hood of the car. My chest tightened. I set the beers down and then sat down on the couch.

Jeremy set the magazine down, stood up, and began to loosen his belt buckle. Mack went to the radio and turned the music up. I wondered why he did that--I hadn't screamed in two weeks.

I stared down at my shoe. I could see Jeremy's naked legs; he'd already taken his jeans off. Behind him, I saw Mack's shirt hit the floor. Jeremy grabbed my hand and pulled me up. I didn't fight when he started pulling my shirt over my head. I'd learned it was easier if you didn't fight. I went numb. I crawled inside of myself.

I started repeating what I said every time I started a new school. "My name is Charli Lauren, I'm 12 years old, and I like pineapples." I kept saying it over and over again in my head. Tears ran down my cheeks, but I never made a sound. "I'm 12 years old, and I like pineapples, I'm Charli Lauren, I'm 12 years old, and I like pineapples. I'm 12..."

"Charli."

I wouldn't let myself come back yet. It was too soon for it to be over. *"And I like pinea..."*

"Charli, Charli." I heard it again. "Charli," said a little voice.

I opened my eyes and Valerie, the youngest orphan in the house, was at my bedside, eyes wide with fear. "You were crying again," she said, "and you said pineapples."

I didn't know what to say. Finally, she said, "Can I sleep with you, Charli?"

I lifted up the blanket, and she climbed in the bed and nestled up next to me. We lay there in silence for a few minutes, then I whispered in the darkness, "What's your name?" She rolled over so she faced me.

"Why do you always ask me those questions, Charli?"

I didn't know how to answer that, so I just lay there quietly. Tears started to escape my eyes. I heard her little voice say, "My name's Valerie Rockwell."

"And how old are you?" I asked her.

"I'm six years old, and I like popsicles," she said.

Kindra

I sat in the waiting room, hands twisting in my lap. A man and a woman walked in and up to the receptionist's desk. There were now four men in the room, including the guy who had just walked in. Three of them were bigger than me, all of them a threat.

I always sat close to the exit; right now, I was two chairs from the door. I touched the keys in my pocket, calculating how quickly I could get out of this office and to my car.

"Kindra." My therapist, Paige, was standing at the other door. The look of concern in her eyes said, "It's ok, you are safe here." I hated when people could tell I was in fight or flight mode.

I gathered my things and followed her through the door, down the hall, and into her office. I loved her office. It was spacious, with a huge green shag rug separating her desk from the couch. Sometimes if our conversations got too intense, I'd sit on the rug and run my fingers through the shag. It always calmed me. The lighting was perfect--not so bright that you felt like you were being interrogated, but not so dark that it made you scared. The couch had throw pillows of different sizes and colors. I usually held onto the blue one with the big goldfish. It reminded me of Nemo. And lastly, a big soft purple blanket that I could wrap up in if the session got really bad.

I sat on the couch.

"How was your week?" Paige always started with this question. I reached over and began twisting the edge of my favorite pillow, thinking about how I wanted to answer it.

"You look tired, are you having difficulties sleeping again?" she asked. I pulled the pillow to my chest and put my chin down on top of it.

"Nightmares," I responded with a sigh. The look in her eyes made me feel like I was letting her down. She was working so hard to make me…normal.

"Do you know what's triggered them this time? Did you see a sexual assault scene on tv or a movie?"

I shook my head no.

"Did you see someone who looked like him or smelled like him?"

Again, I shook my head no and then lowered it in shame. Tears spilled down my face and onto the fish pillow.

"Hey," Paige said in her encouraging voice. "It's okay; you don't always know what's going to trigger you, and sometimes it can be nothing at all that takes you there. It doesn't mean you are doing bad. You're still here; you're still fighting, and that's always a step forward, right?"

I lifted my head slightly and smiled. "Yeah," I said while wiping a tear away. I liked it when Paige said I was fighting. She'd said it in one of our very first sessions: "You may not have been able to fight him off that night, but every day that you get up and move forward with your life, you are fighting him off of you, and that's always a step forward, even on the bad days." I lifted my head a bit more.

"Do you work tonight?" she asked. "Yes," I said. "Today is my Monday."

"And you still like your job, and working the night shift?"

I thought about it for a second. "Yeah, I do; it seems like it's a little bit easier to sleep during the day. Things are still scary at night."

"And how about fundraising for your service dog? How is that going?" At this question, I lit up--any talk about my future service dog made me smile.

"Well, it's going slow." I paused. "Because, in order to ask for donations, I have to tell my story, and that's hard because not everyone wants to hear it. Especially..." I faltered and looked away.

"Especially who?" she prodded.

"My family," I sighed. "I don't know if they are ashamed of it and of me, or if they don't know what to say, but either way, I feel alone and like a burden...like it's my fault."

Paige brought me a box of tissues. "No matter how anyone is feeling," she said, "or how they make you feel, we know it's not..." she stopped and waited for me to complete the sentence.

"My fault. It's not my fault."

I stated this with all the confidence in the world. But inside, I still wasn't so sure.

"How are things with Daniel?" she asked. Daniel was my boyfriend. We had been friends since we were teenagers and now we were in a serious relationship. He was in the military and stationed overseas in Korea. It was hard, but we made it work. Talking about him/us was easy and calming.

Charli

I stared at the clock, counting down the minutes til the lunch bell. What subject was this again? It didn't matter; I rarely stayed in a school long enough for it to matter. The bell rang, and I packed up my stuff and headed outside. I sat a safe distance away from most of the other kids and pulled out my lunch bag. An apple and a fun size bag of Fritos. I put it back in my backpack. I wasn't hungry anyway, I told myself. I sat my backpack down next to the brick planter I was sitting on, pulled my legs up to my chest and laid my head on top of my knees. Maybe I could just rest for a few minutes. I hadn't had a good night's rest in days. I dozed off.

A hand grabbed my arm and shook me. "Charli," a voice said softly. Eyes not open, I wasn't sure where I was or who was touching me, and in one swift motion, I opened my eyes and pushed away whoever it was. I jumped up and ran. I'd left my backpack behind, but now I recognized my surroundings. I ran straight to the girl's bathroom, locked myself in a stall, and bent over. I felt like I was having a heart attack. I couldn't catch my breath.

"I'm going to die right here in this stall," I thought. "Death wouldn't be so bad."

Minutes passed; I didn't die. My heart slowed down, and I could breathe again. I started crying. I wasn't even sure what happened or why I was crying in the bathroom. I sat a little while longer until I heard a bell signaling the end of lunch. I came out of the stall and splashed cold water on my face. Red blotchy eyes would draw attention, and I liked being invisible. I waited a few more minutes in the bathroom until I knew the hallways had cleared and then I walked back to where I'd left my backpack.

Something was sitting on top of my bag. It was a brown paper lunch bag, "Matt" was written on it in big bold black letters. I looked around--no one in the halls. I sat down and opened the bag: a peanut butter and jelly sandwich, a red Jello cup with a spoon, a Hi-C juice box, and a brownie. With real food in front of me, I could admit how hungry I was. I ripped open the sandwich and took two large bites. I polished off the whole lunch, stomach full for the first time in days.

But who was Matt? And why did he give me his lunch?

Kindra

I had plenty of time to stop at the gas station for my work snack--white cheddar popcorn and a root beer--before my shift started at 11 pm.

There were two cars in the Shell gas station parking lot besides mine and one customer in the store. I waited until the customer completed his purchase, exited the store, and left the parking lot before I went in. I said "Hey" to the cashier, whom I saw at least three nights a week but still didn't know his name. He nodded and went back to his phone.

I was back in my car in less than four minutes. No other customers showed up while I was inside.

I pulled into my parking spot at my job at 10:45 pm and called my dad like I did every night. I was 30 years old and still talked to my dad every day. Talk about your Daddy's girl.

"Hey Baby Girl, you in the parking lot?" he asked. "Yes sir," I replied.

"How was your day? Did you get enough sleep?"

He asked the same questions he asked every night, but it did make me feel good.

"Yeah, Dad, I got about six and a half hours of sleep and spent the rest of the day watching "House" on Netflix." I smiled, knowing what was coming next.

"HOUSE!" he sputtered. "I watch Charmed in the mornings. You should watch it too; it's a good show."

"Charmed isn't on Netflix, Dad, and I gotta get into work--don't want to clock in late. I love you." I rushed through my words while trying to gather my belongings.

"Love you too, Baby Girl. Have a good night."

Charli

Most nights I don't sleep. If it's not nightmares that keep me up, it's the other kids crying out in their sleep, having the same nightmares as me. I hadn't had nightmares tonight, but I fought sleep just the same. Didn't want to risk it.

I lay in my bed on the bottom bunk, staring up at the top bunk. Was this what life was like for everybody? It couldn't be…could it?

If my life was going to be like this forever, I figured I should just kill myself. I had been thinking about that a lot lately.

"Suicide." I liked the way it rolled around in my mouth before it left my lips. The dictionary defined suicide as "The act of intentionally causing one's own death," and I liked that too, the way it sounded important.

"Intentionally causing one's own death," I said aloud. I hadn't intentionally caused anything in my life. I had no control over anything--where I lived or slept, what I ate, the clothes I wore, or what happened to me.

I yawned and looked at the clock on the wall. 2:15 am. It didn't seem like I was going to be able to fight sleep much longer. I dozed off, thinking, "Suicide, yeah. I'd have control of that."

Kindra

Floor swept and mopped, check. Boys' and girls' bathroom cleaned, check. Residents' laundry washed, dried, ironed, and placed on hangers for pick up in the morning, check. And breakfast prepared for morning, check. All my work was done, and it wasn't even 4 am yet.

I worked at a place called Village of Hope. It was basically a collection of six houses on a compound that was home to numerous adults of varying levels of intellectual disability. It was one of the nicest group homes in the greater Houston, TX area. I worked nights in House #3 and had a spunky group of residents who kept me smiling.

I walked the whole house and double-checked that all the doors were locked. Safety made me feel calm. Then I sat down on the couch and turned the TV on. "Blue Bloods" would be on for three hours straight on the Ion channel. I set my alarm to go off every two hours to remind me to get up, walk the rooms, and check on my residents. Then, I snuggled into my coat and prepared for my nightly routine of cop shows and checking on residents until it was time to prepare breakfast and go home.

Charli

It had been a week since I'd received the mysterious brown bag lunch. I'd kept my eyes open for "Matt," but it proved to be difficult with so many kids in the school and my social awkwardness. I had started to wonder if I'd imagined the whole thing.

The sound of the bell startled me out of my thoughts. Kids were filing out of the room, so I put my notebook in my backpack and headed out the door.

I didn't have a lunch today; no one had packed me one for three days now. I sat down on the familiar brick planter, pulled my legs to my chest, and tried to ignore the sound of my stomach grumbling. Eyes closed, I listened to the sounds of students on lunch break. Conversations about makeup, sports, and trips to the mall--it was all so foreign. None of it was the world I lived in. None of it made sense to me.

I opened my eyes and saw a boy sitting in front of me on the planter. My heart beat faster, and I looked for an escape.

"Please don't run away," he said. My eyes stopped darting in all directions and settled on him.

He was staring right at me, but it was strange. Lately, when someone stared at me, they wanted to take my clothes off, but he just looked...concerned. I froze under his gaze, and we sat there staring at each other for what seemed like hours. His hair was brown and spiked, and he had these sad, intense brown eyes and the beginnings of a mustache.

"I'm Matt," he said with a smile.

I could tell he was waiting for a reaction, but I didn't know what to say.

Matt reached into his backpack, and I flinched, looking for an escape. “Please don’t go,” Matt said. He pulled out a lunch bag and set it in front of me. I just looked at it. He picked it up and held it out to me.

“Here,” he said. “It’s for you.”

I cautiously took the bag and whispered, “Thank you,” as I looked inside.

A snack bag of Cheez-It crackers, a fruit cup, a Twinkie, and a sandwich with turkey, lettuce, tomato, and cheese. My mouth watered at the sight of all that food. But I didn’t eat; I just looked at him. He pulled out another lunch bag with many of the same things in it as the lunch he had given me. He began to eat his sandwich, so I ate mine, too. I looked up and saw him smiling. As I was eating the fruit cup, he asked, “Your name is Charli, right?”

What did he want from me? Why was he being so nice? I nodded and went back to the lunch.

When the bell rang, Matt put all his trash into his lunch bag, stood up, and looked at me, head tilted.

“So, I’ll see you tomorrow?” he asked. I thought about it. No one had looked forward to seeing me tomorrow in a long time. I could be snatched from this foster home and put in another at any time, even before tomorrow.

I looked him in the eye. “Maybe.”

This seemed to be enough for him, because he said, “OK,” grabbed his stuff, and walked off.

I honestly had no idea what had just happened, but I knew one thing: my stomach was full.

Kindra

I pulled my car into a parking space and stepped out into the evening air. The sun felt good on my arms. I walked to the front door of the women's center and buzzed the doorbell.

"How can I help you?" said a voice from the intercom.

"It's Kindra. I'm here for group."

A loud buzzing rang out, and the door unlocked. I loved that no one could just walk into this place. It was a shelter for battered and abused women, so in order to keep the women there safe, they wouldn't just let anyone on the premises. On Tuesday and Thursday evenings, they had group counseling for victims of sexual assault. I rarely missed a meeting. At this point, I was considered one of the veterans of the group. A lot of the ladies came to me for advice and hugs.

I didn't really come to share my story anymore. Mostly, I came to talk about difficulties I was having (i.e., the nightmares) amongst women who understood because they were experiencing the same thing. I came to support other women who had gone through similar situations. It always made me sad to realize how little support women who had been sexually assaulted got. It made it so much harder to cope. I knew firsthand. So, I made it a point to give these girls the support I never received in hopes that they didn't end up as far off the rails as I did.

I walked into the building, spoke to the girls at the front desk, signed my name on the sign-in sheet, and went into the group room. The room had chairs and spaces in between them in case you wanted to sit on the floor. Soft lighting and ambient beach sounds filled the room.

Most of the girls in the room I recognized as regulars at all different levels in their “healing process.” Also, there were two new faces. The new faces made me sigh. That was two more people who had been victimized and would have to learn how to live the rest of their lives with that victimization. I saw tears run down the face of one of the new girls. I got up, grabbed a box of tissues, and handed it to her just as the group leader walked in.

“Let the healing begin,” I thought. Then, I walked back to my seat.

Charli

I sat on the brick planter waiting for Matt to show up. He had brought me lunch every day for two weeks now and stayed to eat with me. The first week, we didn't say much. Well, *I* didn't say much--he talked every now and then about tests he had taken in his classes, homework, and being on the baseball team. I never spoke about myself. I'd have no idea what to say. I couldn't talk about the things that happened back at the house I stayed at.

This week, though, I had joined in a bit, asking questions about his classes. Becoming more comfortable with Matt was exciting and terrifying. I wasn't used to having friends.

Matt walked up to the planter. He had on black slacks, a white button-down shirt, and a black tie. I think that meant the baseball team had a game today. He sat down, opened his backpack, and started pulling out both lunches.

"Do you have a game today?" I asked, completely unsure of myself. Matt looked pleased. "Yeah," he said. "It's an away game, and I'm going to start."

I wasn't quite sure what that meant, but he seemed happy about it, so I said, "Cool."

He was going through the lunch bags. "You want the turkey sandwich or the peanut butter and jelly?"

"Turkey," I said. "No, wait, what's the dessert with each one?" I asked with a smile. Matt laughed--this was becoming a thing. He dug in the bags again.

"The turkey sandwich has a brownie with it, and the peanut butter sandwich has a Twinkie," he said.

"I want the Twinkie," I said and watched him switch the Twinkie into the bag with the turkey sandwich and hand it to me.

We sat in silence, eating our lunches. Matt finished his first like he always did. Then I caught him staring at me.

"What?" I asked.

"You live with the Kane family, right?" he asked in a bit more serious voice. I stopped mid-bite. How did he know who I lived with? I'd never told him anything about me.

My stomach started tying up in knots. I couldn't eat anymore. I began to pack up the remaining food.

"You aren't going to finish your lunch?" he asked, sounding confused and concerned.

"I'm not hungry anymore," I said while looking around for the fastest way to get away from him.

"But I know you didn't eat breakfast," he said, a bit defensively.

I froze. How did he know so much about me? My heart started to race, and my hands got sweaty. I reached slowly for my backpack.

"I know what happens in that house," he said in a low voice, looking at the ground. My stomach lurched. I grabbed my backpack and ran.

"Charli, WAIT!" I heard him yell behind me, but I didn't dare. I ran straight to the girl's bathroom again, locked myself in the stall again, and bent over…again.

I knew for sure I was going to die of a heart attack this time. I waited for the darkness, but it never came. My heart slowed down, and the tears began to pool in my eyes. What did he want from me? How did he know? Why did I eat lunch with him every day? The bell rang, and lunch was over. I came out of the stall and went to the mirror. Eyes red and puffy…again. I splashed water on my face. I would just have to ignore him, and eventually he would go away…wouldn't he? Unless he wanted something from me.

I waited a few more minutes until I was sure the hallways would be clear. I opened the door and stepped out. I looked left and then looked right. Matt was sitting on the floor on the right side of the girl's bathroom door.

"Charli, please let me--" I jumped back into the bathroom and slammed the door before he could finish.

What was his problem? What did he want with me?

"You can't stay in there forever," he said through the door. I thought about it. I guessed technically I couldn't.

"Please let me explain?" he begged. I stared at the door, trying to figure a way out. I looked around the bathroom--no windows. I was trapped. My heart started racing. *Not again*, I thought as I bent over and put my hands on my knees. I was having trouble catching my breath. I had no idea what to do, so I started to cry. I looked up just in time to see Matt poke his head in the door. One look at me, and he came through the door.

"Charli, are you ok? Try to slow your breathing," he said, panic in his voice. This was the first time I had noticed he was at least two inches taller than me and outweighed me by 20 pounds easily. I backed up against the wall between the stall and one of the sinks.

"Please don't hurt me," I cried between labored breaths. His face took on a look of shock.

"What? Me? No, I wouldn't…" he paused and looked at me, looked around the bathroom, shook his head, and slowly backed out of the bathroom door.

After the door closed, I heard him say, "I'm sorry I scared you; I promise I would never hurt you."

Now, he sounded like he was going to cry. My breathing slowed down to a normal pace, but my whole body hurt like I had been in a fight. I just stood there staring at the door, unsure what to do next.

Matt started speaking through the door again: "How about this, can you just come to the door? You don't have to open it or even come out. I just want to talk to you."

I thought about it. "Seems safe enough, I guess." I walked over to the door and lightly knocked one time on it so he would know that I was there.

"Yeah," he said, all excited. "I will talk. You don't have to--just knock one time for no and twice for yes if I ask a question. Is that okay?" he asked.

I stared at the door. I realized I had spent a lot of time staring at this door today. It couldn't hurt to listen to him. Could it? I could at least find out what he knew. I lifted my hand slowly to the door and knocked twice. I heard him exhale like he had been holding his breath for a while.

"Ok. You remember Elise, don't you?" he asked.

He knew Elise?

A tall girl, two years older than me, with her hair always in braids and amazing green eyes that showed she was wild with a touch of rebellion in her soul. She was moved to another house three weeks after I moved in.

I was still wearing the bracelet she'd made for me, with beads that spelled out "Sis." Two days before she moved, she'd put it on my wrist and said, "You are my little sister now;

this means we are family, and I will look out for you." Two days later, she was gone. We didn't even get a chance to say goodbye.

I opened the door to see Matt sitting on the floor, fidgeting with a bracelet on his left wrist that looked just like mine except his said "Matt" on it. I'd never noticed it before. She'd made him one, too. I came all the way out of the bathroom and sat down next to him.

"She told me what was happening to the kids in that house months ago," he said, looking at the bracelet. "She knew they were going to move her soon, and she asked me to look out for you after she was gone."

"But why me?" I asked, on the verge of tears. "There are other kids in the house."

Matt sighed like this was difficult for him to say: "Because you are older than most of them, she said she knew they would come after you next." One tear slipped down my cheek as I thought about Elise and the time we spent together. She'd left only about two months ago, but that seemed like ages now.

"Hi, I'm Elise," she'd said after the social worker had shown me to the room I would be staying in at this new house.

"Hi," I responded, sitting down on the edge of the bottom bunk bed.

"I know you are sad," she said. "I get sad every time I move to a different house too."

I looked up at her, wondering if she was going to try and steal my stuff when I went to sleep. That happened a lot in different foster homes. I picked up my black trash bag with my stuff and pushed it behind me.

She closed the door, walked over, and sat down next to me on the bed. I made a fist of my right hand. I didn't think she would jump me with the social worker still in the house, but you could never be sure.

“What's your name?” she asked. She didn't seem threatening; she actually seemed a little nice.

“Charli,” I said without making eye contact. She turned and faced me on the bed.

“Listen, Charli,” she said. “I know you are nervous about being in a new home, and I'm not going to lie to you--this one is pretty bad. I don't have long to get you up to speed. I can keep the heat off of you for a while, but you're going to have to learn some things if you want to survive this one.”

She paused and looked back at my trash bag. “And I promise no one is going to steal your stuff.” I looked over at Matt. “I miss her," I said.

“I miss her too, but she wanted me to watch out for you,” he said. “Why did you take so long to talk to me?” I asked him.

“Well, at first, I didn't know who you were--all Elise told me was to look for a 6th-grade girl with dirty blonde hair and that you would be wearing a Bazooka Joe t-shirt.”

“She gave me that shirt!” I said with surprise.

“I know,” he said. “It was her favorite shirt. I used to buy her the gum with the comic strips on them.” He stopped talking and smiled to himself and then continued. “So I had to start keeping an eye out for a Bazooka Joe shirt, which wasn't hard cause no one else wears those.

Then, when I finally saw you, I had to figure out how to approach you. I knew Elise rarely ever had lunch, and she never ate breakfast. I used to bring her lunch, too. So I figured that was the best way to get you to talk to me.”

Matt got really serious and said, “Charli, I tried to get Elise to do something for a while that I thought might help her, and she was really thinking about it. I think you should, too."

"What is it?" I asked. He put his hand in his jacket pocket and pulled out a folded sheet of paper, then handed it to me. I unfolded the paper. It was a flier for the local women's center.

It said that group meetings for victims of sexual assault were held every Tuesday and Thursday at 5 pm.

I didn't know what to say about it. There were words on that page that made me uncomfortable.

"Just think about it," he said.

I said, "OK," without looking up. I could see he was grabbing for his backpack and standing up to leave. I just sat there.

"See you tomorrow for lunch?" he asked. I looked up at him and smiled. "Yeah. See you tomorrow."

Kindra

I pulled into the parking lot at the women's center on Thursday at 5:10 pm, frantically trying to grab my belongings because I was running late (I'd lost track of time watching "House"). That was when I saw her. She couldn't have been more than 13 with brownish-blond hair. She was walking back and forth on the sidewalk in front of the center. She kept gazing up at the building like she wanted to go in. I'd seen her doing the same thing on Tuesday before group started.

I got out of my car, thinking today I should say something to her. She just seemed so young. When I closed my car door, she jumped. We made eye contact for a few seconds, and then she turned and walked down the street and away from the center. I said a quiet prayer for her and went inside.

Charli

"Well?" Matt asked again.

"Well, what?" I snapped back at him.

"Well, are you actually going to go into the group next time?" Matt asked with a hint of frustration in his voice.

I didn't know, so I just stared into the sky. We sat on the football bleachers. Both of us had skipped our last period class because Matt said he needed to talk to me about something. If I had known this was what he wanted to talk about, I would have just gone to class. I didn't know how to make him understand. I couldn't just go tell a group of strange people what was going on in that house because of something a flier said. A flier couldn't help me.

I didn't tell him about the lady I saw when I went to the building where the group was held. Something about her made me feel safe and scared at the same time, and I didn't like it at all.

"Charli," Matt said, snapping me out of my thoughts. "Huh?" I looked up.

"School's out," he said. I looked toward campus and saw a swarm of kids filing out of the building. I hadn't even heard the bell ring.

"Just please think about going," Matt said, his voice tinged with frustration as he picked up his backpack. "They might really be able to help you," he added before walking off towards the parking lot. He seemed angry. I was angry with him, too. Why couldn't he just mind his business? He had no idea what he was asking of me. He stopped about 10 yards away from me, and I watched his shoulders rise and fall like he was taking a deep breath. He turned around and yelled “Hey” back at me.

“See you tomorrow?” he asked with a smile. I smiled back. “Yeah, see you tomorrow,” I yelled back.

I didn’t *really* know about tomorrow, but hey. A girl could hope.

Kindra

The girl with the dirty blond hair had been on my mind for the last two days. I put the car in park in front of the women's center and set a bag of Cheetos and a bottle of Sprite on the passenger seat. Then I waited.

Ten minutes went by, and I began to get discouraged. Twenty minutes.

Then I saw her walking down the street, hands in her pockets, looking down at her shoes.

Charli

Why was I doing this? Was I doing this for Matt? For me? What was I even doing? Was I really considering telling strangers what happens in that house?

I'd seen a kid in another house complain about the beatings. CPS took him out of the house for a few days while they did their "investigation." Then they brought him back--like nothing happened. The fosters were so angry they beat him really badly for the next week.

Thinking about what that kid went through stopped me dead in my tracks. Matt just didn't get it. Snitches get stitches. With that in mind, I turned around to walk away from the women's center. A car door slammed loudly, and I jumped and turned around.

It was her, the woman I'd seen before. She stared me down, never breaking her gaze as she walked around the car and out to the sidewalk I stood on. My legs wouldn't move. I watched her walk to the curb and sit down on it. She set a bag of Cheetos and a Sprite on the concrete next to her; then she pulled out a bag for herself.

She broke her gaze with me and stared out into the street. I wanted to run away. I wanted to sit down with her; I wanted those Cheetos. I slowly walked towards her, feeling like I was making the biggest mistake of my life. I sat down next to her. I opened the Cheetos and began to eat them. We sat there in silence for what seemed like a long time.

"Hi, I'm Kindra," she finally said.

"I'm Charlotte, but people call me Charli," I responded.

We sat in silence a little longer. I picked up the Sprite and turned the cap. The bottle made a loud "tsssssss" noise as the pressure escaped. I lifted the bottle to my lips and took a big gulp. The carbonation burned the back of my throat, but it felt good going down.

"I don't want to go inside," I finally told this lady called Kindra.

"You don't have to," she responded, and then we sat in silence for another few minutes. "Why do you go in there?" I asked her. She looked up at the sky, let out a long sigh, and then said, "Because someone hurt me really bad, and I can come here and talk about it with other people who understand what I'm going through because they've been through it too."

"Oh," was all I could respond. Kindra turned and looked at me, her face very serious.

"Did someone…" she paused, "hurt you, Charli?" she finished. I turned my head away from her. I didn't want her to see the tears that had popped into my eyes. I quickly picked up the Sprite and tried to wash the tears away with the carbonated drink.

"I don't want to talk about that," I said, face still turned away from her. "Ok," she responded. "We don't have to…How old are you, Charli?"

I felt panic starting to rise in me.

"I'm 12," I said in a rushed voice. I wondered why her face turned so sad when I said that. But the panic was building. She was asking too many questions, and I needed to get away.

"I have to go; I have to leave," I said, standing up.

"Charli," she said, halting me in my steps. I turned back around and looked at her. She looked like she wasn't sure what to say, then she said, "I'll be here Tuesday if you want to come back. We don't have to go inside."

I stared at her and heard my voice say, "Maybe."

She smiled a little bit, then looked down at my half-drunk Sprite that I'd left on the ground.

"What's your favorite kind of soda?" she asked. I looked down at the Sprite bottle, too.

What a strange question. I didn't have a favorite soda. I didn't really get to drink it often. "Uhm, I like anything flavored pineapple," I said, and then she smiled.

"OK," she said, and I felt the panic go away a little bit. I turned and began walking to the house, wondering if I should return on Tuesday.

Kindra

I reached back into the car to grab the chips and drink, and when I looked up, she had turned around and was walking away from the center. I went to yell out her name and realized I didn't know it. I had to get her attention, or she might never come back, and something in me said she needed me. I slammed my car door as hard as I could. The whole car shook (maybe that was too hard), but she jumped and turned around. She saw me, and I could see the recognition in her eyes. She remembered me.

I walked around the car, never taking my eyes off her, willing her not to leave, begging her not to leave with my stare. I had no idea what I was doing; I just made it up as I went. All I knew was that she hadn't walked away yet. I walked out to the sidewalk she was standing on and sat down on the curb. Finally breaking eye contact, I set the chips and soda on the sidewalk for her right next to me, an invitation. I opened my own bag of chips, looked out into the street, and waited.

I heard footsteps approaching me and breathed a sigh of relief. She sat down next to me and opened the bag of Cheetos. We sat in silence. Panic raced through me. I had no idea what to say, then finally, I just said, "Hi, I'm Kindra."

"I'm Charlotte, but people call me Charli," she responded, and my heart leapt for this beautiful girl named Charli. Then, a wave of protectiveness came over me. I'd destroy anyone who hurt her.

I was completely caught off guard by these feelings. I didn't even know her, yet I felt like she was mine.

"Tssssss." The sound of Charli opening the Sprite bottle

brought me out of my thoughts. “I don’t want to go inside,” she said.

“You don’t have to,” I replied. “We can stay out here as long as you like.”

“But how will I help her out here?” I wondered. “Am I even equipped to help her?”

“Why do you go in there?” Charli asked me. I looked up at the sky, thinking of the best way to answer her question. I sighed and just spoke from my heart.

“Because someone hurt me really bad, and I can come here and talk about it with other people who understand what I’m going through because they have been through it too.”

“Oh,” was all she said. Maybe that wasn’t a good answer. I turned and looked at her.

“Did someone…” I paused, looking for the right words, “hurt you?” I asked, praying it not to be so. But the second she registered the question, her eyes flashed panic, and she jerked her head away from me. She began taking large gulps of Sprite.

“I don’t want to talk about that,” she said, head still turned away from me. My heart plummeted.

“OK,” I said, hoping to calm her down. “We don’t have to.”

I paused. “How old are you, Charli?” I asked, trying to change the subject but still getting some information about her. I felt like I was losing her.

“I’m twelve,” she said.

“Twelve,” I thought. “She’s just a baby. Who would hurt this baby?”

Charli jumped up, startling me. “I have to go; I have to leave,” she said.

"Charli," I said. She stopped, turned, and looked at me. I had no idea what to say. I didn't want it to end like this. "I'll be here Tuesday…If you want to come back, we don't have to go inside."

She hesitated, then gave her shoulders a little shrug and said, "Maybe." It wasn't a no. We both just stood there. I glanced at her half-drunk soda.

"What's your favorite kind of soda?" I asked, just trying to continue the conversation as long as possible. She looked slightly confused at the question, then she responded, "Uhm, I like anything flavored pineapple."

I smiled.

"OK," I said. We would see each other again. Deep down inside, I knew it.

Charli

I lay in my bed, staring at the bunk above me, and thought about school. I was kind of starting to like my school and some of my classes, and it was because of Matt, the first real, normal friend I'd had in as long as I could remember. I wanted to stay for the first time in a long time, and that scared me because that meant when it came time to leave, I would be heartbroken.

What if Matt showed up with my lunch and I wasn't there? How many days would he bring lunch before he realized I wasn't coming back?

I just had to stay. I had to do everything in my power to stay.

Then I thought about the trips to the shed. I remembered the smell of beer on hot breath falling heavily on me. I shuddered. But that could happen at any home; they could move me somewhere worse. At least here I had a school I was beginning to like, and I had Matt, and there was that lady Kindra…I had no idea what to make of that situation or her, but I wanted to stay and find out. I'd made my decision: I'd do everything I could to stay.

Kindra

It seemed like every time I ironed a pair of the residents' jeans, two more would appear in the pile. How many pairs did they wear each day? Sheesh. I'd washed and dried the residents' clothes and was now ironing them and putting them on hangers, but the jeans weren't bothering me tonight. It was Monday night, and my mind raced with thoughts of Charli and seeing her at tomorrow's meeting. She was pretty much all I thought about since the meeting on Thursday. It was insane how I could spend so much time thinking about a person I hardly knew anything about. I laughed to myself.

"She likes things flavored pineapple," I said out loud.

"Pineapple." I almost jumped out of my skin. Monica, one of the residents, was standing in the doorway in gray sweatpants and an oversized, faded white Houston Rodeo T-shirt that seemed to swallow her whole.

"Monica, you scared me; what are you doing up? It's 2 am."

"Tie my shoe," she responded. I looked down at her feet. She had on white socks with a red stripe across the toes. Every morning, when she got up and dressed for the day, she'd ask me to tie her shoes before heading to the activity shop.

"Monica, sweetie, you don't have any shoes on," I said. I turned the iron off and set it upright on the ironing board. "Let's get you back in bed."

I held out my arm to her. She wrapped her arm around mine and fell in step as I walked her back to her room. I could hear her roommate snoring from the hallway.

"Oh, that's why you couldn't sleep," I said as we entered

the room. Monica climbed in her bed as I picked her comforter up off the floor and covered her with it.

"You all tucked in?" I asked her.

"Pineapple," she responded. I smiled way too hard at such a simple word.

"Yes, pineapple." I gently shook her roommate until she stopped snoring. "Good night, Monica." I left her room and headed back to my ironing board.

"Pineapples," I thought as I picked up the next pair of jeans to iron. The pile finally looked like it was getting smaller.

Charli

The smell of dust and a strange copper-like smell brought me back. I sneezed, and pain ran through my whole body. Tears streamed down my cheeks, and I winced as I sat up to look at my surroundings. I was on the floor in the shed. I brought my hand up to wipe my eyes, which burned from the dust. The shed was empty and dark except for a lamp on a table in the corner with no shade. I wondered how long I'd been on the floor by myself when that weird copper smell filled my nose again.

I looked down. There was a grease-stained blue towel spread across my bottom half. I watched as a red stain on the towel grew. I lifted the towel up. My legs and the ground were covered in a mixture of blood and dirt.

"Don't throw up; please don't throw up." A wave of nausea swept over me. I really didn't need to make more of a mess.

I rolled over on my side, braced myself with my hands, and attempted to stand up. Pain ran through my body, and dizziness swept over me. I rolled back over on my back; my heart was racing, and sweat was pouring from my head.

"This is bad," I thought. "I have to get up."

I took a deep breath, rolled over, and pushed myself up on all fours. I stopped to catch my breath. Then, I pushed myself up into a standing position. I stood panting, looking for something to lean on to steady myself. The closest thing to me was that old black car, and I dared not lean on that. I took another deep breath and reached down to pick up the towel that covered me. I began to wipe the blood and dirt from my thighs. I looked around and saw my jeans in a ball about five feet away. I took one step in the direction of my jeans, and the pain hit with such force I knew I was going to throw up, but again, I didn't. I slowly limped over to my jeans. I saw fresh blood running down my thighs as I put them on. I used the dirty towel to wipe the blood away, pulled my jeans up, fastened them, and began limping towards the door and up to the house.

The cool air welcomed my sweat-drenched body as soon as I stepped out of the shed.

The house seemed so far away. I just wanted to lie down and cry.

Sixty-seven steps to the house. Four stairs onto the porch. I could do that. I started towards the house, moving slowly. I glanced down and saw the blood spreading on my jeans. 7…8…9…10…

Kindra

I couldn't seem to keep my hands still. I was all types of fidgety today. I wondered if Paige could tell.

"You OK?" she asked. I guess she could.

"Yes, I'm OK," I said and glanced at the clock. It was 12:30 pm. Tuesday. I had 30 more minutes of therapy and four and a half hours until group.

"What's on your mind?" Paige asked.

"Well," I said cautiously. I shared everything with Paige, but I wasn't sure if I was ready to share this...Charli...with her. I wasn't even sure what "This" was. There was so much I didn't know.

"I'm just excited about group tonight," I said. It wasn't a lie.

"Really?" she asked in surprise. "I've heard you look *forward* to group--amongst other things--but I have never heard you use the word 'excited.' So what's going on in group?"

Crap.

"Uhm, there is a new member, and I'm looking forward to seeing how she is doing," I said without making eye contact. She wasn't going to get any more information from me. I had already said too much. For some reason, I wasn't quite ready to share Charli yet or tell anyone about her. I know how people responded to me and my trauma in the past, and I didn't want that for her.

"I haven't had any nightmares in a few days," I said to her in hopes of throwing her attention off of Charli.

"No nightmares is good...really good," she said. I smiled,

beaming from ear to ear. I hadn't realized I hadn't been having nightmares. I'd been so preoccupied with thoughts of Charli. Paige eyed me suspiciously.

"Something is going on with you, girl; it's written all over you," she said. I froze.

"But if it's stopping the nightmares, has you happy, and isn't doing you any harm, then I won't pester you about it. It isn't doing you any harm--is it?", she asked. I shook my head "No," very fast, and we both laughed.

"Well, OK," she said. "What else has been going on? Let's talk about fundraising for your service dog."

Charli

"Charli." I heard a voice from far away. I was trying so hard to pull myself out of this groggy place. The sun was so bright that I had to blink several times and shade my eyes with my hand to make out who was standing in front of me. It was Matt.

I looked around. I was sitting on the planter where we always had lunch. Kids were coming out of their classes. I vaguely remember showing up late to school and painfully walking to class. Everything after that was a blur.

"Are you OK, Charli?" Matt asked with a hint of panic in his voice. "Yeah, I'm just tired," I said.

"No, something is wrong," he said as he sat down next to me. "You're sweating really bad, and it's not that hot out, and there's black under your eyes. Tell me what happened," he demanded. I was so tired; why was he yelling at me?

"I'm fine. Can I please have my lunch?" I said. I closed my eyes as he rustled through his backpack. I heard him set a bag down by me. I opened my eyes and picked up the bag. Matt kept glancing up at me. I must look really bad. I reached into the bag and pulled out my sandwich. It was turkey. I couldn't remember when I'd eaten last, but I didn't feel very hungry now. I nibbled on the sandwich and tried to avoid Matt's eyes.

"You aren't even eating; you always eat," Matt said, his panic turning to anger. "What did they do to you?" he yelled. I saw people staring over at us.

"Matt, please," I cried, looking around. He looked around, too, and when he saw people staring at us, he calmed down. He sighed, and his shoulders fell. I set the sandwich down. I didn't have the strength to pretend to eat anymore. His eyes were red with tears that hadn't fallen yet.

"You can't ask me to be your friend and then just sit by and let them hurt you," he said, sniffling.

"Can you just be my friend?" I asked. A large lump formed in my throat from watching him get choked up.

"Could you just sit by knowing someone was hurting me? Would you be ok with that?" he asked me.

"No one would hurt you, Matt; you don't deserve that." "Neither do you," he snapped. "You know that, right, Charli?"

Tears filled my eyes. I just stared at him. Of course, I deserved it. I didn't know why I did, but this was how my life had been for as long as I could remember. Maybe I was a bad baby or something. I never thought about why I deserved it; I just knew I did and tried to make the best of the situations I ended up in.

My stomach started to turn, and my mouth filled with spit.

"You okay, Charli? You really don't look so good." Matt said. I was taking deep breaths, trying to calm myself and my stomach.

"I'm not feeling so great, but I'll be OK," I said between breaths. I couldn't fake it anymore.

"We should get the nurse," Matt said.

"No, I don't need the nurse; just give me a minute," I said, struggling to stand up. As soon as I was on my feet, I collapsed. I saw the ground coming up at me fast, and then Matt's arms caught me.

"Charli, are you OK? *Charli*?!" He said in a panic.

Before I could even try to respond, Matt said, "Crap, Charli, you are burning up; you're so hot. I'm getting the nurse." He gently helped me sit back down on the planter.

“Matt,” I said, my voice barely above a whisper as he walked away. He turned around.

“Please don’t tell,” I begged him, tears streaming down my cheeks. He knew what I was asking. I watched his face go from concern to anger to sadness.

“I won’t say anything” was the last thing I heard him say before darkness took over.

“I’m just going to sleep for a second,” I thought. “I will wake up when the nurse gets here.”

Kindra

A tear rolled down my cheek. I wiped it away with the sleeve of my sweater.

"Stop being so dramatic," I told myself. I looked at my watch. It was 6:15 pm. I had been sitting on the curb for a little over an hour, and she still hadn't shown up.

I looked down at the two sodas and two bags of chips. Feeling defeated, I opened one bag and began eating the Cheeto puffs. I thought I heard footsteps, and I quickly looked up.

It was nothing…again. My imagination, I supposed. At least earlier, there were actually footsteps. Granted, they belonged to other girls showing up for group. I quickly glanced up again, thinking I'd heard something, but the sidewalk was still empty. Another tear slipped out and slowly made its way down my cheek. I didn't bother wiping this one away. I remember Paige saying it's important to be honest with yourself and feel what you are feeling, and right now, I was feeling sad. With that realization came many more tears. What could have happened to her? Did I read the whole situation wrong? Perhaps she didn't need me; maybe she didn't need anything. Did I throw myself wholeheartedly into this for nothing? She couldn't just be gone…could she? Could that just be it?

A floodgate of tears broke through. I was full-on crying, shoulders heaving, nose snotting. But why? If I was being truthful, I didn't manage my emotions well. Paige said it was part of my PTSD, and I also felt like I had lost a friend. Which was completely crazy--she was a child and one that I barely knew. I finally wiped my tears with my sweater sleeve again and began to gather the bags of chips and unopened sodas. I wouldn't miss another group session wasting hope on a fantasy.

I dumped the snacks on the passenger side seat. I glanced at the sidewalk one more time, desperately hoping to see her walking down the sidewalk, hands shoved in her pockets, staring at her shoes, but she wasn't there. I took a deep breath and got in on my side of the car. I sat there thinking. Was I truly giving up on her? Was this really it? Was it worth the heartache? I'd had one conversation with her. Was I doing too much too fast? How had she so firmly planted herself in my life and heart so quickly? I was grasping at straws.

Then I remembered all the times people had given up on me, pushed me to the side, and didn't believe me about the rape. How I'd cried at night and begged God to not let me go through it alone anymore. The pain of that memory, that loneliness, gripped me so unexpectedly. I didn't know why she hadn't shown up, but I wasn't ready to give up on her yet. I couldn't let her potentially go through what I'd been through. It had almost killed me. If I experienced more heartache waiting for her, it would be worth the sacrifice. I'd deal with the pain. The way I wished someone had done for me. Yes--I would be on that curb on Thursday waiting for her. I buckled my seatbelt, started the car, and drove off.

Charli

Something was off. I had never been to the nurse's office at this school, but the smell was familiar...too familiar. It smelled like...my eyes shot open.

I was looking at the bunk above me. I was in my room. How did I get here? What happened? What had Matt told?

Valerie sat on the floor, playing with a doll. She must have heard me move because she looked up at me, smiled, and said, "Charli!!! You're awake!"

"Yep, I am," I replied to her as I stretched and tried to remember.

"You were asleep for a VERY long time, but I've been watching you and taking care of you. Me and my doll are doctors, like Doc Mcstuffins," she said with a grin. I looked up at the window, and the sun was out, so I must have slept maybe a few hours. The house was strangely quiet, though; with a house full of foster kids, it was rarely this quiet.

"Hey Val, where is everybody?" I asked her.

"At school," she said, never looking up from her doll.

"At school?" I repeated. I looked at the window again--the sun was out. I'd only been asleep for a few hours; the other kids should be home by now.

"You didn't go to school with everybody because you're sick. Dad said you have the flu, and I'm supposed to watch you," Valerie informed me.

The flu? "No, Val, I went to school today..." I stopped. "Valerie, how long have I been asleep? How long have you been watching me?"

She seemed to think hard. "Since Tuesday," she said. "Val, what day is it?" I asked her.

"Thursday," she said.

"THURSDAY!" I yelled and sat up way too fast. I was very dizzy.

"Yes, Thursday," she said, startled by my yelling and sitting up. "Dad said to watch you and tell him as soon as you wake up." She paused, then she looked at me and said, "I will be right back."

She then ran out of the room screaming, "Dad, Charli is awake." I swung my legs over the side of the bed. I was trying so hard to remember. Matt had gone to get the nurse, but after that it was all blank. I didn't feel sick anymore, just a little dizzy. I looked down; I had on a diaper. Who put that on me? I got up and slowly walked to the bathroom to clean myself up.

I came back just in time to see Valerie put a tray of food on my bed. She turned when I walked in.

"You need to eat; Daddy says eat," she said to me while pointing at the tray. No one had made food for me like this since I'd moved here, and they definitely didn't bring it to my room. I walked over to the bed.

"Mommy made it," Valerie said with a big grin.

"Mommy?" I thought to myself. The woman of the house who hardly ever came out of her room had cooked?

There was a big bowl of soup with steam coming off of it, a grilled cheese sandwich, and a big cup of orange juice. I sat down on the bed and sampled the soup. Chicken noodle, and it was so good. I could feel my stomach warm up with each bite. I dipped the grilled cheese sandwich in the soup. I thought back to the last home I'd stayed in where they'd actually cooked meals, and I'd felt safe and loved. I thought of the "Mom" in that home…Inissa. I never minded calling her Mom. She always cooked my favorite food. I remember her laughing when she found out I loved broccoli; she said, "No child loves broccoli; you are a special one, Charli Lauren.

Tomorrow, I will introduce you to pineapples."

I'd never had pineapples before her. I felt myself getting lost in the memory of her, and a lump started to form in my throat. I tried to swallow it down with the orange juice. It was cold and refreshing. I couldn't think about Mom Inissa right now. I had to focus and figure out how much trouble I was in and what my next move needed to be. I didn't think I could be in huge trouble, since they'd given me a hot meal and I was still at the house. I stopped eating and thought for a moment.

"Valerie," I said. "Has my social worker been to the house?" She looked up with fear in her eyes.

"No," she said and jumped onto my bed. The soup sloshed over the side of the bowl and onto the tray from the sudden movement. She climbed into my arms and looked up at me with tears in her eyes.

"You aren't leaving, are you, Charli? Please don't leave me," she said as the tears poured out of her eyes. "I will take better care of you, me and my dolly will. Please don't leave," she begged, now sobbing. She always took it the hardest when someone left. I think it was because she was the youngest or maybe because her parents abandoned her. They were druggies, and they just left her in their apartment one day when she was four years old and never came back. I had heard they had a hard time getting her to leave the apartment because her parents had told her they were coming back, and she was scared they wouldn't find her if she wasn't there. Since then, anytime someone would get moved, she would break down.

I wrapped my arms around her. I didn't want to lie to her; any of us could get moved at any time.

"Hey, it's OK," I said while squeezing her in my arms. "I don't think I'm going anywhere; I just asked because I've been so sick, and I thought maybe my social worker came by to check on me."

I handed her my cup of orange juice. She looked up at me like she wasn't sure she believed me. She sipped the orange juice and said, "The social worker doesn't come for the flu, silly."

She set the glass on the tray and climbed back on the floor to continue playing. Maybe it wasn't as bad as I thought. I went back to eating my food, which had cooled a bit but was still good. A few minutes later, Mack walked into the room. My whole body tensed up, and I started breathing rapidly. He rubbed his hand across Valerie's head in a playful manner, messing her hair up. She looked up at him and smiled. My stomach turned. He sat down on the edge of my bed. I couldn't move. I wanted to scream.

"Looks like you're feeling better," he said while running his hands up and down the thighs of his jeans. "You gave us quite a scare there. The school nurse called and said you'd passed out, and one of your classmates ran to get help," he said, not looking at me. Matt hadn't said anything after all. "Thank you, thank you, thank you, Matt," I silently said to myself.

I didn't say anything; I just let Mack keep talking. "When we got to the school, we could see…uhhh…that you uhhh…" he rubbed his hands together like he was attempting to find the words. He looked down at Valerie. "That you had the flu. Valerie, can you take Charli's tray into the kitchen, please?"

Valerie got up, picked up the tray, and headed out of the room. Mack waited until she was out of earshot and continued. “So, uh--we saw you were bleeding when we picked you up; the nurse said it was most likely your period…you got a period yet?” he asked, still refusing to look at me.

“No,” I responded quietly.

“You know what one is?” he asked, looking up at the ceiling fan. I didn’t answer immediately. A single tear slipped down my cheek as I thought about Mom Inissa and her teaching me about a period over hot chocolate. One of the girls in the house had gotten hers, and Mom Inissa thought it would be a good teaching moment for all of the girls in the house. I pushed her to the back of my mind and quickly wiped the tear away, glad Mack wasn’t looking at me.

“Yes, I know what a period is,” I said, voice a little stronger.

“Oh, OK,” Mack said. He seemed a little surprised. “Well, are you still bleeding?” he asked, staring anywhere but at me.

I thought back to taking the diaper off and seeing just a small amount of old, dried blood before I cleaned myself up and put my panties on.

“No,” I said to him, speaking quietly again.

“Maybe I should have lied and said I am,” I thought to myself.

“Guess we need to lay off of you for a few weeks, huh?” he said and slapped my leg. He then stood up. “You don’t have to go to school tomorrow since it’s Friday, but you’re going back Monday. And there’s a big ol’ pot of soup in there; eat as much as you want, but don’t share with the other kids—that ain’t their dinner.”

I just lay there looking at him. He seemed to be uncomfortable with that. He ran his hands through his hair and said quickly, "Why don't you go out and get some fresh air—might make you feel better."

Then he rushed out of the room. I waited a few minutes to be sure he wasn't coming back. I stood up and walked around the room. No dizzy spells. I think the food gave me some strength back. I was still a bit sore when I walked, but for the most part, I felt better.

I walked into the kitchen and fixed myself another bowl of soup. Who knew how long they would feed me like this? I was going to eat as much as I could. I looked at the clock on the microwave. It said 1:45.

"Hmmm… 1:45 on Thursday," I thought to myself. I knew exactly where I wanted to go today. I just hoped she'd be there.

Kindra

I sat on the curb with two pineapple sodas and two bags of Cheetos…again. At this point, I felt a little silly; she hadn't shown up to the last meeting at all. But she had to come today. So I sat--like I had done Tuesday. Girls walked by and asked if everything was OK, then asked if I was coming in.

What could I say? "I can't come in because this girl with dirty blond hair might need me."

It sounded completely crazy.

Instead, I just said, "Yeah, I'm OK," and, "I may come in a little later," then completely ignored the strange glances I got when they noticed the two sodas and two bags of chips.

So there I waited, silently praying, running my thumb up and down the side of the Fanta pineapple soda bottle. Hoping, praying, wishing that when I looked up--oh my goodness! There she was!

She walked down the sidewalk towards me, staring down at her shoes, hands shoved in her pockets. My heart jumped at the sight of her--precious Charli. Then I noticed just a hint of a limp in her walk. Had she gotten hurt at school or practice? What school did she go to? Did she play a sport?

I began to panic. What should I say? How would I help her? What if she didn't want my help? A hundred thoughts raced through my head. I looked up just in time to see her standing over me, looking unsure of herself.

"Say SOMETHING," I yelled to myself in my mind. I watched my arm hold up the pineapple soda and heard my voice say, "Hey, Kiddo, do you want a drink?"

"Kiddo," I thought to myself, "Did I really just say kiddo?" But she smiled down at me and reached for the soda.

Charli

I loved that she called me kiddo, but I had no idea why. It was just a word; it didn't really mean anything. Did it?

A lady walked up; she spoke to Kindra and smiled politely at me.

"Kindra, are you coming in?" the lady asked. "We really missed you at the last meeting."

Kindra looked at me, and I looked away. She was going to go into that building, and what was even worse was that she was going to try to make me go, too.

My chest tightened; I wanted to get up and run. Then Kindra said, "I'm going to stay out here for a while." She put her hand over mine and said, "I might come in later or maybe see you guys next week."

"OK," the lady said and walked off. I sat there in shock. She had decided to stay out here and miss her meeting--when people were looking for her, asking for her--just to stay with me. I slowly pulled my hand away from hers.

"Do you want me to leave?" I asked her. "If so, it won't hurt my feelings; I think it's a good thing if I go," I said, then started to get up. She grabbed my hand.

"Charli, please don't go," she said.

"But those people in there are looking for you; they need you," I said. She turned and looked at the building.

"Nah," she said. "I'd rather be out here with you; you're much cooler." She grinned. "I'm not cool at all," I said with a sigh.

"Most adults kind of suck," she said. I laughed; I'd never heard an adult talk like that before.

"Most kids suck," I said and paused. "Most everyone sucks," I said with a giggle, and Kindra giggled too.

"Tell you a secret," Kindra said to me in a whisper. "Adults are just kids that grew taller; they act exactly the same."

I thought about that for a second and opened the cap on the soda she'd given me. "Pretty much, but adults think they know more," I said, putting the soda bottle to my lips.

"Yep," I heard Kindra say as I took two big gulps, and a blast of flavor hit my mouth. It was easily one of the best things I'd ever tasted.

"Oh, you like that," Kindra said with a laugh. "Duly noted. So, what do you do for fun, Charli?" she asked me. I paused for a moment. No one but Matt ever asked me about myself.

What did I like to do? There had only been rare occasions where I'd been in a home where I got to do things I liked. So I thought about those homes and happier times, and I said, "I like to play volleyball and dance and swim and draw and paint and read."

"Well, aren't you the handful? I bet you keep your parents busy with all those activities," Kindra said.

I looked away from her and responded, "My parents are just foster parents; I'm pretty much on my own."

"Oh my God, I can't believe I just told her that. Why would I say that to her?" I knew better than to tell my secrets. People would start to ask questions and questions led to problems that people wanted to fix but would only make worse. They couldn't know what went on in that house. Kindra couldn't know.

I glanced over at her. She looked like she had no idea what

to say, so I changed the subject. “That lady said you missed group on Tuesday; why did you miss?” I asked her.

“Oh, uhm. I was here waiting for you,” she said.

I felt my eyes go wide with shock. “Me? You didn’t go to your group because you were waiting for me?” I asked her.

“Well…yeah,” she replied with a confused look. “I told you I would be here.” I just sat there, completely surprised.

“But--you gave up something that’s important to you…for me?” I asked. Kindra didn’t immediately answer, she sat kind of wringing her hands in her lap then she looked up at me and said, “Charli…can I ask you some questions and you try really hard not to run away?”

“Don’t run away,” I thought to myself. When things got bad I ran; that was just what I did. I looked down at the pineapple soda (one of the best things I’d ever tasted), then I thought about Kindra sitting out here by herself missing her whole meeting because she was waiting for me, then I remembered I'd decided to do everything in my power to stay, which meant no running.

“OK,” I said to her. “I won’t run.”

Kindra

I beamed. She agreed not to run away, and a little bit of weight had lifted. I could possibly get to know her better now.

I opened my mouth to ask her a question and abruptly closed it. I couldn't think of a single question to ask. I knew nothing about her and had no idea where to start. I didn't want to immediately bring up bad stuff.

"Let's see," I thought to myself. "She lives with foster parents; I believe someone has hurt her in some way; she likes volleyball."

Seconds were ticking by as I desperately searched for something to say.

"Do you know how to make chicken noodle soup?" her voice sliced through my thoughts.

"Well…I can warm up a mean can of it," I said, slightly embarrassed.

Damn it--why didn't I know how to make chicken noodle soup? Why hadn't my mother taught me? Wait, did my mother even know how to make chicken noodle soup? I looked up to see Charli laughing.

"I had some chicken noodle soup today, and it was really good," she said.

"Well, are you going to have some more of it when you get back home?" I asked, glad she was currently steering the conversation.

"I don't know; probably not," she said.

"Why not?" I asked. She paused for a second.

"Lots of kids in the house, so there may not be any left when I get back." Something didn't seem quite right about her answer or the way she was staring at her feet, but I couldn't put my finger on it, so I left it alone. I looked down at her shoes and saw a hole in the big toe of her left shoe.

"Hey, Kiddo, you have a hole in your shoe."

As soon as the words were out of my mouth, I felt stupid. I'm sure she knew she had a hole in her shoe, Captain Obvious. She just responded, "Yeah."

"Are you going to get another pair?" I asked. Another stupid question.

"I don't know," she said. "I don't get new stuff; mostly just hand-me-downs, and it's hard finding shoes that fit good in the hand-me-down stuff. Foster kid problems," she said and shrugged.

"What size shoe do you wear?" I asked her. She slid one shoe off and looked inside. "This says women's 5 ½," she said and slid the shoe back on.

"Is it comfortable?" I asked her.

"Comfortable?" she questioned me back, and I could see her wiggling her feet around in her shoes.

"Yeah, like, are they too tight or too loose? Are your toes curled up in the front of the shoes, or is there space so your feet are sliding?" I asked her.

"Oh. My feet slide a little bit, and my toes don't really reach the front of the shoes, but that's OK," she said. I made a mental note she most likely wore a women's size 5 not a 5 ½. We sat in silence. I watched her finish off her soda, but she hadn't touched her chips. Guess the chicken noodle soup had really filled her up. I handed her my unopened soda. She looked down at it and politely said, "No, that's yours; I drank mine. But thank you."

Someone somewhere had taught her manners.

"That's OK; I could stand to lay off the sugar. You go ahead." "Are you sure?" she asked.

"Yeah, I'm sure," I said and handed it to her. She smiled from ear to ear. I'd buy her all the pineapple sodas in the world if it kept that exact smile on her face.

"What's your favorite song?" I asked her. I felt like you could learn a lot about a person by the songs they liked. Music was a major part of my life, but the rape made it feel unsafe. I was slowly finding my way back to it. She took a swallow of the soda and burped, then giggled.

"Excuse me," she said. I laughed with her. It had been such a long time since I'd had such a carefree conversation, a carefree moment, and here I was having it with a 12-year-old. What would Paige say?

"Same Love by Macklemore," Charli said. I racked my brain. I hadn't heard of that one. I would have to look it up.

"What's your favorite song?" she asked me. "Well…" I said and paused, then laughed at myself. "I don't know, Kiddo; I like different songs at different points in my life for different reasons. Let me think about it, and I will get back to you on that…When will I see you again?"

"Oh…uhm," Charli said, face full of concern. It seemed as if she were carefully choosing her next words. "I plan on being here Tuesday," she said finally.

"Okay," I said. "I plan on being here too."

Charli

"Thank you so much, Matt," I said.

"You're welcome--for like the hundredth time," he said. "I'm just glad you're ok and feeling better."

"Yep," I said back to him. "Feeling much better," I said with a mouth full of Cheez-It crackers.

"I can tell; you ate all of your lunch and half of mine," he said, holding his empty lunch bag upside down. I smiled.

"Sorry," I said, handing him the half-eaten bag of Cheez-Itz that had come from his lunch. "No, you eat them, it's OK," he said.

"I've just been so hungry since I…well, since I woke up," I said.

"I still can't believe you slept for two whole days. I guess I'd be hungry too," he said, laughing.

"It didn't even feel like two days," I said.

"You were really sick, Charli," he said with a very serious look on his face. I didn't like the direction this conversation was going, plus there was something I'd been wanting to talk to him about. I guess now was as good a time as any.

"Matt, I need to tell you something," I said to him. He looked up from his backpack straight into my eyes and said, "OK." I hesitated.

"I went…well, I've been going to the women's center," I said. His face lit up.

"You have? Are they helping!? Are they going to help

you?" he said, full of energy. "Well... I don't know. I've been talking to this lady," I said, trying to figure out how to explain this.

"Oh, is she a counselor or like a caseworker or something?" he asked.

"No...well I don't think so...I mean...I haven't gone in yet," I said to him. He looked so confused. I suddenly realized I had not thought this through at all.

"What do you mean you haven't gone in yet?" he asked. "If you haven't gone in, then who are you talking to?" he continued. He opened his mouth to ask another question.

"Matt," I said, abruptly stopping him. "Too many questions; give me a second to try to explain."

"Too many questions?" he said, starting to sound angry. "Charli. What is--"

"MATT." I cut him off again. "Let me talk." He opened his mouth to say something but then closed it and stared at me. I guess it was my turn.

"OK. I had gone to the place a few times, but I never went in... I was scared," I said. "But Charli, they..." he quickly started.

"Please," I said to him, and again he stopped talking. "It's not easy to just walk into a place full of strangers and tell them what's going on. Plus, it could make things a lot worse," I went on.

"How could it get worse with...?" he started again.

"MATTHEW!" I snapped at him. I'd never used his full name before, but I'd seen adults do it to get a kid's attention. He stopped talking and glared at me. Maybe the whole name wasn't a good idea. Then his whole face broke into a smile, and he started laughing.

"Holy crap, Charli, you sounded just like my mom," he said, still laughing. Now I was laughing too. At least the mood lightened.

"OK, tell me about the lady," he said after a deep breath in a more serious tone. I sat up straight, set the now empty bag of Cheez-Itz to the side, and began talking.

"Her name is Kindra. I'm not sure if she's a counselor, but when the other women walk by, they talk to her like she's kinda important. So the first couple of times I went, I chickened out and left, never made it through the parking lot. I told you about that. But then I saw her. She was watching me like she wanted to talk to me." I got quiet at the end. Matt sighed heavily.

"And then?" he asked. I rubbed my hands together.

"Well, we started talking a little bit, not about *that*, but just talking, and she seems OK, Matt, she seems nice," I said.

"But you don't know anything about her," he said.

"She's not like that, and I do know her a little bit: she can't cook chicken noodle soup, she drives a black Honda Civic, and someone hurt her too."

"Still. She could be dangerous, Charli," he said back angrily.

"SHE BOUGHT ME A PINEAPPLE SODA!" I yelled at him and regretted it as soon as it was out of my mouth. He didn't know what that meant. I barely knew what it meant.

"I'm just trying to look out for you, Charli," he said.

"Well, maybe you shouldn't," I shot back at him. I hoped he knew I didn't mean it. "I'm the only one looking out for you," he said with hurt in his voice.

"Maybe she can look out for me too," I said. "I'm sorry, Matt,

I didn't mean what I said." I was looking at him with unshed tears in my eyes.

"I know you didn't, Charli. You can't get rid of me, 'cause then who would feed you?" he said with a smile, holding up an empty lunch bag. I laughed as one tear rolled down my cheek.

"Just promise me you *will* be careful, OK?" he said.

"I will," I replied.

"I don't know what I would do if something worse happened to you," he said. I threw my arms around him in a hug. He hugged me back, and everything was good in the world--at least for the moment.

Kindra

Oh how I loved my nights off. I had spent the day running errands. I'd driven into Houston earlier in the day to see my mom and spend some time with her, and now I was relaxing in the safety of my apartment. I sat on my couch Indian style with my laptop on my legs. I had just finished responding to an email from Little Angels Service Dogs, the organization I was going through to get my service dog. The email they sent me said that someone made a very sizable donation to the organization and that $500 had been put towards my fundraising, which was amazing and put my current total at $815...out of the $10,000 that needed to be raised in order for me to get a fully trained service dog.

I responded to the email with great enthusiasm and gratitude. I mean, I was obviously excited about the donation, but at this point, raising $10,000 seemed nearly impossible. Feeling a bit defeated, I surfed the Little Angels Service Dogs web page. I loved looking at all the pictures of the beautiful labs in training, working with their handlers, performing tasks to make everyday life easier for people like me. They had dogs trained for all types of things; for people with PTSD like me, the dog would wake me up from nightmares, alert me to oncoming panic attacks, and more. Service dogs can alert children of fluctuations in sugar levels due to diabetes or even prepare for oncoming seizures so people can get to a safe location before the seizure starts--these dogs could be trained to do all types of amazing things.

With the way fundraising was going, it didn't seem likely I would ever get one. Paige was very supportive of it and even wrote a letter to the organization on my behalf, stating why I would greatly benefit from a service dog. I could come up with some great fundraising ideas, but I always came back to the same two problems. First, my anxiety made it a serious struggle to ask for funds. And second, very few people wanted to support survivors of rape and sexual assault. Ask for support for a child with a seizure disorder--that quickly and easily gets support. But mention rape, and people shut down quickly. Instead of talking about the fundraiser, they want to know how much I had had to drink. What was I wearing? And did I somehow lead him on?

After engaging in debates and trying to convince people I wasn't the cause of my own rape, I didn't really have the strength or the courage to speak about fundraisers. Not to mention, those awful conversations usually sent me into an emotional spiral of despair that took days to recover from. It was too much to think about, and it was starting to depress me.

I closed the web page and started trying to think of something that might cheer me up. I pictured Charli's smile when I had given her that second pineapple soda. What was the name of the song she said was her favorite? I knew I had a bad memory, so why hadn't I written it down? I began to get frustrated with myself, and my breathing sped up.

"NO," I said to myself. "We will not go into a panic attack right now. We will control our emotions."

I glanced around the room for something to focus on other than my increasingly sweaty palms. My eyes stopped on the table in the dining area where a Footlocker bag sat. My breathing calmed down a bit. I had toughed out my anxiety and even had fun shopping for the perfect pair of tennis shoes and getting on the employees' nerves with my questions.

"Do you think a 12-year-old girl will like these shoes? What about these?" I picked up pair after pair and finally decided on a pair of white Nike Air Max. I was told they were popular with the kids. Size 5 in women's. No more staring at the hole in her shoe, no more hand-me-down shoes. I couldn't really afford them, but it was worth it.

I breathed in deeply and counted backward from 10. Paige would be proud.

Then, just like she was in the room, I heard Charli's small voice say, "Same Love by Macklemore." I wrote down the name of the song so I wouldn't forget again and grabbed my laptop to pull it up on YouTube with the lyrics.

The song had played over half way through when I paused it and sat stunned. The song was about gay love and marriage but it was written and sung in such a way that was just so much more. What a beautiful and very deep song for a 12-year-old to consider her favorite. I started the song over, set the laptop on the floor, and laid back on the couch. I closed my eyes and absorbed the song. I couldn't help but wonder what had brought Charli to this song and why she loved it so much. I had always felt that for a song to be a person's favorite, it had to connect with them on a personal level. Well, it was a topic that we could discuss, maybe.

I got up and hummed the song as I moved around my apartment, straightening things up.

I took the receipt out of the Footlocker bag and put it in a drawer in the kitchen on the off-chance the shoes didn't fit. I started unloading the dishwasher and let my mind drift.

What was my favorite song? Currently, most of the songs I listened to were about pain because that's what I related to lately. That realization made me sad. Was I a sad person? I didn't feel like I could honestly answer that question. I put the last dish away, turned the light off in the kitchen, grabbed a journal off of the bar, and went back into the living room. I lay across the floor next to the laptop and opened the journal. I rarely wrote in the thing, but sometimes it helped. I opened Windows Media Player and my most frequently-played songs and played the first song. A small child's voice came over the speaker.

It was "Only Human" by Joe Budden. I knew the song forwards and backwards. I started writing the lyrics in my journal as the song played. The song paused a few minutes in and switched to a commercial, just as tears dropped onto the page, blurring the last few words I'd written. I hadn't even realized I was crying.

It was one thing to listen to the words, but writing them and having them come from my hand made me connect with them so much more. Paige always said writing really helped bring out your emotions. I had never really listened to her about writing before, but I guess she was right. I began to wipe my eyes when I heard my cell phone ring.

Dad. I contemplated not answering, but I hadn't talked to him since yesterday, and if he couldn't contact me, then he would call my mother, who would then call the FBI, and I didn't need that headache tonight. I quickly wiped the last of my tears on my shirt sleeve, took a deep breath, and answered the phone.

"Hey, Daddy," I said, trying to sound more cheerful than I felt. "Baby girl, what are you up to on your night off?" he asked. "Nothing. Just relaxing," I answered.

"What's wrong?" Man, he knew me well.

"Nothing, Daddy, just tired," I answered with a yawn, hoping to sound believable. "Your voice sounds funny. You sure you're just tired?" he asked. I smiled…a true smile. "Just tired, Pop," I said.

Charli

"Charlotte Lauren."

I looked up from the book I was reading to see a student standing next to my English teacher with a hall pass.

"Charli, the nurse would like to see you," my teacher said. My chest tightened. What could the nurse want? Had Matt said something after all? Would a case worker be waiting for me in the office? I slowly gathered my things and walked to the front of the class.

I grabbed the hall pass and followed the student out of class and into the hallway, making a mental note of the nearest exits. I calmed down a bit when I saw there was only one person in the nurse's office. I guessed it was the nurse. I wasn't really awake the last time I was here.

"Charlotte!" she exclaimed, very chipper. I weakly smiled at her.

"Come in and sit down," she told me. I walked in and sat in the chair next to her desk. I checked out my surroundings--some posters on the walls about the proper way to brush your teeth and wash your hands, a scale against a wall, two rooms with beds in them, and lots of containers with cotton swabs, wooden sticks, and band-aids. Only one way in or out.

"How are you feeling, Sweetie?" she asked. I looked at her for a moment; this felt like a set-up.

"I'm OK," I said cautiously. She was busy typing something on the computer, so she didn't look up when she said, "Well, that's good because you gave us quite a scare the other day. Your parents were very concerned--your father made it here in record time."

I sat quietly, not sure what to say. She continued, "So I just wanted to check in, make sure you are feeling better, and make sure everything's OK with you." She stopped typing and looked up at me.

"Is everything OK with you, Charlotte?" Time froze. I yelled to myself, "OK? No, everything is not OK."

I wanted to tell her everything. Could she help me? Could she keep me safe? I imagined her and a case worker taking me out of that house and to a home with my own room--a room painted purple, with stuffed animals on the bed and a soft blanket.

But thoughts like that were dangerous; I snapped back to the real world. They would put me in another house just like the one I was in or send me back to that "concerned father." A real home was a nice thought, but this was my reality. I put on my best smile and said, "Yes, I'm feeling much better. I'd just never had a period before." She must have bought it because she said something about becoming a woman and sent me to lunch.

The bell for lunch hadn't rung yet, so I sat in my normal spot and waited for Matt. It was a sunny Tuesday. The sun felt nice on my skin, and I felt relaxed. The nurse didn't know anything. I was really looking forward to seeing Kindra tonight. Could I say she was my friend?

Maybe not a *friend,* but she was something; she cared about me, and I could count the people who cared about me on one hand. Speaking of friends, I saw Matt finally walking towards me.

"You're early," he said, setting his backpack down.

"I got called to the nurse's office," I told him. He set my

lunch in front of me and sat down.

"What did the nurse want?" he asked with obvious curiosity in his voice. "Just to see if I was OK," I said. He looked away from me.

"What?" I asked him.

"You're not OK, Charli. None of this is OK; it's the farthest thing from OK. Why didn't you tell her so she could help you, so someone could help you?" he pleaded with me.

"Matt, I told you: telling people could…" I tried to say, but he cut me off:

"--make it worse, I've heard you say that a hundred times, but how could it be worse?

How could it be worse than it already is?" he asked.

I sighed. "It's not as easy as we tell adults, and they fix things--they don't. They may "investigate," but the fosters know how to say all the right things, and then they put you back in the house with fosters who are now mad because you almost got them in trouble, which gets you in more trouble. Or maybe they move you to another house where they abuse you worse, and the other kids beat you up and take your stuff. At least here, I know what I'm getting. I can deal with it. I just keep my head low. Plus, you're one of my only friends; if they move me, then I lose you, too."

"We could keep in touch," he said.

"When's the last time you talked to Elise?" I asked him, already knowing the answer. "Not since she left," he admitted. We sat in silence for a few moments and ate our lunches. "Is it really that bad…everywhere?"

"Most places, yeah. Every once in a while, you might run across a good home, but that doesn't happen often, so you don't get your hopes up," I told him sternly. I really wanted him to understand so we didn't have to talk about it anymore.

"I guess I get it," he said, "but I don't like it." He crossed his arms across his chest. "Me neither," I said. "You gonna eat that brownie?"

He shook his head, laughed, and handed me his brownie.

Kindra

I was in such a good mood before I came into therapy today, but then I walked in, and Paige said, "Let's talk relationships today." If we were talking about Daniel, that would have been fine but it was when she brought up my ex-husband, Jack, that I got anxious, angry, and sad all at the same time. We had discussed him a few times before. It never went well. Why today?

"I don't want to," I said firmly back to her. She wrote something down on her pad. "Don't write that down!" I wanted to yell.

"OK, let's take a couple deep breaths and try to relax again. You've completely tensed up. Unclench your fists," she said to me. I hadn't even realized my hands were fists. I opened them slowly, fingers sore from clenching them so tight. I took a few deep breaths to settle myself then I asked her, "Why do we have to talk about him?" I grabbed the pillow sitting on my lap and roughly threw it to the side of the couch.

"Because even the mention of him still elicits very strong negative emotions from you. We very rarely talk about him, the things he did, and the pain he caused. I think it's time to start unpacking some of those feelings so that hopefully you can move on from them."

What she said made perfect sense. I just didn't want to. However, Paige was the best therapist I'd ever had. She'd gotten me farther along than any others, and there had been quite a few. I'd decided a while ago to follow where she led me for my healing, even with hard topics. Especially the hard topics.

I sighed heavily. "OK," I said, already feeling deflated.

"Tell me about him," she said. I grabbed the discarded pillow and brought it back to my lap. This was going to be difficult. I grabbed the blanket, too.

"I met Jack two weeks after the rape. I was in Mississippi. My mother had wired me money so I could come to South Carolina, where she was living then, and start over. He was in line in front of me at the Wal-Mart money center. I asked him if he had a pen so I could fill out the money order paper. He didn't, but he struck up a very innocent conversation. So soon after the rape, though, I wanted no part of strangers, let alone strange men. Awkwardly enough, he wrote his email address on the back of a receipt and said, 'Why don't you email me sometime,' then left. I thought nothing of it, put the receipt in my pocket, and went on my way."

I stopped talking for a moment, thinking about how everyone had said the way we met was a sign that we were "supposed" to be together.

"You're doing well," Paige said, urging me on. I continued: "I left the next day driving` to South Carolina, starting my life over. A few days after I arrived, my mom had to leave on a business trip to Russia. She left me in a place where I knew no one and had no support system. I didn't even know where the grocery store was, and she left me. I was petrified to go out. I wanted to talk to someone, but I didn't want to talk at the same time. I especially didn't want to talk to someone who knew me--the people around me seemed to care the least about the

rape--but I remembered the guy at Wal-Mart. It seemed safe enough. So I emailed him, and we began emailing regularly, and over the next week, I poured everything out to him. It was two weeks before we even exchanged phone numbers. He was there during such a difficult time for me.

When my family wasn't, he was. It wasn't long before he started coming to visit me. He was safe and supportive; my mom loved him. Within six months, he had moved to South Carolina to be with me. About nine months after that, we were married."

I stopped again. I knew what was coming next. My heart hurt, and my pulse raced just thinking about it.

"Let's take a break for a moment," Paige said. She could see I was struggling. "Can I get you a bottle of water?"

"Yes, please," I responded. She got up and left the office. I took the moment alone to compose myself. "I can get through this," I told myself. I had nothing to be ashamed of; this was not my shame. I tried to convince myself, but it wasn't working well at all. Paige walked back in and handed me a cold bottle of water. I drank some and set the bottle on the floor by my feet.

"Are you ready to continue?" she asked.

"Yes. The relationship was a little bit rocky, but we got married anyway. A family emergency caused us to move to Florida, where my sister was, and we were doing OK at first, but then the nightmares began to come more frequently. I'd wake up fighting and screaming. The rape was happening over and over, and the nightmares seemed so real…so incredibly real." I stopped talking. My eyes filled with tears. I took deep breaths, trying not to cry. Not to let the tears flow. This was not my shame, I told myself again. Paige sat quietly, waiting for me to compose myself.

"One night," I continued, "I woke up from a nightmare. I wasn't fully awake, and he was on top of me…my husband was having sex with me while I was having a nightmare about being raped…I didn't want it. I didn't know what to do, so I pretended I was still asleep."

The dam broke, and the tears poured over. I sobbed as I tried to explain: “He was the only one I felt was there for me after the rape; I couldn’t lose my only support. I didn’t know how to go through it alone, so I let him. I pretended to still be asleep. I let him do it, I let him.”

I cried it out to Paige between sobs: “I let him.” I stopped talking and waited for the judgment to come down, waiting for Paige to confirm my fears that I’d LET it happen to me, that this time it really was my fault. It never came.

Instead, she rushed over to the couch with a box of tissues. “Kindra, that was not your fault,” she told me.

“I didn’t tell him no,” I said, still crying.

“But you didn’t tell him yes either,” Paige said, and her statement stopped me cold. I hadn’t said yes. I didn’t say no, but I didn’t say yes either. “You didn’t give him permission,” she went on. I thought about that. “Let’s take some deep breaths," she said.

I started breathing deeply, in rhythm with Paige and felt myself calming down. “How long did it go on?” Paige asked once she could tell I was calm.

“It happened a few more times that I awoke for. I don’t know how many times it happened before the first time I woke up. One night, I woke up from another nightmare with him on top of me. I couldn’t take it anymore, so I opened my eyes and just stared at him. When he saw I was awake, he scrambled off me and onto the floor; he sat in the corner, crying and apologizing. I didn’t say anything, and we never talked about it. He never did it again. A year after we were divorced, I was going through another really rough spell. I got in touch with him and asked him why he did it. He said he didn’t know and all he could say was that he was sorry. His apology meant nothing to me.”

"I'm really proud of you for getting through that. I know it was not easy to share, and I can see that you think it's your fault. This was not your fault, either. It sure does explain a lot, though. Kindra, you have one of the more severe cases of PTSD from rape that I have treated, but it's because you were retraumatized at the hands of your own husband. You already had trust issues stemming from the rape, trust issues from where your family failed you after the rape, and then the one person you thought you could trust and depend on violated you and that trust in the most horrendous way."

When she said it like that it really didn't sound like it was my fault. Maybe it wasn't?

"How did you and Daniel deal with the nightmares?" Paige asked. I smiled at that question.

"It was a bit difficult at first, but we figured it out together. When I am having a nightmare, he takes my hand and interlocks his fingers in mine."

I locked my fingers together, giving her an example. "Then he gets as close as he can to my ear and says in a very calm tone, 'It's Daniel, you're safe, I got you,' and he keeps saying it until I come out of it. It used to take a while to come out of it, but now it's like my mind recognizes him, and his voice and everything he is doing to wake me up is contrary to the horrific dream. He isn't yelling, he's holding my hand, he's telling me he's here, no matter what bad is going on, he's here."

"That's a really great tool you guys have come up with," Paige said. I smiled, proud of us. "How are you feeling?" she asked me.

"Tired," I responded truthfully. I was completely drained.

"Well, I think this is a good stopping point for the day. We ran a little over, but I didn't want to cut you off in the middle. We can pick up here next week," she said. My mind was barely listening after she said the words "ran over." I looked at the clock, and it was 4:20 pm.

"I'm late," I yelled and jumped up. In the middle of the session, I'd forgotten about everything, about group, about Charli. I still had to go by my place and pick up her shoes. I grabbed my purse and was yelling, "OK Paige, see you next week!" as I bolted out of the door.

Charli

I guess technically Kindra wasn't late, but she was usually here by now. I paced up and down the sidewalk in front of the women's center. Ladies were going into the building. I saw some of them glancing my way. What did they want? What were they thinking? Where was Kindra?

I shoved my hands in my pockets and looked down at my shoes. The hole over my big toe was getting bigger. Maybe I could put some tape over it. I would have to ask Matt if he had some duct tape. Another lady stared at me as she walked up to the building.

Why do we meet here anyway? I wonder if Kindra would be OK meeting somewhere else.

Unless she still wants me to go into that building. I sighed and looked up just in time to see Kindra's black Honda Civic whip into the parking lot. I laughed to myself. She thought she was late too.

She jumped out of the car and ran to the trunk, pulling out a bag with black and white stripes on it. Our eyes locked, and she smiled. I smiled too. She started walking towards me with the bag. I had the sudden urge to run up and hug her. I didn't, but the thought definitely crossed my mind. It was weird. I never really wanted to hug people; I didn't get many hugs. She walked up and paused. I think she wanted to hug me too, but she didn't. She sat down on the curb, and I sat next to her.

We sat quietly for a moment, neither one of us saying anything. I glanced over at her. "You're late," I said with a smile, and she just unloaded: "Oh my gosh, I know; I'm so sorry, Kiddo. I lost track of time in a really intense therapy session today, then I had to run home and pick up something I bought for you, and then I was racing here but they were doing construction, but it's Houston, they're always doing construction, right? Sheesh, sorry I'm late kiddo."

She had said all that so fast I had to pause when she stopped talking to process it all.

She called me Kiddo. I caught that. I tried to respond in the order of what I'd heard her say.

"You weren't really late, just later than you normally get here. It's not even 5:00 yet, I don't think," I said. She smiled at me and looked relieved. "You go to therapy?" I asked her. I think I caught her off guard because she looked surprised at the question.

"Oh, yes, I do," she replied.

"But isn't coming here like therapy?" I asked her, pointing at the women's center.

"It's therapeutic coming here because I get to talk with the other girls, but when I see my therapist, I can get deeper and talk about everything down to the nitty gritty, even the stuff I don't want other people to know about." She paused. A look of sadness came over her face for a split second, and then it was gone.

Kindra had things she didn't want people to know about too? I wondered what type of things. I looked up to her staring at me. I caught sight of the black and white bag and remembered she'd said she'd bought something for me. That made me feel strange. I wasn't used to people buying me things. I think she saw me looking at the bag because she got really excited, like she forgot it was there.

"Oh!" she yelled. "Yes, I bought this for you!" She put the bag in front of me and started talking really fast again.

"So I got these for you, and I hope you like them, but if you don't, we can get something else, and I'm pretty sure they are the right size…oh, just open it," she said, pushing the bag towards me. I opened the bag and pulled out a shoe box that said women's size 5 on the side of it. I opened the box, and I knew my eyes were as wide as saucers. I was looking down at the most beautiful tennis shoes I think I'd ever seen. They were so white it seemed like they lit up the box. I had seen kids at school with shoes like these, but these seemed better, brighter. Then it clicked. She bought these shoes for me.

"Oh no," I whispered to myself as tears began to run down my cheeks. I looked up at Kindra, and she had the biggest smile on her face until she saw my tears.

"Charli, what's wrong? If you don't like them we can get something else; we can exchange them. Please don't cry," she said. I closed the lid on the box and pushed the shoes toward her.

"I can't take these," I said quietly, not making eye contact.

"But why? I got them for you, it's OK," she said, her voice shaky.

"I just can't!" I snapped back at her and quickly got up to leave. I had taken two steps away from her when her voice came at me firm.

"Charli," she said. I stopped but didn't turn around. "You promised you wouldn't run." I could hear the tears in her voice. I turned around, ran back, got down next to her on the curb, put my arms around her, and cried. She put her arms around me, and she cried too, right into my hair. What a strange sight we must have been. I wasn't even sure why I was crying. The tears slowed and then stopped, but I didn't want her to stop hugging me. She lifted her head out of my hair but didn't move her arms from around me. She sighed.

"Charli, why can't you keep the shoes?" she asked. I didn't answer at first, wanting to soak up as much of her hug as I could. I finally let go and put a little space between us so I could talk. She seemed reluctant to let go. Scared I was going to run, I'm sure. I didn't want her to cry. Not because of me. I took a deep breath.

How could I explain this? She deserved my honesty. I wanted to be honest with her. So I was. "Foster homes aren't the greatest places, and you can't really have new or nice things

cause other kids will beat you up and take it from you." I knew there weren't kids like that in the home I was in right now. I needed to be honest without being too honest. I kept talking.

"And sometimes foster parents don't want you to have nice things either or they want to know where it came from, and it could cause trouble," I said, looking straight at her.

"Is that how your parents are?" she asked me slowly.

"Sometimes," I said back. "Kindra, these shoes are beautiful. I don't think I have ever had a pair of new shoes that I can remember, but I know these will get taken away from me and maybe get me in trouble. They are too pretty." I pushed the box in her direction again. Kindra looked sad.

"It's OK though! I was thinking before you got here that I could ask Matt for some duct tape to put over these, and they will be fine," I said, talking as fast as she was earlier.

"Matt?" she asked. Oh right. She didn't know Matt.

"He's my friend from school, my only friend...well, besides you," I said sheepishly. She smiled big and wrapped her arms around me again.

"Of course, I'm your friend," she said, and the whole mood lightened. I melted into her arms.

"OK," she said, letting go way too soon. "I will take the shoes back." She put the shoe box back in the bag and on the other side of her. She didn't seem sad or upset.

The sun had set and it would be getting dark soon. "I guess I gotta get going," I said to her. We both stood up.

"See you Thursday?" she asked me. "Do we have to meet here?"

She paused. "Uhm, I guess not. Where would you like to meet?" "There's a park not too far from the middle school," I said.

"Yeah, I know where that is. OK. I'll see you there Thursday," she said.

"OK," I said, and I just stood there with my hands shoved into my pockets. I guessed she sensed there was something else because she said, "Charli?"

"Can I have another hug," I blurted out.

"Oh! Of course," she said with a laugh and drew me into her arms. I wanted to remember this feeling, remember what she smelled like and how I felt in her arms. She held me for a moment and then let go. It was OK; I had soaked up as much of her as I needed.

"See you Thursday," I said and turned to walk away. My arms were swinging at my sides, and I didn't look down at my shoes. I didn't need to. I had a new pair of shoes--even if I couldn't keep them.

Kindra

I sat at my desk at work, tapping my pen on the side of the chair, deep in thought. It was a little after 2 am on Wednesday morning. So far, I'd gotten laundry done, cleaned the house, and had things ready for breakfast. I was pretty much done for the night except for room checks here and there. Normally, I'd be watching TV at this time, but tonight, I had so much on my mind. I'd met with Charli at the park earlier that day. She seemed so much calmer there. I had never realized how tense she was at the women's center.

She told me about school and was very excited to show me the silver duct tape wrapped around her shoes that Matt had brought for her to cover the hole. I was glad she had Matt; she seemed very fond of him in a big brother way. But I wasn't pleased with the duct tape shoes.

The shoes I had brought her were still in my trunk. I couldn't bring myself to return them. I'd spent days trying to figure out this shoe situation. She was a child; she should have decent shoes, and what was up with this foster situation? I hadn't been able to sleep properly, thinking that precious Charli had been beaten up and had her stuff stolen by other kids. And who were these foster parents that would punish her for nice shoes? All of my thoughts on the foster system were now confusing. Was it really that bad? My experience with foster homes went as far as Oliver Twist, and that was just a story.

My phone buzzed. Time to check on my sleeping residents. I made my rounds, stepping into each room and listening to the heavy breathing (and, in some cases, snores) of people sleeping comfortably. I looked at their shoes, some right at the foot of their beds, some haphazardly thrown about their room. They didn't have expensive name-brand shoes, but none of them had holes. The group home would never allow it. They may not have much, but it was our job to make sure they had dignity. No shoes or clothes with holes, nothing too old or faded. Back in the front, I looked over at all the clothes I had ironed to make sure they looked presentable. How could her foster parents not care at least that much? I sat back down at my desk. My anxiety was starting to build. I took some deep breaths and closed my eyes.

Nothing the residents had was new. When their clothes were run down, where did they get new stuff? And then it came to me. My eyes shot open, and I knew what I was going to do.

Charli

"Like those?" Matt said, pointing at a student's shoes as they walked by.

"Kinda like that, but way better and a brighter white," I said. Matt understood why I couldn't keep them. He even said he felt like Kindra was a good person to have in my corner and that he was starting to trust her. That made me feel good.

"Geez, Charli, they must have been the brightest white shoes ever made."

I shrugged. "Maybe," I said. I knew he was thinking I was being dramatic about the shoes, but I didn't care. They were the most beautiful shoes I'd ever seen, and they were mine.

"So I was thinking," Matt said. I was shuffling through my backpack to make sure I had my book for my next class. For the first time in a long time, I was doing my schoolwork and getting good grades, and I liked it. I zipped up my bag and gave Matt my full attention.

"Maybe I could meet Kindra," he said to me. I didn't say anything at first. "Well?" he asked after I'd been silent for a moment.

"Why?" I asked him "Why do you want to meet her?" I was diverting his attention while trying to figure out my feelings about this.

"Well, she's important to you, and I'm important to you. So we should meet...right?" he asked, smiling. I just stared at him.

"You want to tell her, don't you?" I finally said in a very defensive way. "No! Well...maybe she can help," Matt responded.

"I don't need help; I'm fine, better than I have been in a long time, and they aren't even bothering me much at home right now, and my grades are better than yours, so maybe you need some help," I yelled at him. He was looking down at the ground.

"I didn't mean to upset you. I know things are good right now, but what if they change again? What if it gets really bad again?" he said. I knew he didn't mean any harm; he'd been my friend long enough for me to know that. I scooted right next to him so we were sitting shoulder to shoulder. I laid my head on his shoulder and sighed.

"Things always change; they always get bad again. Can you just let me have this while it lasts?" I asked him.

"Yeah." He sighed. "I still want to meet her, though. I promise I won't say anything about…that."

"OK," I said. Then the bell rang. We gathered our stuff. Just as Matt was about to head off, he said, "You get two good test scores, and now I'm the one who needs a tutor, sheesh."

I laughed out loud and headed to my class.

Kindra

The picnic table at the park was our new meeting spot. I had a white shopping bag next to my feet, and I was so excited about what it contained that I thought I would burst. Two people were walking towards me. I thought one was Charli, but who was the other person?

As they got closer, I could tell it was a male. I guessed it had to be Matt. I was a bit surprised she would bring anyone. They walked right up to the table. Charli smiled at me, and I smiled back.

“Kindra, this is my friend Matt. I hope it’s OK that I brought him,” she said to me. “Of course it’s OK. Nice to meet you, Matt. Charli speaks very highly of you,” I said. “Nice to meet you too,” he responded as they both sat down.

“Hey, I didn’t get my hug,” I said to Charli as she sat down. She jumped back up, ran around the table, and gave me a big hug. Since she’d asked for one the other day, I made sure to give her a hug whenever I saw her. Matt smiled when she sat back down and nodded in what I guessed to be approval of me. I nodded back. I reached down into the bag at my feet and brought out two pineapple sodas. I pushed one in front of Charli and the other in front of Matt.

“I know you weren’t expecting me; it’s OK,” Matt said and pushed the soda back in my direction.

“No worries, I’m good,” I told him. He picked up the soda and examined the bottle. He took a quick sip and then looked at Charli.

“I told you!” She’d already finished half of her bottle. Matt laughed. "So I've been thinking about our problem," I said to Charli.

"What problem?" she asked.

"The problem with your shoes," I said. She swallowed a large gulp of her soda, and I could see her eyeing Matt's. He was drinking his slowly.

"But my shoes are fine now," Charli said, lifting her foot onto the bench and showing off the duct tape wrapped around the toes. I cringed at the shoes. I couldn't allow this to go on.

"I know, and that was really sweet of Matt to get the tape for you, but I think I have a better solution," I said while lifting the bag onto the table.

"Goodwill," Charli said, reading the name on the bag.

I reached into the bag and said a silent prayer—*"Oh Lord, please let her like these"*--as I pulled out a pair of used black New Balance tennis shoes with pink trim and set them on the table in front of her. Her eyes got wide.

"They're for me?" she whispered with awe in her voice.

"Yeah, well, I knew we couldn't do new shoes because they would attract attention. I had to go to four different stores to find your size in a shoe that was actually cute. I hope you like them, Kiddo. I just really didn't want you walking around with holes in your shoes."

"I like them," Matt said. Charli was still just staring at the shoes.

"Well…what do you think?" I asked her. I was starting to get nervous. "I…I love them," she said with tears running down her cheeks.

"Well, try them on," I told her, trying to hold back my own tears. She quickly kicked off the duct tape shoes and put on the New Balances. She bent down to tie them.

"My toes reach the front, and my feet don't slide," she squealed as she stood up. "Are they too tight?" I asked her.

"No, they're perfect," she responded as she walked around the table modeling her slightly new shoes. The second time around, she stopped and hugged me really tight.

"Thank you, Kindra. Thank you so much," she said with her arms still wrapped around me.

"You don't think these will cause a problem with your fosters or other kids?" I asked her. "No, they are perfect," she said. Matt pulled out his cell phone.

"Let me take a picture of you in your new shoes, Charli," he said. She came back around to his side of the table, put one foot on the bench, leaned her elbow on her knee, and smiled a smile bigger than pineapple soda. Matt took the picture.

"Can you send me that picture, Matt?" I asked him.

"Sure," he said and handed his phone to me so I could input my number. A moment later, my cell phone pinged, alerting me that Matt's picture had come through.

"Thanks, Matt," I said.

"I can't believe they are mine, and I can take them with me, and my feet don't slide," Charli said in a sing-song way. I smiled.

"Charli," Matt said. "I hate to ruin your good time, but I have to get home so I don't get in trouble."

"That's OK, you guys get going," I said to them. The evening was a success, and it was perfectly fine if she left early. I stood up from the table and began to gather my stuff when Charli ran around the table and hugged me again. She looked up and locked eyes with me while her arms were still wrapped around my waist.

"You're welcome, Kiddo," I said to her, never breaking her gaze. She eventually let go and walked around the table again. I could tell Matt was ready to go.

"It was nice to meet you, Kindra; I'm glad Charli has a friend like you," Matt said to me. "Ditto," I said back to him.

"Matt, are you going to drink the rest of your soda?" Charli asked, and we all laughed.

Charli

“It’s like the blue goes on forever,” I said to Matt.

“Yeah, if I keep trying to look deeper into it, I get dizzy,” Matt said, sitting up. We were lying on the bleachers staring into the sky. School had ended for the day. I wasn’t meeting Kindra, and I was in no rush to get back to the house. So Matt and I were hanging out on the bleachers. It had become a semi-regular thing. I put my feet in the air, still admiring the shoes. Even after a month, they still looked new.

“They don’t look dirty to you, do they?” I asked him.

“No, Charli, you clean them like twice a day,” he said, pushing my legs out of the air and laughing when I fell over. I sat up and dusted the shoes off with my hand anyway, just in case. I’d told Matt that I had thrown away the duct-taped shoes since I’d gotten these from Kindra, but I hadn’t. I had them in with my stuff, just in case.

“I gotta get home early today,” Matt said to me. “I have a project that’s due tomorrow.” “Oh.”

“You don’t want to go home, do you?” he asked.

“I never want to go to that place, Matt--you know that,” I said back to him. We both sat in silence for a moment. Matt broke the silence first:

“They’ve started on you again, haven’t they?” he asked. I didn’t immediately answer. “Why do you say that?” I asked him purposely, staring down at my shoes.

“Sometimes, in the mornings, you have a little bit of a limp. But it usually goes away by lunch. And you hardly ever want to leave lately,” he said. I hadn’t realized I was limping in the mornings, but if Matt noticed it, other people could have too. I'd have to do better.

"Things aren't as bad as they have been before, Matt. I promise," I told him, hoping he would drop it, but deep down, I was glad he noticed, glad someone noticed. Maybe I wasn't so invisible.

"OK, see ya later," he said as he picked up his backpack and headed down the bleachers. I sat confused. That was it? No argument? No talk about how we needed to get help? This was not like Matt at all. Had he given up on me?

Kindra

I smiled to myself as I rinsed my dishes and put them in the dishwasher. I was off work tonight, and I'd just had an amazing Skype date with Daniel. He'd said yesterday that we should both get pizza and eat it together while Skyping. It would make it feel like we were on a real date, and he wasn't on the other side of the world. It worked. Even though his pizza was from the mess hall on base and mine was a frozen Totino's, it was still great. I'd wanted to order a pizza, but it wasn't in the budget. We chatted for a little over two hours, just catching up. I'd told him about work and therapy and how I'd started the TV show "The West Wing" over again for the umpteenth time. I loved the show so much that he bought me the whole series on DVD for Christmas. It was one of my favorite gifts because it showed that he listened when I talked to him about things I loved.

I hadn't told him about Charli. I wasn't ready to share her, and I was nervous about what his opinion would be of the whole situation. We did discuss fundraising for my service dog, though. He'd come up with the idea that I should reach out to famous people via Twitter and tell them my story--maybe they would help. I thought the idea was silly.

"My own family didn't much care about my recovery or my need for a service dog, so why would a famous person that didn't even know me?" I'd said to him. He said the worst they could do was say no, and I'd be no worse off than when I started. Then he made me promise I would at least try.

"Time to beg some famous people," I muttered to myself as I dried my hands on a dish rag and went over to the table where my laptop was. I pulled up Twitter and began the process of creating an account. It was pretty straightforward. Once it was set up, I began looking for people to follow. I'd followed about seven people when my phone alerted me from across the room that I'd received a text message. Why did it seem like that thing was always so far away from me when it went off? I got up, grabbed the phone off the couch, and returned it to the table. I unlocked the screen and saw the message was from a number I didn't have saved on my phone.

I opened the message. It said simply, "Kindra?" I looked at it with no idea who it was from. I then scrolled up on the phone because it looked like I'd received a message from this number before. It was a picture of Charli staring back at me with her knee on a bench, showing off her new shoes.

"Hey, Matt." I stored his name in my phone. The phone pinged again.

Matt: Can I talk to you about something?

I looked over at the time on the microwave. It was 11:15 pm. "Pretty late for him to be up," I thought.

Kindra: Sure, what's up?

Beads of sweat dotted my brow as I waited for him to respond. I wondered, was something wrong with Charli? Had they moved her? I knew that was a major fear of hers; we had talked about it before. What could be going on? *Ping:* The phone went off.

Matt: This might be strange, but the whole situation is kind of strange right? lol

I just stared at the phone.

"Get to the point, kid," I said out loud. *Ping.*

Matt: I know Charli isn't your child or anything, but I know you care about her.

Kindra: Yes, I do very much.

Matt, you are killing me here.

Matt: Do you think you could help me get Charli a cell phone?

I stared at the message. A cell phone? I hadn't seen that coming at all.

Kindra: Why do you think she needs a cell phone?

A cell phone? I sighed. I couldn't afford to order a pizza. How was I going to get her a cell phone? I shut down the laptop and closed it. I was definitely done with Twitter tonight. Matt was taking quite a while to respond. I just sat lost in my own thoughts. *Ping*.

Matt: Well, she's one of the only kids at school without a phone, and what if she gets moved? We could lose her forever.

I wasn't too concerned with her being the only kid at school without a phone, but he did have a point about her moving. I'd be devastated if I lost her like that. But how would I do this? Matt ask if I could help him, so maybe he had an idea.

Kindra: How do you propose we do this?

He responded immediately.

Matt: I have two old phones. When I get a new one, I just put the old one in a drawer. They are good phones; they just need a SIM card to make them work. I could give her one."

Well, at least I wouldn't have to buy a phone--that made the task a little less daunting.

However, the thought of taking on another monthly bill made me want to cry.

Kindra: Ok, that's a start

Matt: If we get a prepaid plan, then the bill would only be $40 a month. I get a small allowance, so I could help with $10 a month.

I sighed. $30 a month. I would have to come up with it, but how?

Kindra: Ok, that's doable.

Matt: Great! I will get it all set up and then give you the info. Kindra: Sounds good. Thanks for being such a good friend to her.

Matt: That's what friends do, right? I will get you all the info for the plan once I get it. Thanks, Kindra! Good night.

Kindra: Ok. Night, Matt.

I stared at the phone after my last message had gone through. What had I done? I put my head in my hands.

"Lord, please help me figure out how to pay for this," I whispered. All of a sudden, I was drained.

Charli

Hot water from the shower poured down on my head. I had been standing here for a while now. Tears and shower water mixed, running down my face and eventually down the drain. I wished I could go down the drain. I turned around so the hot water could hit my back. My lower back was hurting pretty bad. Mack had thrown me down when he was done with me tonight. I'd landed hard on my bottom, and pain shot into my lower back. The hot water helped the pain a bit.

Things were getting bad again. Matt was right. I quickly soaped up and rinsed off twice before getting out and drying off. I put on my night clothes and went to the sleeping room. I climbed into my bottom bunk bed and got under the covers. I wondered what it would be like to die. I hadn't thought about it in a long time, but there it was. I thought I believed in heaven, but I wasn't sure, and I wasn't sure I'd get in anyway. Mostly, I hoped it would be dark and cool and quiet, and you just kinda float in the darkness forever. That didn't seem so bad. Maybe dying wouldn't be so bad. It couldn't be worse than this, could it?

Kindra's face flashed into my mind, then Matt's. I didn't want to leave them. Didn't want them to be sad because of me. I loved them, but I still felt so alone. The tears began again, making paths slowly down my cheeks. I quickly wiped them away, sat up, and grabbed the shoes Kindra had bought me. I put them on, tied them tight, and lay back down in the bed. I pulled the covers up to my neck.

Kindra

I pushed back from my desk in frustration. I was at work--had been there for over an hour but hadn't started on anything yet. I looked towards the back of the house where all my residents' dirty clothes for the day sat staring at me. I had no urge to get started. It had been a rough day. It started with a really bad night's sleep. Nightmares. I hadn't had a night that bad in a while. So, the morning started out slow. Then, I spent the first portion of the day trying to figure out how to come up with money for Charli's phone bill, to no avail. I had a session with Paige; we discussed the nightmares, and she asked me if I had anything on my mind that could have triggered them. I told her I had a financial problem I was desperately trying to work out, and that had me stressed, but nothing rape-related. She asked me if the financial situation had me a little stressed or a lot stressed. I thought about Charli and her getting moved and me never seeing her again with no way of getting in touch with her. I told Paige I was very stressed.

"That's what has triggered the nightmares," she said.

"No, but I wasn't thinking about that, about the rape," I told her angrily.

"The way PTSD works is basically when you were raped, it was so traumatic and so stressful that your brain got stuck like a needle stuck on a scratch on a record that keeps repeating. Your brain got stuck in the moment. All the things you were feeling, your brain got stuck on them, and anytime you do anything that triggers similar feelings or emotions from that night, your brain goes back there. For instance, remember you told me after the rape, you went to the hospital, and it was freezing cold. It was cold because it was two days after Christmas in Louisiana, and it was just cold in the hospital," she said.

"Yes," I said, remembering. "They took my clothes for evidence and gave me a thin hospital gown, and I was freezing." I wrapped my arms around my shoulders at the thought.

"Now, what happens anytime you get cold?" she asked me.

"I get scared," I said. We'd discussed this at length some months ago.

"Right. Because your brain associates being cold with that night and how scared you were. Because your brain got stuck there," she said. I remembered all the nights Daniel complained I'd had the "heater on Hell" because I'd rather have a room so hot that my skin almost felt like it was burning than risk the chance that I might get cold. He'd sit there and sweat it out until I fell asleep, then he'd adjust the temperature to a normal setting.

"Your brain is doing the same thing with stress. You are really stressed about this financial situation, and your brain is just recognizing the stress and not the cause of it and going back to that night. Hence the nightmares," Paige said. I sat there in frustration and anger.

Every time it seemed like I was doing better, something else came to knock me down. It seemed like the rape continuously touched on every corner of my life.

Paige said she was going to send an email to my psychiatrist, Brandon (they worked in the same office), recommending he increase the dosage of my anxiety meds and the meds that helped with nightmares. I wasn't happy with that--an increase in meds meant I wasn't doing better--but I agreed.

After therapy, I felt so broken, but I pulled my broken pieces together because it was the day I met with Charli. I don't know if it was just me, but even she seemed out of it and not

herself today. We discussed the book they were reading in her language arts class, "The Adventures of Huckleberry Finn." She told me they had to go around class with each student reading a paragraph. She told me the n-word was in her paragraph and how the teacher hadn't given any instructions on what to do when they came to that word.

"So I just skipped over the word when I came to it," she said, looking at me for approval. "Is that OK?" she asked.

"That's perfect," I told her.

"I know it's not a regular bad word, but it hurts people's feelings. I saw some kids get in a fight over it in a group home I was in once," she said. I wrapped my arms around her.

"You did a good thing by not saying it. Your teacher should have given more directions, but you did good, Kiddo," I told her. I held her in my arms a little longer. I really needed this hug today. We talked a bit more about this and that. It seemed like she didn't want to leave, but she eventually said, "I guess I should get going."

We parted ways, and I went home to take a nap before work, and now here I was an hour in and no work done. I pushed my chair back to my desk and looked for what felt like the hundredth time at the paper I had been writing on. I had all my bills written out for the month. The only thing that might be considered a luxury was my Netflix account, but I didn't have cable, and Netflix really helped distract me during the rough times. Plus, the cost of my Netflix was nowhere near enough to cover $30 a month. I gave a heavy sigh and opened the root beer and then the white cheddar popcorn that was my at-work snack for the night. I got up and sorted the laundry and started the first load, then went to clean the bathrooms. After the bathrooms were cleaned, I sat back down at my desk and just stared into space. I was staring in the direction of the white cheddar popcorn bag. There was something about it, something right on the edge of my mind. And then it clicked.

I jumped up and pulled the receipt from the gas station out of my pocket. One root beer soda and one bag of white cheddar popcorn totaled out to $4.72, which rounded up to $5.00. I got the same snack about 3-4 nights a week. If I didn't get my snack twice a week, I could put that money towards Charli's phone bill. Over the course of a month, it would be $40. I could get my girl a phone and wouldn't even need Matt's help to pay for it. I cried real tears of joy and made a mental note to call Paige and not have my medication dose increased.

Charli

My class had gotten out a little early so I'd beaten Matt to our lunch spot. I sat there, eyes closed, soaking up the sun. I'd just taken a pretty difficult test in my math class, but I thought I'd done OK on it. I opened my eyes and saw Matt walking up. He had a huge smile on his face. He sat down next to me and went into his backpack for our lunches.

"What's up?" I asked him. He looked up at me, realized he was smiling, and quickly made a straight face.

"Nothing," he said and handed me my lunch.

"Did you get a good grade on a test or something?" I asked him.

"What? No," he said, pulling his lunch out. He had been acting so strange lately. I took a bite of my sandwich, and he was smiling at me when I looked up.

"What is it, Matthew?" I snapped at him. His face fell at the sound of his whole name, but he quickly regained his composure.

"Your lunch doesn't feel heavy?" he asked with a sneaky smile.

"Heavy?" I asked, setting my sandwich down and looking inside the bag. There was something black at the bottom. I reached into the bag and wrapped my hand around it. It felt like…but it couldn't be. I didn't bring it all of the way out of the bag but opened my hand so I could look at it. It was a cell phone!

I looked up at Matt with total surprise on my face. Now he was laughing with delight. "SURPRISE!" he said.

“Me and Kindra got it for you!” he continued. “Kindra?” I said. I was so confused.

“Yeah, I talked to her, and we agreed…” he started saying, but I cut him off.

“You didn’t tell her, did you, Matt? You didn’t say anything? Did you tell her?” I asked. “No, no, and no. I promise I didn’t tell her. I just said you needed a phone in case they moved you-- so we didn’t lose you forever. And she agreed,” he said, beaming. “How did you get in touch with her?” I asked him accusingly.

“I had her number from when I sent her the picture of you in your new shoes. Can you just be excited about your phone, Charli?” he asked. I sneaked a look back in the bag. I had a cell phone! I had never had a cell phone of my own before. A slow smile spread across my face. I looked at Matt, and he was smiling again too.

“OMG, I have a cell phone!” I squealed.

“Shhhh,” Matt said. “Cell phones aren’t allowed at school. If you get caught with it, they will take it away and call your parents, and that can’t happen, right?”

“Right,” I said. I couldn’t imagine the school calling Mack and then me trying to explain where the phone had come from. I guess I could say I stole it.

“No, the school *can’t* call the fosters,” I said firmly.

“So you really have to keep it hidden, especially at home,” he said. I hadn’t even thought about the house yet, but I wasn’t going to let anybody find my phone or take it from me.

“OK,” I said.

“Meet me at the bleachers after school, and I will show you how to use it,” Matt said. “OK!” I said excitedly.

"I already programmed my number and Kindra's number into it," he said.

"OK!" was all I could say. I was so excited. We ate the rest of our lunch in silence, occasionally looking at each other like we had a great secret. I guess we did!

Kindra

Ping. I grabbed the phone immediately--for the fourth time so far today. Excitedly waiting for my first text or call from Charli. Matt told me he was going to give her the phone today, but he hadn't specified when. I thought about texting her first, but if the phone went off in class, she could get in trouble.

I unlocked my phone; the message was from my sister asking what I was doing. I responded, "Sleeping," which I could have been. Working the night shift allows you to be asleep any time of the day. I love my sister. I just didn't feel like talking. I didn't particularly feel close to anyone in my family except my Dad since the rape and after my divorce. I was going through a world of turmoil just trying to exist, and I couldn't seem to get them to understand how the rape had completely altered my life. I tried, for the most part, to keep a smile on my face for them so my issues didn't make them uncomfortable, but that made me tired. My mom would always say "I don't know how to help you," and that broke my heart. There were books and articles on how to love/help someone with PTSD, but my family never took the time to read them. I guess they were busy. I was trying to let go of that anger. Paige said I needed to work on making peace with the fact that I may never get what I need from my family regarding the rape and PTSD, but I still had to live. The best way for me to make peace was by not dealing with them too much. I felt like they were getting off easy with all of this. I felt like I was drowning in the ocean most days, and they were relaxing on the beach. Occasionally, one of them would look over at me, wave and yell "swim," then go back to what they were doing. So I didn't feel bad telling my sister I was sleeping when I wasn't.

It had taken about a week for Matt and I to get the phone going and ready to give to Charli. He did all the legwork--getting a SIM card and a number and getting it activated. He just sent me the number, and I called and paid the bill once a month to keep it on. I wanted to mention the phone to Charli every time I saw her during the week, but I kept it a secret just in case we weren't able to pull it off.

One message from my mother saying I had some mail at her house. Two messages from Walgreens informing me it was time to refill two prescriptions. And the last, of course, from my sister. I set the phone on the floor next to the couch I was lying on and hit play on my remote to continue watching the episode of "House" on Netflix. It was Friday, and I didn't have to work tonight. I'd switched shifts with a coworker who needed a different day off. I hadn't had a Friday off in months, and I had no plans for this one except to wait to hear from Charli. So she could tell me about her new phone.

Ping. The alert sounded so far away. I hadn't realized I'd dozed off. I opened my eyes and looked at the TV. "Are you still watching?" was printed across the screen. How long had I been asleep? Then I remembered the *ping* and grabbed the phone. I unlocked it, and the message notification said Charli. I opened the message to one little word: "Hello."

And I lit up like a Christmas tree.

Charli

What was taking her so long to respond? I looked at the time I sent the message, and then I looked at the actual time. It hadn't even been a full minute yet. I laughed to myself. School was out for the day. Matt had spent the last 45 minutes showing me the ins and outs of my new cell phone. How to store numbers in my phone, send text messages, take pictures, send pictures, how to use my navigation in case I got lost somewhere or just needed directions, how to set alarms, and most importantly, how to keep the phone on silent so no one would hear it. We decided I would hide my phone inside my shoes when I was at the house. He'd shown me everything he could think of that I might need. Then he gave me a phone charger and said he had to go. Friday was family pizza night at his house. I wondered what it would be like to have a family to have a pizza night with. *Bzzz.* The phone vibrated in my hand. It was Kindra.

Kindra: A little birdy told me you got a phone :-)

What? A smiley face. Matt hadn't shown me how to make smiley faces. I would have to ask him about that.

Charli: Well, you're a pretty big little birdie.

Kindra: Do you like it?

Charli: Do I like it?

Sometimes, I realized with a jolt that Matt and Kindra had no clue what life was like for me.

Charli: I LOVE IT, IT'S AMAZING, THANK YOU THANK YOU THANK YOU!

Kindra: You are so welcome. You have to make sure you keep it hidden. I don't want you getting in trouble, but I couldn't risk you getting moved and disappearing on me.

Charli: I will hide it and keep it on vibrate or silent. I promise.

Kindra: Well, the phone was Matt's idea. He came to me with it and did most of the work in getting it for you.

I'd thought he was giving up on me for the last two weeks, but he was trying to figure out a different way to look out for me. I felt guilty for doubting him. I clicked his name on my phone and sent him a message.

Charli: Hey Matt, thanks for being my best friend.

I figured he was eating pizza or doing something with his family, so I didn't wait for a reply. Speaking of waiting, it was getting kinda late and I should probably be heading to the house. I sent Kindra another message.

Charli: I'm going to put my phone on silent and head to the house now. I will text you when I can.

Kindra: OK, pretty girl. I look forward to your next messages.

I put the phone on silent and slid it into my pocket. Then I thought better of it. If Mack called me to the shed as soon as I got there and the phone was in my pocket, it could be found, and then I would be in a world of trouble. I opened my backpack, pulled out my binder, slid the phone into the front pocket, and put the binder back in my bag. Then I started my walk to the house.

Kindra

Frustration turned to panic and anxiety. I felt my chest tightening. I took a deep breath and moved my laptop off of my legs and onto the bed. I needed to walk away for a minute. This Twitter thing was kicking my butt. I walked to the kitchen and poured myself some juice. Took a sip, then took a deep breath and counted backward from ten to one. I really hated my PTSD and how it made just about every emotion turn to panic. I was frustrated because I couldn't get any famous people to respond on Twitter. It had been two weeks and nothing. I think that's a fair reason to be frustrated, but not to have to do grounding exercises in my kitchen.

"Ugh," I sighed. Now I was angry, and there went my chest tightening again.

"OH COME ON!" I yelled as I started to take calming breaths. A tear rolled down my cheek. Was this really what the rest of my life was going to be like? I had been asking this question more and more lately. The tears flowed at the thought. This was no way to live. I didn't even attempt to wipe the tears away. I went back into my room, pulled the comforter off of my bed, and dragged it into my walk-in closet. I sat down on the floor and wrapped myself in the blanket. This was, in my mind anyway, the safest place in my apartment. I could control everything in this small space (or at least I told myself that). The tears kept coming, but at least I felt calmer in here. The intro to Macklemore's song "Same Love" played somewhere in my bedroom, alerting me that Charli had sent me a text message. I jumped up from the floor and ran back into my room, looking for the phone.

I thought I'd seen it last on my bed. I looked back at the comforter on the floor of my closet. I got down on all fours and spotted the phone on the floor at the foot of my bed. It must have fallen when I pulled the comforter off. I crawled around to the front of the bed, picked up the phone, and unlocked the screen.

Charli: Hi

I looked at the time. It was well after midnight, and she had already sent me my nightly "good night" message hours ago. I wondered why she was up as I responded.

Kindra: Hey Kiddo, you ok?

She responded quickly:

Charli: I can't sleep

"Well, I guess that makes two of us tonight," I thought to myself.

Kindra: What's keeping you up?

Charli: Bad dreams.

I hated the thought of her having bad dreams. Life seemed hard enough for her without torment during sleeping hours as well.

Kindra: Do you want to talk about it?

Charli: I have bad dreams that people are hurting me.

I froze. Hurting her like how? It was always in the back of my mind that I met her at the Rape Crisis Center and that she never went in the building...ever. There had been plenty of times I'd wanted to ask her about it, but I had seen her shut down and run from me before. So, I'd always tried to let her lead the conversations since then. Now I feared my beautiful girl had PTSD too, from whatever had happened to her. I prayed it was just bad dreams.

Kindra: I have bad dreams about people hurting me too.

I responded to her. I didn't want her to feel alone in this, not like I did when it all first started.

Charli: Really? Do you have bad dreams too?

Kindra: Yes, and sometimes they are so bad I wake up crying.

Charli: Me too! I was crying, and now I'm scared to go back to sleep.

I knew those nights all too well. *What happened to her?* I wondered and tried not to think the worst.

Kindra: Do you want to tell me about what happens in the dreams?

Charli: No.

That was all that she replied. I knew better than to push.

Kindra: OK, you don't have to.

I responded, and then I sat there for a moment. I was not quite sure what to say next, but I felt sad. So I got up with my phone, went back into my closet, and wrapped myself up in my comforter. Just as I was getting comfortable, her text alert went off again.

Charli: Did I wake you up? I'm sorry if I did. I shouldn't be bothering you.

I'd seen her do this before. She was beginning to shut down on me, and I needed to stop her.

Kindra: I wasn't asleep, Kiddo, and even if I was, I'd wake up to talk to you.

Charli: Oh.

She loved using that "Oh."

Charli: What were you doing up? It's kinda late, and you aren't at work tonight?

I loved that she kept up with my schedule. I thought about how to respond to her and decided I was just going to be honest and hope I didn't lose her like I'd lost so many other people when I spoke about this topic.

Kindra: I was working on getting my service dog.

Charli: What's a service dog?

What was the easiest way I could explain this to her?

Kindra: It's a dog that's trained to take care of people with different illnesses.

Charli: You have an illness?

Kindra: Yes. I have something called PTSD because someone hurt me, and my brain won't let me forget. I have nightmares really bad, and sometimes when I get scared or angry. I have panic attacks, and it feels like I may have a heart attack or something. So, my service dog would wake me up from nightmares and help calm me during panic attacks or even alert me that I'm going into a panic attack. Does that make sense?

I waited and waited for her to respond. Nothing. I'd said something wrong. My chest began to tighten. Not even the closet felt safe right now. I had to get out. I stumbled into the bathroom. My breath was coming in gasps. "This is nothing you can't handle," I thought to myself. I turned on the faucet and splashed cold water on my face. I tried to focus on the feeling of the cold water and the sound of the water coming out of the faucet and hitting the sink. I squeezed my nails into my palms until it hurt and then tried to focus on the pain. Nothing seemed to be working, and I was starting to feel lightheaded.

Charli's ringtone sounded from inside my closet. I ran to it and dug the phone out of the blanket on the floor. I unlocked the screen, and her message appeared.

Charli: I think I have PTSD too.

I sank into a heap on the floor and cried.

Charli

"Only military people have that," Matt said to me. I'd stayed up really late researching it on my cell phone, and I was sure that I had it too. I was trying to share my thoughts with Matt, but he wasn't much help.

"Matt, do you even know what PTSD is?" I asked him.

"Well...yeah. It's like...uhm. It's what military people have when they come home from overseas, and you aren't in the military, so how could you have it?" he asked in a very know-it-all way.

"Not just military people get it, Matthew," I said, using his full name so he knew I was serious. "Anybody can get PTSD if they have been through a traumatic event, like a car accident, or a natural disaster, or if they experienced horrible things in the military, or if...they have stuff like me." I got more quiet at the end while looking down at my shoes. I leaned down and dusted them off with my hand.

"Really?" Matt asked. "Yeah," I responded.

"Well, why do you seem so happy about it?" he asked, crumbling up his lunch bag and putting it in the trash can next to him.

"Because I thought I was having heart attacks!" I said a little too loudly. Matt looked around to see if anyone was looking at us.

"Shhhhh," he said.

"Sorry, it's just there have been so many times," I said, then paused and thought for a second. "Remember when we first met, and you chased me into the bathroom?" I asked him.

"I *followed* you into the bathroom," he quickly corrected me. I laughed. "Yeah, remember I was crying and bent over?" I asked him.

"Yeah," he said with a pained expression, remembering that day.

"I thought I was having a heart attack; I thought I was dying, but it was a panic attack because of the PTSD, and I have had a lot more since then, and the nightmares are all because of the PTSD," I said, completely out of breath.

"So what do you do about it?" he asked very seriously.

"I don't know that part yet, but I see Kindra today so I'm going to ask her about it. She did say something about a dog," I said while trying to remember what she had said.

"A dog?" Matt asked.

"Yeah," I said. Then the bell rang.

"Well, tell me what she says," he said as he grabbed his stuff and headed off to class. "I will," I yelled behind him.

"Kindra has answers--she always has answers," I thought as I headed to class.

Kindra

I pulled a blanket out of my trunk, tucked it under my arm, and grabbed the grocery bag with items I'd purchased throughout the day. I was at the park where Charli and I met. I had gotten there early so I could set up and attempt to get my mind right. I knew we'd be talking about PTSD today. I didn't want to sit at our normal picnic table. I felt like we needed something more intimate for today. So I brought a blanket so we could sit picnic style.

I laid the blanket out on the grass near the table we usually sat at so she wouldn't have trouble finding me. Then I set the bag down and began to remove its contents: two pineapple sodas, two bags of Cheeto puffs, a bag of M&M's with peanuts, a bag of Skittles, and a hair brush. I purchased the hairbrush special today from Dollar Tree. I hoped she would let me brush her hair while we talked. The world had always seemed a little bit better of a place when my mom brushed my hair. Once everything was set up to my liking, I sat in thought. What could have caused her to have PTSD? What had happened to her?

Whatever it was, I blamed these foster homes. They were obviously way worse than I thought. I guess I'd always assumed they were decent places for kids to stay while in transition--not places where the adults didn't even care if your shoes had holes and people stole your stuff. I shifted my thinking. I was getting upset. I wondered how Charli was feeling about the PTSD. To be quite honest, I was worried. I didn't get much time to dwell on the worry before I saw her walking down the sidewalk towards me. Her head was up, and she had a smile on her face. I took that as a good sign. I also was glad she'd stopped staring at her shoes. I saw her look at the table, then stop walking and look around. She spotted me a few feet away from the table, sitting on the blanket. She smiled even bigger and ran over. She dumped her backpack on the blanket, dropped to her knees, and gave me a big hug.

“Hi, Kindra,” she said with her arms still around me.

“Hey, Kiddo,” I responded, giving her a good squeeze before she pulled away and sat down.

“We are having a picnic today!” she said excitedly.

“Yeah, I thought we’d do something a little different today,” I said back to her.

“I’ve never been on a picnic” she said while grabbing a bottle of soda and a bag of chips.

She stopped at the two bags of candy and looked up at me.

“You can have whichever one you want,” I told her with a smile. She stared at both bags for a few seconds then grabbed the M&M’S.

“Can I take my shoes off? They do that at picnics right?” she asked.

“I’m not sure who ‘they’ are but we can take our shoes off at our picnic. How was school today?” I asked her.

“It was fine. I talked to Matt about PTSD at lunch today,” she told me. Well she’d just jumped right in. I regrouped.

“Come sit here in front of me,” I said and patted the space on the blanket in front of me.

She looked up from her bag of M&Ms.

“Why?” she asked with genuine curiosity.

“I want to brush your hair,” I said, holding up the newly purchased brush. She didn’t move.

“But why?” she asked again.

“Well…my mom brushes my hair when serious things are going on or we are going to have a serious conversation.” I responded.

“Oh” she said. “Are we going to have a serious conversation?” I could tell she was worried.

“I was hoping to talk with you about PTSD,” I said.

“Oh, OK!” she said and quickly plopped down in front of me. I smiled, relief washing over me. I began brushing her hair.

“So what do you know about it?” I asked her.

“I researched it on my phone last night so I feel like I know a lot about it. It’s when something bad happens to you, something really scary and your brain can’t get over it and then you have nightmares and anxiety and panic attacks and flashbacks and you think about it a lot because your brain won’t let you forget, is that right?” she asked.

“Yeah, that's pretty spot-on. Do you want to talk about what may have caused you to have PTSD?” I asked cautiously, preparing for her to bolt on me. I saw her shoulders tense at my question. I just kept calmly brushing her hair, although I was panicking on the inside. She said, “No,” very quietly.

I said, “OK,” and kept brushing. Eventually, the tension in her shoulders relaxed, and I smiled just a little bit to myself. *“Thanks, Mom, for brushing my hair so I could know to brush hers,”* I thought to myself.

I wasn’t quite sure where to go next with our PTSD conversation, so I asked her, “Well, do you have any questions about it?”

She quickly turned around to face me.

“Yes, now that I’m pretty sure I have it, and it is the reason for the nightmares and stuff. How do I make it go away?" she asked with a very serious look on her face. I felt a lump in my throat form, and I wanted to cry for me, for her, for the truth I was about to tell her. I sighed heavily, opened my soda, and took a sip. I patted the spot in front of me again.

"Turn back around, Kiddo," I told her, and she did. I started brushing her hair again. "Healing from PTSD is not linear."

"What does that mean?" she asked. Right, she was a child. I set the brush down and drew a straight line with my finger across her back. She giggled a bit.

"OK, that's a straight line, and I could put steps one, two, and three across the line," I said as I drew a 1, 2, and 3 along where I had drawn the line on her back. "When I say it's not linear, I mean there is not a straight path with easy directions on how to heal from PTSD. Instead, it's more like this." I put my finger on her back again and started to draw another straight line, then I curved it way up her back, then way down, then I doubled back and made a loop and then just went crazy with it, drawing the line all over her back in no pattern--just chaos.

She giggled more and fell backward into my lap. She lay there for a moment, then looked up at me.

"That seems hard, Kindra. It never just goes away?" she asked.

Oh, how many times I had wished it would just go away, prayed for God to take it away. "Nope, it doesn't just go away, but you learn things to help you deal with it. You learn things to help calm you during panic attacks and tough times, and you work on healing, and over time, the panic attacks and nightmares and things become less and less, and sometimes they can go away for good. Eventually." She lay quietly in my lap. I could tell she was processing what I said.

"How long have you had it?" she asked me.

"Six years," I said. Her eyebrows rose in surprise.

"What kind of things did you learn to help deal with it?" she asked. "Now, this I can do," I thought, smiling to myself.

"Okay, sit up. I'm going to teach you a grounding technique," I said to her. "What's grounding?" she asked as she sat up.

"When you have a panic or anxiety attack, there are things you can try to do to help you calm down or 'ground' you. Does that make sense?" I asked, wanting to be sure she understood.

"Yes," she said.

"OK, it can be difficult to ground yourself in the middle of an attack when you feel like you are dying. So it helps to practice when you aren't having an attack," I said to her. She nodded.

"First," I continued, "I want you to take some deep breaths. When you are anxious, you may feel like you can't breathe, so deep, slow breaths are important." I watched her take a few deep, slow breaths.

"The 5-4-3-2-1 technique helps to distract you from your feelings of panic. So, if you were in panic mode right now, you would stop and look for five things you can see and name them out loud. Any five things. Go!" I said.

"Uhm," she said, looking around. "I see the picnic table, that tree right there, I see your car, uhm, the bag of Skittles and..." she looked around for one last thing to name. "MY SHOES!" she said excitedly. I laughed.

"OK, now, four things you can touch, and you have to actually touch them. Remember you'd be doing this to distract your mind from the fear and panic, so it's OK to really feel and focus. Is it hard or soft? Hot or cold? You are attempting to force your mind onto something other than the fear. Four things you can touch. Go!" I said. She looked down on the blanket and picked up her bag of M&M's. I watched her finger caress the bag.

"It feels lumpy from the M&M's inside, and the paper feels hard," she said. "Good," I responded. "Pick something else."

She reached down and grabbed a handful of the blanket.

"It feels soft, but I can feel things under it like the grass and a tree root," she said. "Good, what's next?" I asked her. She picked up her soda bottle and ran her hands up and down it.

"It's cold, and it feels a little wet. The bottle is smooth, though," she said and set the bottle down. Then she reached for my leg and ran her hand against my calf.

"Your jeans feel kinda smooth and not hard but not really soft," she said, looking up at me with a smile.

"OK, you're getting it. Now, three things you can hear," I told her. She closed her eyes, and I could tell she was listening.

"I hear the cars on the road," she said. I sat quietly, watching the intense look of concentration on her face. I didn't want to interrupt her.

"I hear birds chirping," she said. I smiled, but it was bittersweet. I was glad I could teach her things to help her cope and fight the bad times, but I hated that she even had bad times like this. She was just a kid. She shouldn't have to be learning this.

"The wind! I hear the wind!" she said.

"Yep, that's three. OK, now two things you can smell," I said. "Sheesh, this is getting hard," she said.

"Well, it's a distraction, and the harder you can focus on

something else, the less you focus on the fear and panic. Two things--GO!" I said. I watched her breathe in and out and in and out trying to pick up the scent of something. I picked up my soda bottle and took a sip but left the cap off. I may need to help her on this one. She closed her eyes again and took a deep breath.

"Are you wearing perfume?" she asked me. I laughed. "Lotion," I said.

"It smells really good, but I can't name the smell," she said.

"It's called Love Spell from Victoria's Secret," I said. My sister always sent me Victoria's Secret lotions and body sprays; she kept me smelling good. I smiled at the thought of my big sister. I looked over and saw Charli's eyes still closed. She was taking deep breaths in an attempt to smell something else. I lifted my open soda and held it beneath her nose. She sniffed and sniffed and then:

"PINEAPPLE SODA!" she yelled, and her eyes shot open. We both laughed. "OK--last time. One thing you can taste," I said.

"Taste?" she asked.

"Yep, one thing you can taste," I said. She sat still, but I could see her tongue moving around in her mouth. She was so focused.

"Peanuts from the M&M's!" she shrieked.

"Well, OK," I said, laughing. I couldn't remember the last time I had laughed so much in one day.

"That was kinda hard, but I liked it," she said.

"It's really hard when you are in an attack, but that's why you practice. And over time, you find you don't have to do all five if certain ones work better for you," I told her.

"Which ones work better for you?" she asked. I thought back to last night.

"Things I feel, like splashing really cold water on my face and then focusing on how that feels," I said. Then I thought maybe I should tell her the other one. Did I want her to try this? Was it fair to keep it from her, knowing that she experienced these things too?

"OK, sometimes it gets really, really bad, and most of the stuff I do isn't working. So I will make a fist like this," I said, holding my hand out in a fist for her to see. "And I will dig my nails into my hand until it hurts, and the pain sometimes stops the panic." I paused. I held my head down in shame.

"Sometimes it's the only thing that stops it, that brings me out," I said. I felt horrible telling her how to inflict pain on herself. Was I no better than those foster parents who didn't care if she had holes in her shoes?

Charli

I never realized it was so bad for Kindra too. I felt sad for her as she sat there, her head hung down and her hands in fists. I reached over and took her hand, unclenched her fist, and locked my fingers in hers.

"Tell me about the dog again, please?" I asked her. "The one that helps with PTSD." She smiled and lifted her head. That was good. I didn't want her to be sad.

"Right, it's called a service dog, and they help people with all kinds of illnesses, but for PTSD, they are so much better at helping you come out of an attack than grounding. They can wake you up from nightmares. They are specifically trained to your needs," she said.

"So why don't you have one already?" I asked her.

"They are really expensive to get, but Daniel told me to ask famous people on Twitter for help raising the money. That's what I was doing when you messaged me last night. Being ignored by famous people," she said with a slight laugh.

"Who's Daniel?" I asked. Kindra never really mentioned other people like friends or anything. She talked about her Dad and sometimes her Mom, but that was about it. I sat quietly, waiting for her to tell me who Daniel was. She seemed to really be thinking about it. Then finally, she said, "Daniel is my boyfriend," and she blushed a little bit.

"I didn't know you had a boyfriend," I said. We had been friends for a couple of months now, and she never mentioned her boyfriend. I wondered why.

"Is he nice to you?" I asked her.

"He is really nice to me, and he is very patient and understanding about my PTSD," she said.

"Oh," I said. Then, we both sat quietly. "Does he love you?" I asked her. Now, she was smiling from ear to ear.

"Yes, he does," she said.

"How do you know?" I asked her. I didn't want anyone to trick her or hurt her. She sat quietly for a moment. I could tell she was thinking again.

"Daniel is in the military, and he is really far away in another country right now. While he's been gone, he's been taking a class to be trained to help people who have been hurt like I was, but in the military. He took the class and helped other people so he can better understand what I go through and get direct training on how to support me through it," she said. "He didn't have to do that. Most of my friends and family won't even read an article on PTSD, let alone take a class. But he did it because he loves me." She nodded her head.

"Yeah, I think he loves you cause sometimes I hate being in my classes, but I think I could do it for someone I love," I said. We sat silently again. Kindra had that slight smile on her face again. "He must make her really happy," I thought to myself. I smiled at that. I wanted her to be happy.

"Do you think you will marry him?" I asked her.

"I really hope so. I'd marry him in a heartbeat if he asked!" She smiled so big it took up her whole face.

"And then you guys will have kids?" I said, attempting to join in her excitement. "Oh no, no, no, I don't want kids," she said.

"Oh," I responded as my heart fell to the bottom of the shoes she bought for me.

"I think kids are great. I just don't know how good of a mom I would be. Plus, childbirth scares me," she said, laughing. I wanted to tell her what a great mom she would be compared to some of the moms I'd had, but I just sat quietly and focused on the sound of the cars going by. It was getting late, and I knew I needed to go.

"Will you brush my hair a little bit more?" I asked her.

"Sure," she said and patted the space on the blanket in front of her for me to sit on.

Kindra

Can we talk later?

Love, Me

I finished typing the quick email on my phone and clicked send. I imagined it traveling on some electric current all the way to the other side of the world and popping up in Daniel's email. He was usually pretty quick about replying if he was at his computer, and he usually was about this time of day. I waited a few moments, and sure enough, an email from him arrived in my inbox. I found such comfort in the reliability of his schedule.

Hey Beautiful, I was just thinking about you. One of my favorite songs for you just played on my playlist. "Let Me Love You" by Neyo. "Can we talk later?" sounds serious. Are you ok? Do you want to talk now?

Daniel

I could feel the love and worry in his email. I'm not sure what I did to end up with someone who loved me so much, even through all of my "stuff," but I'd learned to stop doubting his love and embrace it. That song by Neyo definitely helped enforce that.

I'm OK, and it can wait until I get off work and have slept.

Me

I clicked 'send' and waited. A new email appeared.

OK, I know it's not our usual Skype night, but do you want to Skype and talk?

Daniel

I responded:

Yeah, that sounds good. Talk to you then. I love you.

Send. I got an immediate response.

Can't wait to see that beautiful face. I love you too.

Daniel

I closed out of my email, set the phone down on my work desk, and went over to the ironing board. I had already ironed all of my residents' shirts. I just needed to iron their jeans and put them on hangers.

It had been two days since I'd told Charli about Daniel. I hadn't told anyone about Charli, and I wasn't really sure why. Did I feel like I was protecting her? Maybe I was protecting myself. Everyone already thought I was crazy--they didn't fully believe me about the rape or just acted like they didn't care. I felt so small and insignificant in regard to them. I wouldn't let them make my relationship with Charli insignificant. She mattered as much as I did. Even if it was only us mattering to each other. But Daniel wasn't like that. I never felt small or insignificant with him and I never kept anything from him. So tomorrow, when we Skyped, I was going to tell him about Charli, and hopefully, he wouldn't think I was crazy. Hopefully, he'd still love me. I glanced at the clock. It was 12:30 am. I went back to ironing.

Charli

I sat at the lunch spot with my head held down. I had been crying off and on since my last visit with Kindra, and today, I really couldn't seem to hold it in. I was angry at myself for letting it get here. I knew better.

"Hey," I heard Matt say as he walked up. I looked up to say hey back, but before I could speak, his face turned to anguish when he saw my face.

"Charli, what happened?" he said, running up to me. Crap. I had forgotten that Mack had busted my lip last night because he'd said I'd made a noise when I normally didn't make any. I'd told my teachers (as instructed by him) that I'd busted it playing baseball with my "siblings," and they didn't ask any more questions. I looked away from Matt and said my rehearsed line.

"I got it playing baseball with my siblings," I said and held my head down again. I don't know why I said that to Matt. I felt so tired and defeated. Matt was quiet for a moment, and then he said, "Hey, Charli, you're my best friend. You don't have to lie to me. You can lie to them, and I know why you do..." He put his arm around my shoulder. "But you don't have to lie to me."

I laid my head on his shoulder, and a dam inside of me broke. The tears poured out. I couldn't control it at all. Matt turned and wrapped me in a bear hug, which just made me cry more.

"She doesn't want me, she doesn't want me," I cried out between sobs. Matt pulled back with a confused look on his face.

"What?" he asked. I was crying so hard now I couldn't breathe. I felt the panic coming, but I couldn't stop it.

"Kindra," I sobbed out between breaths.

"Kindra did this?" he asked with his voice rising. I cried more because he didn't understand me. I couldn't breathe, so I violently shook my head "NO." The panic was getting bad.

"Charli, try to calm down," he said.

Calm, I thought. I grabbed Matt's hand and thought to myself: *Five things I can see*. Matt's backpack on the ground, the red bricks of the planter we sat on, Matt's hand in mine. I stared at our hands for a second, then kept looking. A girl walking by had a blue SpongeBob t-shirt on, and there was a Dr. Pepper soda can on the ground. I calmed a little bit; I could breathe a little easier.

I said out loud, "Four things you can touch." I didn't want to touch anything at that moment, so I moved on.

I said out loud, "Three things you can hear," and I closed my eyes and focused on the sounds. It was loud and chaotic. I never realized how noisy lunchtime was. The noise began to drown out the panic in my brain. I tried to focus and separate some of the sounds, so they made sense and not just noise. I heard a girl having a conversation near me about going to her friend's after school. I was getting calm. I heard an announcement over the P.A. system asking for Harper Lightener to come to the front office. Calmer. And finally, I heard Matt.

"Charli, please talk to me. You're scaring me, and I don't know what to do," he said, then squeezed my hand. Calm. I opened my eyes and looked at him. My breathing was close to normal. I sniffled a bit as my words came out.

"Kindra doesn't want me; she won't ever adopt me," I said.

Matt looked confused again "Wait, she was going to--"

I cut him off: "I don't know, but I thought maybe," I said. "And now?" he asked, still a bit confused.

"She doesn't even want kids," I said with no sobs, no panic, just a steady stream of tears running down my cheeks. "I'm going to be stuck with the Kanes...or worse--forever," I said, and he hugged me again.

Kindra

I heard my laptop begin to ring, alerting me that a Skype call was coming through. It was Daniel. I told myself that telling him about Charli was a good idea, but as the day progressed, I began to think it might not be, and now that he was calling, I was petrified to share her. What if he didn't accept her?

I sat down in front of the computer, took a deep breath, and clicked the accept button.

His beautiful face came into view on my screen. He was smiling all the way up to his eyes. I loved him so much.

"Hey, Beautiful," he said. I blushed and looked away from the screen. After all this time, he still gave me butterflies. Beautiful, colorful butterflies that filled my insides with nervous energy.

"Hey," I responded.

"How was your day?" he asked me as he pulled a gray hoodie sweatshirt over his head and threw it on the floor. I just stared at him, sitting there in a white t-shirt in a room that looked like a college dorm room all the way on the other side of the world. He was so handsome, muscles in his arms peeking from beneath the shirt sleeves. There was a gap between his two top teeth that showed every time he smiled and deep, intense brown eyes that seemed to look clean into my soul--like he was doing now. Wait, had he asked me a question?

"Huh?" I said, realizing I hadn't answered whatever it was he had asked. He laughed that amazing, deep laugh.

"I said *how was your day*?" he repeated. "Oh, it was fine,

uneventful," I responded. "Well, we like the uneventful," he said.

"How was your day?" I asked him. *He loves me; I know he loves me. So I shouldn't be afraid to talk to him*, I thought to myself.

"My day was good," he said and pulled out a bag of sunflower seeds.

"So, what did you want to talk to me about?" he asked, throwing a few seeds in his mouth. I wasn't ready yet.

"What did you have for lunch today?" I asked him, completely ignoring his question.

"Hmmm, so you aren't ready to talk about it, so it's pretty serious," he said. I looked away from the screen with a smile, blushing again. He knew me really well.

"But you are smiling, so it's not bad. OK, I'll go along. I had a burger and fries for lunch in the mess hall," he said.

"Was it good?" I asked. He paused and looked at me for a second; he knew I was buying myself time.

"As good as a burger and fries from a military cafeteria can be," he said with a chuckle. I knew he was laughing at me but in a loving way.

"And for breakfast?" I asked. He took a deep breath and looked up at the ceiling, trying to remember breakfast.

"Uhmm, an egg white omelet with..." I cut him off and word-vomited my next sentence.

"I met a young girl outside the rape crisis center, and she's an orphan, and I think someone hurt her, and I just want to protect her, and I know that I love her, and I thought you should know cause I love you too," I said and then finally took a breath. He set the bag of sunflower seeds on his desk and sat up straighter. I think he was processing what I had said. I grew nervous in his silence. He finally spoke.

"What's her name?" he asked. It was such a simple question, but in it my fear melted away. With that question, he was telling me that it was OK.

"Her name is Charli," I said, smiling.

"Charli, huh? That's a pretty name. Why don't you tell me about her," he said. I smiled, ready to talk about my girl.

Charli

I stared at the bunk above me, tears streaming down my cheeks. My whole body hurt, and even though I had taken a shower and did my best to wash them off of me, I still felt like I had dust in my nose from the shed. My body hurt, my heart hurt, my nose hurt. It seemed really bad. It felt worse than usual. I didn't know if it was because they were rougher with me or because my heart was broken since Kindra didn't want me. I didn't know, but I knew one thing: I didn't want to do this anymore. I was tired. So very tired. And things weren't getting better. I wanted out, and I knew exactly what that meant.

I sneezed, then sneezed again through my tears. I got up and ran to the bathroom to get some tissue. I blew my nose, and the snot was dust-colored. Dust from when they threw me down into the dirt when they were done with me. I sat on the floor in the bathroom and cried and cried and cried. I pulled out my cell phone, typed the message "I want to kill myself," and hit send. As soon as the message was sent, I panicked. Why had I done that? What was I thinking? I stared at the phone. At this moment, I hated it. Stupid phone. I dropped it on the floor in front of me, pulled my knees up to my chest, and cried while rocking back and forth. I didn't know what else to do. I just rocked and cried, lost in my own pain. Drowning in it. That's what it felt like. Like I was drowning in an ocean of pain, and every time I started to get a little better, here came a wave drowning me with more pain.

I stopped rocking. It had been a while since I had sent that text message, and there had been no response. No response. No one even cared if I died. I thought I had reached the bottom of my pain, but realizing that no one even cared if I died took me to a whole new bottom. I'd never felt so alone. I kicked off the shoes that Kindra had bought for me. I'd started sleeping in them regularly to feel less alone, but right now, they just felt heavy on my feet. I lay down on the floor, tucked myself into the fetal position, and put my thumb in my mouth. I used to suck my thumb when I was little and afraid--usually when I would get moved to a new foster home. A fresh stream of tears ran down my face, and I started thinking of how I would do it. What would be the quickest way to kill myself? I could get a knife from the kitchen. Everyone in the house was asleep, and Mack and Jeremy were still in the shed. I could get a knife right now and cut my wrists. I'd heard older girls in another home talking about how a girl in the house had killed herself by cutting her wrists, and that was how a spot in the house had opened up for me to be there.

I needed a knife. I got up, thumb still in my mouth, and headed for the bathroom door. It would all be over soon. I felt a bit of relief at that thought. I reached up, and just as my hand touched the doorknob, my cell phone vibrated on the floor. I looked back at it but didn't move. I just looked at it. I didn't know what to do. Part of me wanted to run from the phone. Run straight to the kitchen, get the knife, cut my wrists, and fade away right there on the kitchen floor. But another part of me wanted to know what the message said. I knew if I looked at the phone, I wasn't going to kill myself. Not tonight, anyway. Killing myself was my out, and I wanted out. I wanted out badly.

Hand still on the doorknob, I stared at the phone. It looked like it was getting farther and farther away. I looked at my hand on the knob then back at the phone again.

"I'm sorry," I whispered to the two people whose names were stored in my phone. I turned back to the door and twisted the knob to open it. The phone vibrated again, indicating another message. I turned and ran to the phone, fell down on my knees, and snatched it off of the floor. I frantically put in my code to unlock it and went to messages. There was a "2" on the message icon. I opened it up.

Kindra: I sometimes want to kill myself too

Kindra: Kiddo, are you there? Please talk to me.

I felt like my whole world shifted, and the pain didn't seem so bad anymore. Kindra felt this way too? She walked around with these feelings inside her too? I looked at the messages and pictured Kindra on the floor with her thumb in her mouth and tears streaming down her face. I didn't want that for her. The phone vibrated in my hand. I read the new message as it appeared.

Kindra: Kiddo?

I quickly typed in a response.

Charli: You feel this way too?

Kindra

Oh, thank God she responded. I let out a breath I didn't realize I had been holding. When her first message came through, I was so stunned that I froze. I had no idea how to respond. I realized that texting me that she wanted to kill herself was a cry for help. I hadn't texted anyone before I'd tried suicide. She was brave.

I initially went into a panic, trying to figure out what to say back to her, but not my usual anxiety panic. I wasn't having trouble breathing, and my hands didn't get sweaty. The feeling was more protective than anxious, maybe like a Mama bear protecting her cub. I know my response took so long, but I was desperately trying to think of the right words to say. What did I want to hear when I was in that moment? I thought about it, and I remembered the pain. I remember sitting on my bedroom floor with a bottle of sleeping pills. My bedroom door was locked, and my oldest nephew unaware in the other room (he was about 22 at the time). I remember feeling alone. Even though there were people who loved me, one just in the other room, I still felt alone because they didn't understand what I was going through. They didn't know what it was like to feel so low that suicide seemed like the only escape. I wanted someone who'd been where I was and could talk to me about that pain.

And that's when I knew what to text her back. It seemed risky, but it would have been what I wanted to hear. I said a quick prayer and responded. "I sometimes want to kill myself too." A flood of shame washed over me as soon as the message was sent. That's not something I readily told people. Only Daniel knew I used to keep razors on standby for when I built up the courage to end it. I'd broken down one day and told him about it. I'd cried something fierce that day. It was the same day I called my mother in the middle of an emotional breakdown, and she responded to me saying, "Oh, that really happened to you? We thought you made that up."

I went and bought the razors that day and placed them in sporadic places: my car, my bathroom, on my windowsill. So wherever I was when I found the courage to do it, I would be prepared. I'd told Daniel about what my mom had said later that day and felt myself break into several pieces while telling him what had happened. I'd held myself together just long enough for the two-hour ride to the military base where he lived. Daniel didn't have many words for me that night; he just hugged me tight as I cried and forced those broken pieces to stay together with that hug. He was so mad at my mom. I didn't want him to be mad at her. She was my mom, but it did feel really good that someone had my back. I told him about the razors. Maybe that was my cry for help. Over the next few weeks, he steadily took all my razors. I never saw him do it, and he never said anything about it. Just one day, they were there, and then they were gone. They slowly disappeared from all the places I'd put them, so I never had time to build up the courage to use them.

Two days after Daniel held my pieces together, I told my therapist I wanted to kill myself.

She felt I should be committed to a mental hospital for my safety. That was a year and a half ago. The sleeping pills on my bedroom floor incident was about a year ago, and the rape itself was six years ago. I was honest with Charli and told her my truth, and she'd finally responded.

Charli: You feel this way too?

Kindra: Not as much as I used to, but yes, I feel that way too.

Charli: What do you do when you feel that way really bad?

That was a really good question. I thought for a moment, and I just kept being honest with her.

Kindra: Sometimes it gets really bad, and I can't think of anything else except how much my life hurts, and I just want the pain to stop. I want to end it. In those moments, I tell myself that I need to survive until morning because tomorrow might be better.

Sometimes, though, morning seems too far away to live with that type of pain. So I tell myself if I can just survive the next hour, but sometimes that hour seems too long. So I just try to survive the next 30 minutes, but sometimes that's too much. So I just try to survive the next 10 minutes, but even that can be too long. Five minutes can be too long; one minute can be too long. Thirty seconds can be too long, but ten seconds. I can always survive for the next ten seconds. So, on nights when it's really bad, I tell myself to try to survive for ten seconds, and after that ten seconds, we will see how I feel. Then I set a timer on my phone for ten seconds, and when the timer goes off, I'm a little bit proud of myself because I managed to keep myself alive for ten seconds. So I try for another ten seconds, and sometimes I can only live for ten seconds at a time, but I keep living. Does that make sense?

Oh, I hoped I hadn't put too much on her. These were secrets I'd learned in the mental hospital in group therapy, and they'd kept me alive. I prayed they'd keep her alive too. My cell phone chimed in her ringtone.

Charli: I think I can survive for ten seconds.

Kindra: And I will survive with you for ten seconds.

I sat quietly and watched the second-hand tick by on the clock on the wall at work.

3...2...1.

Charli: I did it; we did it. Ten more seconds?

Kindra: Ten more seconds.

This went on in increments of ten seconds up to five minutes for about half an hour.

Then:

Charli: Kindra, I know you don't want kids, but do you think maybe you could be my big sister?

A single tear rolled down my cheek. I didn't remember telling her that I didn't want kids.

Kindra: I would love to be your big sister.

Charli: Really?

I was kind of surprised at how important this was to her. How could I make it so she knew it was important to me too? I thought for a moment.

Kindra: Yes, really, and since you're going to be my little sister now, you are going to need a nickname. I'm going to call you Charli Bear.

Charli: OK, and I can call you Sissy!!!

I laughed.

Kindra: Yes, you can call me Sissy.

Charli: Sissy, will you survive with me tonight? Will you stay up with me?

Kindra: Of course I will, Charli Bear. I will stay up with you all night if you need me to because that's what big sisters do.

Charli

It was Thursday after school, and I was power walking to the park to see Kindra. I didn't see her on Tuesday because she wasn't feeling well. She told me she was sick but wanted to meet me. We hadn't seen each other since my suicide scare, but I'd promised her it was OK. I was so excited to see my big sister today. It felt like something had definitely changed for me. Someone wanted me...sort of. It was enough.

I saw Kindra's car in the parking lot, but she wasn't at our table. She was sitting on a blanket.

"SISSY!" I yelled out and started running to her. I saw her head lift in my direction; she stood up when she saw me running. She smiled big and opened her arms wide as I ran full speed into her. Her arms wrapped around me, and I melted into her. I inhaled her scent; she smelled like her lotion and...cough drops. I held her tight just a little longer, then pulled away and said, "You smell like cough drops."

She laughed and looked down at me. I could see tears running down her cheeks. "Sissy, why are you crying?" I asked her. She pulled me into another hug.

"I'm just glad you are OK," She said, squeezing me so tight. I thought something had changed for her too. I hoped so. I sat down on the blanket and started taking my shoes off. Kindra sat down and did the same.

"No shoes on our picnics," she said. I giggled and looked over at her. She had on the most colorful pair of socks I'd ever seen--they had all types of purple and gray and blue and orange with no rhyme or reason. I burst out laughing.

She smiled and said, "Oh, you like them?" Then she reached behind her and grabbed another pair of socks with the same crazy pattern and threw them at me. They landed in my lap. I picked them up.

"For me?" I asked her.

"Of course," she said. "Socks are the cure." She smiled. "Cure?" I asked with what I knew was a puzzled expression.

"It's hard to be sad when you look down at these socks-- the cure for sadness, right?" she asked. I held my new socks up with a big smile and said, "Socks are the cure," and we both laughed.

Kindra laid back on the blanket and stared up into the sky. I laid next to her and looked up too.

"It's a really pretty day, isn't it?" she asked. "Yeah, it is," I said, looking into the clouds.

"I'm glad you are still alive... still here to see this pretty day," she said, stumbling over her words. The comment caught me off guard. I had come really close to not being here to see

any more pretty days, to not smelling Kindra's lotion and cough drops, and no one knew that but her. I hadn't even told Matt.

I looked over at Kindra. Her eyes were closed, but I saw a single tear running down her cheek. I pulled out my cell phone, typed a message, hit send, and put the phone back in my pocket. A second later, I heard music and saw Kindra reach for her phone and then look at me.

"Did you just send me a text message?" she asked with a smile. I smiled back. She pulled out her phone and read out loud, "I'm glad you're still alive to see this pretty day too." She sat up and wrapped her arms around me.

"How did I end up so lucky to have you as a little sister?" she said. I just smiled. "Hey, was that 'Same Love' that played when I texted you?" I asked her.

"Yeah! It's your favorite song, so it plays whenever you text me," she said.

"I didn't know you could do that on the phone; Matt never showed me that," I said.

"Well, he's going to show me tomorrow--that's for sure," I thought to myself.

"Why is that your favorite song?" she asked me. I lay down next to her. She was my sister now, so I could share some things with her. That's what I told myself.

"In the house I was in before this one. There were a lot of us. There's always a lot of us, but there were these two older girls in the house--Maya and Michelle. They were really close. They did everything together. They took care of each other; they looked out for each other; they

loved each other. They wanted to get married one day. I hadn't seen love in so long; it made me happy—even if I wasn't the one being loved. Watching them made me think someone could love me too. There wasn't love in that house. It wasn't a horrible house; it wasn't like there was a lot of abuse or anything, but no one cared for us either. We were all just paychecks. Those two girls brought love into the house, though, and "Same Love" was their favorite song. They danced to it all the time. It was nice, but then..." I paused and took a deep breath.

Kindra sat up. I think she could tell I had started to struggle because she pulled out the hairbrush and patted the space in front of her. I quickly sat up and scooted over. She began brushing my hair, and I just sat quietly with my own thoughts.

"Sissy?" I finally said.

"Yes, Charli Bear?" Kindra responded, still brushing my hair. "How can love be wrong?" I asked her.

"What do you mean?" she asked.

"All that most foster kids like me want is to be loved and wanted. More than we want new clothes, or our own room or even..." I looked down at my feet. "Even new shoes," I said, dusting off the shoes with my hand. "And there was no love in that house, Sissy, and Maya and Michelle? They loved each other, so they had what we all wanted. Someone to love them, and it was good and pretty and warm." Tears began to spill down my cheeks. I kept talking, though. "They loved each other, and they played that song, and they were happy, but then one of the fosters caught them kissing, and she got mad. She said that it was wrong, and she called

the case manager and the case manager said they couldn't do that because they were sisters, but they weren't sisters; they just lived in the same house. They all said it was wrong, and they moved Maya to another house, and Michelle had no way to find her. So she just cried all the time, and there was no love in the house anymore, and no one played the song and no one danced. I just don't understand--if all we want is love, and we find someone to love us when no one else will, then how can it be wrong? Especially if it's the only love we have? How can it be wrong, Sissy? Why did they take their love away?" I was full-on crying and shaking at this point. Kindra dropped the brush and pulled me into her lap. She wrapped her arms around me.

"I don't know, Kiddo, but I love you, I love you, Charli...Charli...What's your full name?" she asked me.

"Charlotte Victoria Lauren," I said into her shirt. "I love you, Charlotte Victoria Lauren and no one can take that love away,

OK? Do you understand?" she asked me. I nodded my head in her shirt. She loved me…Kindra loved me.

My whole body felt warm--was that the love? I just lay in her arms, in her love. I didn't know what to say.

"I hate my middle name." It popped out of my mouth before I could stop it. I did hate my middle name, but this probably wasn't the time to mention it. I pulled my face out of Kindra's shirt. She lifted my chin with her finger so I was looking eye to eye with her.

"Victoria is a beautiful name," she said. I sighed. "I don't like it," I said, pouting. She laughed at me.

"But you like 'Same Love,'" she said. I smiled a bit.

"It reminds me of when there was love in the house. It reminds me of love," I said quietly. Kindra picked up her phone; she pressed a few buttons on it, and "Same Love" started to play. I hummed along to the song while being loved.

"I love you too, Sissy," I said to her.

Kindra

I had been home about an hour from my picnic with Charli. My emotions were completely raw. I had "Same Love" playing on repeat on my laptop. The song had taken on a whole new meaning after seeing it through her eyes (or ears). I couldn't help but get emotional thinking about all those kids that just wanted to be loved. My Charli just wanted to be loved, and here I was, worried about the holes in her shoes.

Charlotte Victoria Lauren--such a beautiful name. I laughed to myself--even though she was an orphan, she still hated her middle name like most kids did. She was different in so many ways and yet still so similar, still just a kid.

I opened my Twitter account and checked the notifications. MC Spinner had responded to my message. A real celebrity had responded to me. I forgot how to breathe. I finally took a breath and climbed off of the bed, and backed away from the laptop slowly. I didn't want to break it. MC Spinner was in there. Well, he wasn't in there, but I didn't want to risk hurting the laptop. I backed into my bathroom and sat on the edge of the bathtub. I put my head in my hands, trying to wrap my mind around what was happening.

MC Spinner was a well-known hip-hop artist in the late 80's early 90's. He was huge--he was a big deal, and he had responded to me. Oh, crap--I needed to respond back. What should I say? What if I messed this up? I felt my chest tighten just a bit.

"NO!" I yelled out in the bathroom. The noise startled me as it bounced off of the walls.

"This is a good thing," I told myself. No need to panic. My

palms were already sweaty.

"Ugh," I said as I got up. I ran to find my cell phone. It was on the counter in the kitchen.

I needed Daniel. I opened my email on my phone.

I need to talk. Are you busy? It's important.

Love, Me

I hit send and stared at the phone, hoping for an instant response. No such luck. I looked up and peeked into my bedroom at my laptop, still sitting on my bed. It looked OK; it hadn't blown up or anything. Wait, was I being ridiculous? Spontaneous combustion was a thing, and today would be the day my laptop exploded. I looked down at the phone again. Nothing. I sent another email. HELLO was all it said. I hit 'send' and began pacing in the living room.

Every time I passed my bedroom door, I took a quick glance at the laptop, but I didn't go back in the room.

What was taking him so long? What time was it in Korea right now anyway? My mind couldn't process numbers to calculate that in its current state of stress. Wait, did I smell smoke? I dropped the phone and ran to my bedroom door. I stood in the doorway, staring at the laptop. There was no smoke coming from it. There was no smell of smoke. I was losing it.

"Calm down," I said out loud to myself. I walked into the kitchen and got a container of juice out of the fridge. I set it on the counter and reached for a glass from the cabinet when I heard my phone alert me to a new email.

"Daniel!" I yelled and ran and picked the phone up off of the floor. I opened the email.

"I'm here, are you OK?" it said.

I paused--*was* I OK? Yes, I was OK. So I responded, "Yes, but I need to talk, are you busy?" and hit send.

An email came right back: "I have a minute, let's Skype."

Yeah, Skype! I got up to go get the laptop and stopped in the doorway. Crap--the laptop.

"I can't Skype; I can't touch my laptop." I hit send.

"Why not? What's wrong with your computer?" he quickly responded. At that moment, something clicked in my head. Perhaps this thing with the laptop was overblown. It wasn't really going to self-destruct...was it? Somewhere in my mind, I knew I was being irrational, but in my current reality, I wasn't so sure. I couldn't always trust myself to make the best decisions. I'd allowed myself to trust someone who raped me, and people told me it was my fault, so I didn't always trust myself. But I trusted Daniel. He always reigned me back in.

So I typed, "MC Spinner responded to my message on Twitter, and I don't know how to respond back, and I'm scared my computer is going to spontaneously combust, and I will lose him forever before I get any help." I clicked send.

He responded, "THE MC Spinner?"

"Yes," I typed back to him. I was starting to see a bit of the lunacy of my thought process. His message came through.

"A few things. First, have I told you lately that I love your smile? ..." I smiled from ear to ear. He did that on purpose. I went back to the email. "Second, you remember what my job is, right? I am an I.T. guy for the United States Navy, so I know a bit about computers. I know everything about your computer because I set it up before I left. So I know with 100% certainty that it's not going to blow up, and if on the -10% chance that it did, you can access your Twitter account from another computer so you won't lose MC Spinner. So, are you ready to

Skype now?"

He had a way of making things make sense without making me feel completely crazy--even if sometimes I was.

"YES," I responded and hit send. Not five seconds later, my laptop was ringing, a Skype call coming through. I accepted the call, and his picture came into view, but he had a pillow in front of his face. He peeked his head out from the side of the pillow and said, "Just in case your computer blows up." He smiled that smile I love so much.

"Don't make fun," I responded, laughing at myself. "It could happen." He laughed. "So, MC Spinner, huh?" he asked.

"I know--it's crazy, right? "I said back. "So?" he said.

"So what?" I asked back.

"So, what has the conversation been? What did he say? What did you say?" he asked. "Oh, right!" I said. "Well, I sent him a message that said, 'Hey, can I ask you something? 'And he responded, 'Sure, what's up?'"

There was this awkward pause where Daniel just stared at me. Finally, he asked, "Then what?"

I looked at him, perplexed.

"Then I freaked out and emailed you," I said. He laughed so hard I was almost offended. "Baby, you're so cute," he said.

"There is nothing cute about this; what do I say next? How do I not scare him off?" I said in a frenzy.

"Easy, beautiful, take a breath. You just tell him your story like you tell me your story," he said.

"But why would he want to help me?" I asked, already feeling discouraged. "Why wouldn't he help you?" Daniel responded.

"Because I'm a nobody," I said.

"He's a nobody," he shot back. I just looked at him.

"OK, OK, maybe he's not a nobody, but he's just a person. Just tell him your story." "And what if he says no?" I asked.

"Then you keep trying, but who knows, this could be it." "OK, I guess I will tell him my story," I said reluctantly. "When?" Daniel asked. Ugh, he knew me way too well.

"Fine, I will do it when we hang up," I said.

"Good--do it now, and we will chat later, OK?" he said. I just sat there, ignoring him, wanting to keep him on this Skype call as long as I could because A) I missed him, and B) I didn't want to respond to MC Spinner yet.

"Come on," he said. "This is for your future; this could be it, and you're gonna potentially miss it just to sit here and look at my face?" He smiled.

"It's a nice face," I said back sheepishly. "Babe, you got this; go get your dog," he said. "OK, I love you," I said to him.

"I love you too," he said. Then the screen went black. I took a deep breath, opened my Twitter account back up, and began to type.

"MC Spinner, my name is Kindra. I am a survivor of rape who suffers from PTSD, and I was wondering if you would consider helping me?"

Charli

"Hey, you want to come over?" Matt asked. It was Friday after school and we were sitting on the bleachers. I looked up at him because I'd obviously misunderstood his question.

"What?" I said.

"Do you want to come over?" he repeated without making eye contact. I waited, thinking that after a few seconds, my brain would work out what he'd just said. Nothing changed.

"Do I want to come over?" I repeated back to him to see if I was hearing him correctly. "Yeah," he said. OK, so I had heard him correctly.

"No," I responded sharply.

"What do you mean, 'No?'" he asked. I truly didn't understand what was going on. "Isn't it family night?" I said, grappling for excuses. I knew Matt was my friend, but his parents? Adults can be weird.

"Yes, it's family night, that's why I invited you, because...I consider you my family."

I quickly turned away. I didn't want him to see me tear up. He considered me family.

Now I wanted to go. I wanted to be with "family."

"But your parents..." I started, and he quickly cut me off.

"They don't know about that stuff. They just think...well...that you are poor. Because I bring you lunch every day."

I laughed. "I guess I am poor though, huh?" I said.

"We can take you home after. I mean, what time do you have to be home?" he asked. "Uhm, he doesn't start looking for one of us until a little after dark, so I just always make sure I'm back by then," I said. It was weird talking about stuff like this out loud. "So you will come?" Matt asked again.

"I guess so!" I said with excitement in my voice.

"OK, great, grab your stuff. My mom will be here in a few minutes to get us," he said. "Wait, don't you have to ask?" I said while picking up my backpack and following him down the bleacher steps.

"I asked last night; Mom knows you're coming," he said. I stopped on the steps.

"Hey, how did you know I would say yes? And why didn't you ask me earlier today?" I asked him. He stopped and turned around to face me with a kind of guilty smile on his face.

"I didn't know you would say yes. I just hoped you would, and I didn't tell you earlier because I knew if I told you at lunch, you'd have talked yourself out of it by the end of the day. Now come on." He turned back around. I guess he did have a point. I mean, should I really even be going to his family's house? Could this lead to something bad?

"There's her car. Oh, and if she asks, your mom said, 'Yes, it's ok for you to come over.'" He grabbed my arm and dragged me toward a gray minivan.

"My mom?" I said as he opened the sliding door and pushed me into the back of the van.

"Shhhh," he whispered in my ear and climbed into the van next to me. He threw his backpack on the floor and began to buckle his seat belt, so I did the same.

"Hey, Mom, this is my friend Charli. Charli, this is my mom," Matt said.

"Nice to meet you, Mrs…uhm. Mrs. Matt's mom," I said with a laugh. I was nervous and couldn't remember Matt's last name. Matt's mom laughed.

"You can call me Mrs. Lindsey or Mrs. Alexander--whichever you like--and it's so nice to meet you, Charli. Matt has told me so much about you."

I cut my eyes towards Matt, but he was already shaking his head no. Letting me know he hadn't told them anything. I calmed down a little bit.

"Matt, honey, did you give the note to your teacher requesting the opportunity to retake that math test that you failed?" Matt's mom asked. The look he gave her looked like he was shooting darts out of his eyes at the back of her head.

"Yes, ma'am," he responded between gritted teeth.

"Matt, you didn't tell me you failed a math test," I said to him. He rolled his eyes at me.

"Everyone isn't great at math like you," he said, clearly agitated with the whole conversation. I was definitely starting to relax until Matt's mom said, "Charli, your mom did say it's OK for you to come over, right?"

"My mom?" I said out loud, then stopped. I thought about the lady in the house that we were told to call Mom. She hardly ever came out of her room. I might see her once or twice a week and always in passing. She never spoke to us kids--she just kind of looked through us. We knew she knew what was happening because she always left fresh towels in the bathroom after Mack had his way with one of us. She always looked sad and had on pajamas. I couldn't imagine asking her anything.

Matt nudged my arm, bringing me out of my thoughts and back to the conversation. "Uhm, yes, my mom said it was OK,"

I quickly responded.

"Good. Matt, your dad should be just ordering the pizza. Did I hear him right? He said you asked for ham and pineapples on one of them?"

I smiled and looked at Matt; he was smiling too. He'd remembered I loved pineapples. "Yes, ma'am," he said.

"Well, OK," she responded. I settled into my seat and finally relaxed fully. Is this what family was like--them remembering your favorite things? I couldn't believe I was going to be a part of a family pizza night. I imagined what it would be like to have a family pizza night with Kindra, but then I got sad because that would probably never happen. She wasn't my mom. I pushed that thought out of my mind. I wanted to enjoy tonight. I wanted to remember every detail of the family pizza night with Matt.

Kindra

The night was going smoothly--laundry done, bathrooms cleaned, breakfast prepped. My life was better than it had been in a long time. Daniel loved me, MC Spinner had agreed to help me get my service dog, and Charli had called me from family pizza night at Matt's house. All was right in the world. Well, at least in my crazy little corner of it.

I sent MC Spinner the link to the Little Angels Service Dogs page that told my story and requested a donation. I wanted him to know that my request for help was serious and not a scam. He'd said he wanted to help. The prospect of getting my service dog no longer seemed impossible. I could really get my dog with his help. I was basking in the joy of it all when my phone alerted me to a text message from Charli. I glanced at the clock. This was about the time she messaged me every night to tell me good night. I looked at her message.

Charli: Hey, Sissy.

Kindra: Hey Charli Bear, you all ready for bed?

Charli: Yes, but I'm too excited.

Kindra: Excited?

Charli: I had such a good time at Matt's. It was so great to be a part of a family. Sissy, do you think that maybe one day we could have a family night?

Kindra: Sure, Bear, I think we could work that out.

Charli: OK, good.

Kindra: Guess what?

Charli: What?

Kindra: A famous person on Twitter said they will help me get my service dog!!!

Charli: What? That's amazing! Who is it?

Kindra: MC Spinner!

Charli: Who's that?

I had to chuckle to myself. She definitely made me feel old. *Kindra: A big deal rapper from the late 80's early 90's.*

Charli: Oh.

Kindra: He's a pretty big deal.

Charli: And he wants to help you.

Kindra: Yep.

Charli: That's awesome, Sissy. Is he just going to give you the money?

Kindra: I don't know. He said he needed to check out the organization and that he would get back to me.

Charli: That is soooo cool. This is happening for you!

Kindra: Yep. Pineapple sodas all around!

Charli: Cheers!!

I laughed at her response. My precious, silly Charli. About 30 minutes went by. Then I realized that Charli had told me she was excited but hadn't told me goodnight. So I messaged her back.

Kindra: Hey Bear.

Charli: Yes Sissy.

Kindra: You didn't tell me goodnight, Kiddo.

Charli: Cause I'm not going to sleep yet.

Kindra: Well, what are you doing?

A couple of minutes passed with no response.

Kindra: Bear…

Charli: I'm building up my courage.

Building up her courage? What did that mean?

Kindra: Building up your courage for what?

Charli: To ask you something.

What on earth could she want to ask me that she would have to build her courage up for? My mind raced through things like boys and dating or, heck, girls and dating. As her big sister, I guessed I needed to be ready to talk with her about these things.

Kindra: You know you can talk to me about anything.

"Or," I wondered, "Is she finally going to talk to me about what happened to her?" Oh boy, was I ready for that conversation? I took some deep, calming breaths. Whatever she wanted to talk about, I was going to be here for her. A message came through.

Charli: I had such a good time at Matt's for family night, and I know you said we could have a family night one day, but I don't want to have it for one day with you. I want to have it every Friday with you, and I know you don't want kids, so you don't have to be my mom, but you could be my foster sister. Sissy, could I come live with you?

I wasn't as surprised at her question as I should have been or as I felt I should have been. I think deep down inside, I knew this day was coming. Deep down, I knew I wanted her safe with me as much as I knew she wanted to be with me. I was scared to be honest with myself about those thoughts, about all that getting her would entail. How hard it would be. Deep down, I knew she had been thinking about it too. Here she was, being the one brave

enough to bring it up. She's so strong, and she shouldn't have to be. I thought about how to respond and decided I didn't sugarcoat things with her, and I wasn't going to start now.

Kindra: Charli I would love for you to come live with me. I've thought about it, and I'm sorry I never brought it up. I was scared. I still am. Scared I won't be enough, scared they won't let me have you, scared that you deserve better than me, but if you want me, then I'm here.

I paused from typing the message to gather my thoughts. This was going to be difficult, and I needed her to know that. I went back to the message.

Kindra: Charli, I don't have myself together the way I would need to in order to foster you right this minute. I'm not exactly sure what the qualifications are, but I know I'm barely making enough money to keep myself afloat. I'm going to find out what I have to do to get you. It's going to take some time, probably a while, but I'm going to do my best to figure this out. So I need you to be patient with me. So we can figure this out together. Deal?

I hit send and waited. I thought I'd be freaking out and feel like: *what have I done*? The same way I'd felt when I'd agreed to get Charli a cell phone with no idea how I'd pay for it. I had no idea how I would afford this, but I still felt a sense of peace and calm. Like this was the right thing to do. I'd just have to figure it out. My phone went off on my desk.

Charli: You really want me?

Oh boy, here come the waterworks. I felt the tears building in my eyes. This beautiful girl had spent most of her life believing no one wanted her. I had my issues with my family--feeling abandoned by them when I needed them most, misunderstood by them, and even completely alone in my struggles with the aftermath of the rape. But I never felt like they truly didn't want me. That no one wanted me, I couldn't imagine the hole that would leave inside a person.

Kindra: Of course, I want you, my beautiful girl.

Charli: :-) OK, I'm going to sleep now. I love you.

I laughed. She'd gotten what she needed and was ready to go to sleep. I hoped she slept lighter tonight.

Kindra: I love you too, Charli Bear.

Charli: Oh, and goodnight.

Kindra: Goodnight Princess.

Charli

I left the house early, hoping to catch Matt before school started. We never saw each other before school, but I was determined today. I had waited all weekend to talk to him. This was not a conversation that could be had by text. I was looking around where the baseball players hung out, but I didn't see him. I didn't really know who he hung out with besides me. Then the bell rang.

I stopped and weighed my options: should I go to class and catch up with Matt at lunch, or should I go try to pull him from his first-period class and potentially get us both in trouble? Hmmm. There was absolutely no way I could wait until lunch to tell him. I started heading in the direction of his first-period class when the bell rang again. I was now late, but this was worth it.

I saw a few other kids speed-walking through the halls, late as well. I got to Matt's class and stopped before going in. How was I going to get him out of class? I peeked my head in the window and saw him sitting off to the left. He looked up just in time to lock eyes with me, his eyebrows raised. I just smiled. I know he was wondering what I was doing there. I devised a plan in my head, took a deep breath, and walked into the classroom. The teacher stopped speaking and gave me full attention when I came through the door; the rest of the class did the same. I looked over at Matt again. He had a look on his face that screamed, "WHAT ARE YOU DOING?" I had to look away from him to keep from laughing. I looked at the teacher and said, "We need Matthew Alexander to come to the attendance office."

As soon as the words were out of my mouth, the students looked away and went back to what they were doing. The teacher looked over to Matt, said, "Go ahead," and then went back to teaching. Matt grabbed his backpack and followed me out the door. Once the door closed behind us and we were a few steps away from it, I whisper-yelled, "Holy crap, I can't believe that worked!"

"Charli, what are you doing? What's going on? Is everything ok?" Matt said. I could see the worry forming in his eyes. What I had done *was* extremely irregular.

"Yes, everything is OK. I just need to talk to you. Come on, let's go over by the gym," I said and started walking. He grabbed my shoulder. I turned around and saw the worry sketched all over his face.

"I promise it's not bad," I said and gave him a big smile. Then, I grabbed his arm and dragged him in the direction of the gym. "Come on," I said.

"OK, OK," he said, but I could still hear the concern in his voice.

We got to the gym and went around the side to an area that was mostly hidden from view. I took a deep breath and froze. I was scared to say it out loud. I was scared it was real, scared it wasn't.

Matt looked at me. "Well, what is it?" he said. He was really nervous.

"Kindra wants me; she wants me, Matt, she really does," I blurted out. Matt looked confused.

"What?" he said. I looked around to make sure we were alone, then pulled out my cell phone, opened it to Kindra's and my conversation, and handed the phone to him. He took the phone, glanced around, and began reading the messages. I watched his face slowly transform from worry to excitement. He finished reading and looked up at me with the biggest smile I'd ever seen on him and before I knew what was happening he grabbed me around my waist and picked me up into the air.

"She wants you! You're going to have a home!" He yelled.

"Shhhh," I said. "Right," he said and put me down and glanced around again to make sure we were still alone. Then he pulled me into a bear hug.

"You're going to get a home," he said again over my shoulder. I pulled back from the hug, smiling, but saw that Matt was crying.

"Matt…" I said, and he cut me off, wiping his tears on his sleeve.

"No, it's OK. I just…I just thought you were coming to tell me they were going to move you or something. I thought you were coming to say goodbye. I mean, we had such a good time on Friday, and my mom told me you were welcome to come back anytime, and then the way you popped up, I thought they were taking you away, and you wouldn't be able to come to family pizza night, and I was going to lose you, but you aren't; you can stay forever and come to family pizza night all the time." He pulled me into another hug. "I'm always worried they will take you away, and you wouldn't even have gotten a chance to say bye. I worry when you are late for

lunch that they took you away or worse, that they hurt you really badly, but we won't have to worry about any of that anymore!" he said.

All I could do was smile, even though part of me was so sad that being my friend was so stressful for him. But I wouldn't dwell on that now. Now, I would just be happy.

"We need to get back to class. I'm probably going to get

detention for being late, but this was totally worth it," I said, smiling ear to ear.

"Yeah, I'm going to research how to foster a kid in Texas in my computer class today so we can help Kindra out," he said.

I felt the tears start to fill my eyes, but I wasn't going to cry. Not right now. I just smiled and said, "Thanks, Matt, I'll see you at lunch," and headed towards my class. I felt like I was floating on air.

Kindra

It was Monday, a little after 1 pm, and I was just waking up. I had worked the night before but was off tonight, which was great because I needed some time to process and research. I pulled out a pad of paper and wrote on the top.

Things Needed to Foster Charli 1.

I stared at the number one for a while. Just the idea of fostering Charli seemed so huge. Would they find me acceptable? Could I be the best thing for her? I couldn't be any worse than the people who didn't care if her shoes had duct tape on them. I looked around my apartment. It was nice, but it was small--a one-bedroom that was a little over 550 square feet. There was no way they would let her live here with me, would they?

I pushed the pad aside and got up to brush my teeth. I all of a sudden noticed how small the bathroom was. I imagined her trying to get ready for school and me trying to get ready for work at the same time. "Good thing I work night shift," I said out loud and rinsed my toothbrush.

I needed to talk to Daniel, but I was scared. I'd just agreed to take on a child without even discussing it with him first. Was our love strong enough for this? What if he didn't want her?

What if he made me choose between the two of them? We had a Skype date coming up this week, so maybe I could talk to him about it then.

My phone beeped, a text from Matt. He was supposed to be in school.

Matt: www.dfps.state.tx.us/adoptionandfoster_care/get

started/steps.asp

I clicked on the link, and my phone took me to a web page that said "Steps to become a foster/adoptive parent." I laughed out loud. I guess Charli had told him. I did a quick

read-through of the page. It didn't seem super overwhelming; the requirements didn't seem too daunting. However, two things stood out: "Be financially stable" and "Must have a bedroom of at least 80 square feet for a foster child."

Technically, I was financially stable. I mean, all my bills were paid on time, but I definitely didn't make enough to take Charli on, and my apartment was not going to suffice, either. I shot Matt a text back.

Kindra: Thanks Matt, now put your phone away! :-)

He quickly responded:

Matt: OK.

What a sweet kid he was. I picked up the pad I had been writing on and wrote two things on it.

Things Needed to Foster Charli

1. A second or better-paying job
2. A bigger apartment

I tossed the pad aside. I would come back to that. I pulled out my laptop and opened it to Twitter. MC Spinner had connected me with his manager, Darla. Thus far, she had been really nice. She'd asked my story, so I'd told her. I told her the benefits of a service dog and how I expected it to change my life. I was glad she was kind of a go-between of MC Spinner and myself. It's always been a bit easier to share in depth about my rape with women than men. I had been trying to find a happy medium when reaching out to her and MC Spinner. I didn't want to annoy them, but I didn't want them to forget about me either. So, I'd regularly started commenting and retweeting MC Spinner's tweets. He commented back sometimes, which was cool, and I would send Darla a message here and there. Today I sent her a message that said "Hey, hope you are having a great day. I have some questions for you, hopefully we can talk later." I didn't really have any questions, but I would by the time she responded. I just wanted to keep myself relevant to them. I closed down the laptop and got up to start getting dressed. I needed to go get a newspaper. I had to start looking for another job.

Charli

"When are you going to tell her?" Matt asked me. We were sitting at a table in his kitchen doing homework after school. This was my third time at his house. I liked coming over; his house was peaceful.

"Tell who what?" I asked him, looking up from my math homework.

"Tell Kindra about what happens in that house," he said with a look on his face that showed he had no intentions of backing down. I accidentally knocked my cup of water over when I started frantically looking around to make sure his parents were out of earshot. Matt jumped up and got a towel.

"My dad is still at work, and my mom is in the backyard in her garden. No one can hear us, Charli," he said as he wiped the table down.

"Why would I need to tell her anything?" I asked him. I felt heat rush to my face. I was so mad at him. Why was he doing this now? His house was one of my few places of peace and happiness, and he brings this up.

"So she can help you," he said. His voice had lost its edge and sounded more like he was pleading with me.

"She's trying to foster me, doesn't that count?" I asked him while trying to soften my voice, trying not to be angry with him.

"Once you move in with her, do you think everything is just going to magically go away?" he asked.

"Yes," I responded. I'd be in a safe house with love. Kindra wouldn't hurt me, so what was he getting at? He sighed.

"What about the PTSD?" he asked. I was becoming so confused. "What about it?" I asked him.

"It's not going to just go away," he said.

"When did he become an expert on PTSD," I thought to myself. "I've been reading up on it," he said, as if reading my thoughts. "Oh," was all I could say.

"Charli, I think you have it bad, and you don't even realize it," he said.

"I'm the one that told you about PTSD, and you didn't even believe I could have it," I said back to him.

"I know, and I was wrong, but I've been researching it," he said. "Matt, I'm OK," I said, unsure what else to say.

We both just stared at each other, neither of us breaking eye contact. Then he said, "I read that 40% of adolescent girls who experienced stuff like you had thoughts of suicide." I looked away from him immediately. I'd never told him about that night, about those thoughts, about how close I came. He kept talking.

I interrupted, "I would never do something like that if I lived with Kindra." But I couldn't meet his eyes.

"Are you sure? Because PTSD doesn't just go away," he insisted. I thought about Kindra saying she had been dealing with her PTSD for six years. "When we walk past the football team at school, you always get really quiet and look down at your shoes, and you get tense. I've

seen you do it for a long time, so I try to walk between you and them when they pass," he said. I didn't know he'd been doing that.

"Isn't Mack's son on the football team at the high school?" he asked. I nodded. Anyone in a football jersey made me feel nervous. I was surprised Matt remembered Mack's name. We'd talked one day after school on the bleachers, and I'd told Matt everything. I'd told him about Mack and Jeremy and the shed. I'd cried, and Matt sat and listened with hard eyes and his hands in fists. After I got it all out, he hugged me, and we never talked about it again. I'd felt so much better being able to talk about it out loud. Maybe that was why Kindra went to those meetings. I was still surprised Matt remembered the details.

"When you get nervous around football players, that's PTSD," he said. I thought about it.

I guess it made sense.

"What about in your classes? Where do you sit?" he asked. "What do you mean?" I asked him back.

"Like, do you sit in the front or the middle or to the left?" he asked. I thought about it and realized what he was getting at.

"In any of my classes that don't have assigned seating, I sit as close as I can to the door," I said.

"Why?" he asked.

"So I can get out quickly if something goes wrong," I said.

"What could go wrong in your classroom?" he asked. I thought and thought, and I couldn't really come up with anything. Nothing had ever happened to me in a classroom for me to feel that way.

"That's the PTSD," he said. "That's why you have to tell Kindra so she can help you."

"She can help me without knowing all of that stuff, Matt. She's getting a service dog to help her with her PTSD, so when I live with her, it can help me too. She just has to raise enough money to get it," I said.

"How much money does she need?" he asked. "Like ten thousand dollars," I said.

"Whoa!" he said.

"I know, but she's talking to this famous guy named MC Spinner, who might help her," I said.

"Who's MC Spinner?" he asked.

"I dunno," I said and shrugged my shoulders. "She needs a GoFundMe page," he said.

"What's that?" I asked just as Matt's mom opened the sliding glass door and walked in.

We both fell silent. She walked over to the sink and began washing the dirt off of her hands. "How's the homework coming along?" she asked over her shoulder.

"Fine," Matt and I said in unison. "You guys hungry?" she asked.

"Charli's always hungry," Matt said. I cut my eyes at him, but we all laughed.

Kindra

It was Friday, and I was at the park waiting to meet Charli. It wasn't our normal day to meet, but I needed to see her. I needed to talk to her about something important. I'd messaged her earlier in the day and asked if she could meet me at the park even though we'd just seen each other yesterday. She told me she'd planned on going to Matt's after school for their family pizza night. I told her it was pretty important that I see her, and she agreed. I'd stopped at Little Caesars and grabbed a $5 pizza. It was the least I could do since I'd taken her away from family night with pizza. I had been running errands all day and had forgotten to put the blanket we used for picnics back in my car after I'd washed it yesterday. So we would have to sit at the table. I'd made sure I grabbed the brush though, just in case.

I had the table all set when I saw her walking up. She looked so much more confident and happy than the girl I'd met outside the women's center. I smiled. She walked up to the table and set her backpack on the ground. She smiled big when she noticed the pizza box.

"Family pizza night!" she said. I just smiled back at her and silently prayed this went well. "No picnic today?" she asked as she sat down.

"I forgot the blanket," I told her.

Charli put two slices of pizza on her plate. I put one on mine. I wasn't super hungry. I was nervous. About halfway through her second slice, she looked up and asked me, "What's wrong, Sissy?" I guess I was acting a bit out of character, hardly talking. I hadn't even asked about her day, but I guess it was time to talk.

“Nothing’s wrong; I just need to talk to you about some things,” I said. She set her slice down and put her hands in her lap. I could tell she was becoming anxious, and that was not what I wanted. I saw her glance over at the hairbrush.

“I don’t think we need it, but if at any point you feel like you do, you just come sit next to me on this side OK?” I said, and she nodded. “OK, so you know how we have been talking about the things I need in order to foster you?” I asked her.

“Yes, you need more money and a bigger apartment,” she said. I’d been very honest with her about the process. I needed her to know it was going to take a while but that I was trying.

“Yes, that's right,” I said back to her. “Well, yesterday morning, I had a job interview,” I said.

“You didn’t tell me that when I saw you yesterday,” she said. “I know; I didn’t want to get your hopes up in case it didn’t go well.” She eyed me suspiciously.

“But it went well, right?” she asked. I smiled.

“They called and offered me the job this morning,” I said. “Yaaaa!” She jumped up and ran around the table to hug me. “What’s the job?” she asked after pulling away.

“Well, it’s part-time, and I would be a caregiver for a 13-year-old girl who has Down’s Syndrome and some other health issues,” I said.

“I think you will be great at that,” she said, smiling.

I took a breath. “I hope so, but Bear, listen, I have to work this job in addition to my night job. This new job will be Monday through Friday from 2:30 pm to 6:30 pm,” I said and waited.

She was smiling and nodding, and then…it clicked. “But that’s during our time,” she said.

"I know Kiddo, but I need to take this job so I can be more financially stable so I can get you," I said, hoping she understood. "Bear, this isn't permanent. I just need more income, and in a few months, I should be able to move into a bigger place, and we will be that much closer, OK?" I asked. I needed her to be okay with this. I needed her to know I wasn't abandoning her. She sat quietly.

"Bear, when we get our new apartment, what color should we paint your room?" I asked. She lifted her head slowly.

"My room?" she said in awe.

"Yes, pretty girl, that's why I'm taking this job so you can have your own room," I said. "I don't need my own room, Kindra; it's OK," she said.

"Well, the state of Texas says you need your own room, and I agree. I know it's going to suck not seeing me very often for a little while. It's going to suck for me too, but I'm doing this so you can be with me, OK?" I said.

"OK!" she said and smiled, then leaned in for another hug.

"I start my new job on Monday, which is why I wanted to see you today. I'm not sure when we will be able to do this again just yet, so I need you to be strong and remember I'm working to get you, and you still have your phone, so you can call or text me anytime, OK?" I said. I was getting emotional as I spoke. Charli reached over me and grabbed the hairbrush and held it up in front of me. I smiled and nodded. I pulled my hair out of the ponytail and ran my fingers through it a few times to get the kinks out. I turned a bit on the bench with my back to her.

Charli stood up behind me and began brushing my hair. A single tear escaped my eye.

"How did I end up with such an amazing girl?" I was

thinking when she leaned in my ear and whispered, “I want to paint my room purple, Sissy.”

Charli

I walked up to our table and looked around. It was strange being at our meeting place, knowing Kindra wasn't coming. It felt cold and lonely, and yet I felt close to her here at the same time. It was Thursday, almost a week since the last time I'd seen her. Even though this was only the second day I would miss seeing her, it felt like so much longer--maybe because I didn't know when I was going to see her, maybe because I really missed her hugs. I mean, I got hugs from Matt sometimes, but it wasn't the same. I couldn't get lost in Matt's hugs the way I did in Kindra's. He didn't smell like her. Like Lovespell from Victoria's Secret, I remembered when she told me when she was teaching me grounding techniques. I closed my eyes and tried to conjure the smell of her up, but I couldn't. I felt the tears start to build behind my eyes. I really missed her. I pulled out my phone and sent her a text message.

Charli- I miss you, Sissy.

I set the phone down, pulled my notebook out of my backpack, and set it on the table. I reached back into my bag to pull out a pen when my phone vibrated. I picked up the phone and read the message.

Kindra- I miss you too, Bear. You ok?

The tears started to flow. I quickly wiped them away with the sleeve of my shirt and responded.

Charli- Yes, I'm fine, just missing you.

I knew she needed to do this for me, and I didn't want her worrying about me. Another message came through.

I love you.

More tears. I didn't even attempt to wipe these away. I responded,

I love you too.

Then I picked up my pen and flipped to the sheet of paper I had been working on at school today.

Things I want in my room

- Purple walls
- My new shoes
- A service dog

Kindra

I sat in the waiting room at Paige's office, waiting for my name to be called. I sat by the door like always but wasn't quite as ready to bolt as usual. I wasn't as scared. It was an unfamiliar but nice feeling. Almost a sense of calm.

"Kindra," I looked up and saw Paige at the door. I smiled at her, gathered my things, and followed her to her office.

"So, how's the new job?" she asked as I was making myself comfortable on the couch.

"It's good, I like it. The girl I take care of is a sweetheart except when she feels like she isn't getting my attention, then she throws things at me. I nicknamed her chipmunk because her cheeks are big," I said, laughing, and then yawned.

"Are you getting enough rest? Between the two jobs, you are pulling 60 hours a week now, right?" Paige asked.

"Yes. It's an adjustment, but I'm doing OK," I said back.

"OK, let's talk about fundraising and MC Spinner, how's that going?" She asked. "Well," I said and broke into a shy smile, "Things are going good, I think. I talk to his manager more than him, she's really nice. They haven't confirmed exactly how they are going to help me yet, but I'm being patient." I said. "OK, all seems good there, and how are things with Daniel?" she asked. I paused. I usually light up at the mere mention of him. Today, a sliver of fear arose. It wasn't major, barely noticeable, but it was foreign in regard to my feelings for him, so I felt it. I needed to talk to Paige about this without fully talking about it. I still hadn't told Paige about Charli. I hadn't told anyone but Daniel.

"We had an interesting conversation about two weeks ago, and I feel like things are a bit...different between us now," I said, placing my hand on the pillow next to me with the fish on it.

"OK, should we talk about the conversation?" Paige asked. How do I do this without putting it all out there? I didn't want Paige's opinion of my situation with Charli. I didn't want Charli rejected by another person just because I wasn't perfect. I took a deep breath.

"I've been thinking about becoming a foster parent, and I shared that with him," I said, carefully choosing my words. Paige picked up her pen and started taking notes.

"STOP THAT," I wanted to scream at her. I just squeezed the pillow.

"We've never talked about fostering kids before. Where is this coming from?" she asked.

"She's not lying," I thought to myself.

"Just something I've been thinking about," I responded. She wrote more notes. I grimaced. I could feel myself becoming defensive.

"You've always said you didn't want kids; what's changed your mind?" she asked. Crap. She was right. I'd been adamant that I didn't want kids.

"It's just something I started thinking about," I said and hoped she bought it.

"And you shared those thoughts with Daniel?" she asked. I loosened my grip on the pillow. Calming a bit now that she'd moved off of my reasoning for considering fostering.

"Yes," I said.

"And what were his thoughts?" she asked.

"Well, he wasn't against it really, but..." I struggled to find the words.

"You and Daniel had both decided that you guys weren't going to have kids, correct?" she asked.

"Yes," I said, tightening my grip on the pillow again. "He didn't say he was against it; he said taking on another human being was a huge responsibility, and he wanted me to think about if this was truly something I wanted to take on. He said he wanted me to really think about it, and we would talk about it more later." She was taking more notes. I wanted to snatch her pen and throw it across the room.

"He makes some good points," she said when she'd stopped writing. Of course, she'd side with him.

"Kindra, I've definitely seen a lot of progress in you in the last few months, and I'm very proud of the work you are putting into owning your mental health. Fostering a child is big and comes with a lot of things I think we should discuss. For starters, the idea to foster really seems to have come out of nowhere. Let's unwrap that," she said.

"I don't want to unwrap anything; this isn't a gift, it's therapy," I sat there thinking as she talked.

"Are you lonely?" she asked. I had stopped fully listening to her, but those words snapped me back. Of course, I was lonely. I hadn't seen my boyfriend in six months, and it would be at least another six months before I saw him again. I barely saw my mom because of my work schedule and the strain on our relationship. I had very few friends. So yeah, I was lonely.

"I'm OK," I responded. I didn't want to foster Charli because I was lonely.

"OK, so let's come up with some productive ways to combat loneliness," Paige said. I sighed. That wasn't what this was about.

"Also, over the next week, I want you to really think about all of the things that could possibly go into fostering a child. Make a list of the good and the bad, and be honest with yourself. You have come really far. I wouldn't want the stress of some of those things to set you back. So write that list, and we will talk about it honestly next week." Paige said with a smile. I forced a smile back and said, "OK."

Paige and I had reached the end of our road; I thought to myself as I walked out of her office without stopping to schedule my appointment for next week.

Charli

"So why don't you have to work your second job today?" I asked Kindra as she unpacked a bag full of Chinese food onto the blanket for our picnic. It was Wednesday, and she had sent me a text this morning saying she didn't have to work her second job and to meet her at the park after school. I was so excited to see her that I could hardly focus in my classes all day.

"The girl that I take care of," she started. "Chipmunk," I said, cutting her off. She laughed.

"Yes, Chipmunk had a doctor's appointment today so her mom picked her up from school and took her so they didn't need me," she said.

"Good cause I needed you today," I said back to her. "Did you really, now?" she asked me back with a smile.

"I haven't seen you in 19 days, Sissy," I said very seriously. She stared at me for a moment. Her eyes seemed sad, and then she said, "I missed you too, Kiddo. Now, enough with the Hallmark. Let's eat!" She handed me a plate.

"What is all this stuff? It smells good," I said.

"OK, that's chicken fried rice, those are egg rolls, that's broccoli beef, that's teriyaki chicken, and that's lo Mein. Eat as much as you want of whatever you want," she said. It looked like so much good food. I got a little nervous.

"Sissy, can you afford all of this?" I asked her.

"Well, I am working two jobs now, and if I can't splurge on my little sister a bit, who can I splurge on?" she said and heaped a spoonful of rice onto my plate. I went straight for the broccoli beef and saw Kindra smile at me.

"What?" I asked her, picking around the beef to get to the broccoli. "I spent the day thinking of what we could eat. I know you love pineapples, and you love broccoli. I knew you'd probably have pineapples on your pizza with Matt on Friday, so I got Chinese so you could have broccoli, and it was the first thing you went for. So I think I did good," she said.

"Very good," I said with a mouth full.

We finished eating and were lying on the blanket. I don't remember ever being so full. It was great! I reached over and grabbed Kindra's hand and locked my fingers in hers. She gave my hand a quick squeeze.

"Sissy?" I said.

"Yes, Bear," she said and turned her head towards me.

"I had a really bad nightmare two nights ago," I said. Kindra rolled onto her side, facing me, but didn't say anything. "And when I woke up, I felt like I couldn't breathe, but I grounded myself the way you taught me, and I was OK, but then when I went to school, I didn't feel good. I was nervous and stuff. That's PTSD, right?" I asked.

Kindra sighed heavily. "Yep, and it sucks," she said, reaching into her bag. She pulled out the hairbrush.

"No, I don't need it," I said. She looked at me for a second with questioning eyes. "I'm sure," I said. So, she put the brush away.

"But Sissy, do you think when I come to live with you and after MC Spinner helps you get your service dog, that maybe it could be OUR service dog, and it could help me too?" I asked. I'd been thinking about this for a while now--ever since Matt said I needed to tell Kindra about what was happening. I couldn't tell her that, but maybe the service dog could help us both.

“I definitely think it could be OUR service dog, and you know how he would wake you up from nightmares?” she asked me.

“How?” I responded.

“Well, he would lick, lick, lick your face!” she said and started tickling me. I laughed and squealed and squirmed, trying to get away. When she stopped, I sat up, and so did she. I wrapped my arms around her in a big hug. She lifted my chin so she was looking straight into my eyes.

“I love you, Charli Victoria Lauren,” she said. I scrunched up my face at the sound of my middle name and then smiled.

“I love you too, Sissy,” I said.

“OUR service dog?” she said with a smile. “Yeah, OUR service dog” I said back.

“OK, let’s look at these fortune cookies,” Kindra said, grabbing one of the bags.

Kindra

There had to be a kink in the line somewhere or something. I had just gotten Chipmunk off the school bus and was attempting to set up her feed. She had a g-button in her stomach. So, all of her meals were liquid that went straight into her stomach via a feeding machine and a bag that held a very enriched type of PediaSure. I could usually set up her feed with no problem, but today, the machine kept beeping every time I turned it on, and I couldn't figure out why. I turned it off, waited a few seconds, and turned it back on. (My best friend from college was an IT guy, and that's his answer to everything. Turn it off and turn it back on). Then I started it up. Within 15 seconds it was beeping again.

"What is wrong with you?" I said out loud to the machine in frustration. I guess Chipmunk was getting frustrated too, because she threw the plastic music box she was playing with across the room. It hit the wall with a loud smack, and the nursery rhyme it was once playing now sounded distorted and high-pitched. It was an annoying sound. I looked back at the feeding machine that was still beeping and began to run my fingers down the tubing to check for kinks or whatever may have been causing the malfunction when my cell phone started ringing. All the noises combined were too much. The beeping machine, the broken music box, and my cell phone, mixed with the frustration of the feeding machine not working, sent me into sensory overload. My heart started racing, and I threw my hands over my ears. I took three slow, deep breaths. "I can handle this," I told myself. I hit ignore on my cell phone, turned off the feeding machine again, and went and got down on my hands and knees to see where the busted music box landed. I followed the piercing noise it was making and found

it behind the TV--glad it hit the wall and not the TV. Chipmunk's parents would not have been pleased with that.

I picked up the toy, opened the back cover, and took the batteries out. A beautiful silence fell over the house, and I immediately felt calm. I took a few more deep breaths and looked down at Chipmunk, who was reaching her hand out for the music box I had just taken the batteries out of. I put the batteries in my pocket and handed her the toy. She put it to her ear, she then looked at it, turned the switch off and back on, and put it back to her ear. Then she shook it. When still no sound came out, she raised her arm to throw the toy again. I grabbed it just before she released it at full speed across the living room.

"No more of that for right now," I said while putting the toy and its batteries in a cabinet in the kitchen. I grabbed the remote and put on a "Head, shoulders, knees and toes" video on YouTube, at which point she smiled, and I went back to the feeding machine. I decided to take the whole thing apart and put it back together. I finished taking the device and its tubing apart when my phone alerted me to another notification.

"Where's the fire?" I said out loud as I put everything back together and turned it on. No beeping and the PediaSure was running through the line just fine. I hit pause on the machine and took it over to where Chipmunk was sitting on the floor. I connected the tubing to the button in her stomach and pushed the run button. I took a breath and sat down on the floor next to her to make sure no issues arose. She paid me no attention as the video changed from "Head, Shoulders, Knees and Toes" to "The Wheels on the Bus." I pulled out my cell phone. One missed call from mom, one new voicemail, and two new messages on Twitter. I hit the button to play the voicemail and put the phone to my ear.

"Hi, Honey, it's Mom. I haven't heard from you in a few days and just wanted to check on you. I can't remember your new work schedule. Call me when you get a chance and let me hear your voice. Love you." Click. I smiled and glanced over to Chipmunk, whose eyes were now getting heavy. I jumped up and grabbed her blanket and pillow off the other couch. I covered her with the blanket and put the pillow between her back and the couch. I couldn't let her lay down while the feed was going because it could upset her stomach, but she frequently fell asleep sitting up, and I would just lay her down a little while after the feed was done. I sat back down next to her, picked up my phone again, and opened my Twitter. There were two new messages from Darla, MC Spinner's manager. The conversations between us had slowed down lately, and I was getting worried, but I didn't want to push, so I left it alone. The messages read:

Darla- Hey Kindra, you live in Houston, right?

Darla- Spinner is doing a show in San Antonio in two weeks, and he wanted me to invite you and give you two VIP passes. Do you think you can make it? Let me know.

I read the messages over and over. They were inviting me. I was going to get to meet him and get to tell him my story in person. He was going to help me! I wanted to scream and jump up and down. I turned and looked at Chipmunk; her head had fallen backward onto the seat of the couch, her mouth was wide open, and her eyes were closed. She was breathing evenly.

Sleeping like a princess to the hum of the feeding machine and "Twinkle Twinkle Little Star, now playing on YouTube. I couldn't celebrate the way I wanted to right then, but I would definitely be dancing all the way to the car once this shift was over.

SECTION 2:
NIGHTMARES

Charli

"Thank you, Mrs. Lindsey," I said as she placed a cup of hot chocolate with whipped cream in front of me and a cup in front of Matt. Since I wasn't meeting with Kindra so much anymore, I'd been spending more time at his house after school--anything to keep from going straight back to that house.

"So Matt tells me you may be getting your own room soon and are trying to think of ways to decorate it," Mrs. Lindsey said to me while drying a pot she'd just washed.

"MATT," I said with mock frustration.

"What do I know about decorating a room?" he said, holding his hands up in defense.

We all laughed.

"Well, that's very true. I can barely get you to keep your room clean, let alone decorate it," Mrs. Lindsey said.

I laughed, picked up my cup, and took a sip of hot chocolate. It was so good I closed my eyes and felt the liquid warm my insides up. I heard Matt whisper, "Charli." I opened my eyes and looked at him. He was pointing at his nose.

"Huh?" I said to him; I didn't understand what he was trying to tell me. "You have whipped cream on your nose," he said and laughed.

"Oh," I said and grabbed a napkin off of the table to clean my nose.

"The secret to good hot chocolate is to use milk and not water, and almond milk is even better because it's thicker," Mrs. Lindsey said. I made a mental note of that. I wanted to have good hot chocolate with Kindra, and I would have to tell her about the milk, not the water. I smiled to myself, picturing us having hot chocolate at our home.

"Now, Charli, do you know what color you want your room to be?" Mrs. Lindsey asked me.

"Purple," I replied.

"Like a violet purple or a lavender purple?" she asked. "Uhmm…" I said, confused. Mrs. Lindsey laughed.

"Light purple or dark purple?" she said.

"Oh! I don't know, I just like purple," I said sheepishly and took another sip of the hot chocolate.

"Hmm, maybe lilac then; it's not too light or dark purple. I'm sure you could find a lovely lilac comforter at JCPenney's and some lamps at Ikea," she said.

"Lamps?" I said, looking at Matt for help.

"Yeah, I got to pick out some cool lamps for my room from Ikea," Matt said. "What's Ikea?" I asked.

"It's a huge store with arrows on the ground telling you which way to go, and they have all types of furniture and stuff, and you can get an ice cream cone for a dollar from the snack bar," Matt said.

"That's the only reason you ever go with me, isn't it, Matthew, for the ice cream cone?" Matt's mom said with a smile. Matt shrugged his shoulders while laughing.

"They have good ice cream," he said.

"Charli, you'll have to let us help you decorate your room when the time comes. I have to go make some phone calls. Matt, please put yours and Charli's dishes in the sink when you are done, and don't leave them on the table." We waited silently for a moment until we heard her talking on the phone.

"You told her about my room?" I accusingly asked Matt.

"It's all you've talked about lately. I thought she could help. She's good at that stuff. She got me that really cool Star Wars picture that totally sets my room off. You've seen it," he said. It was a nice picture. It did make his room look cool. I looked around the kitchen, and it was decorated really nicely. Matt's mom had good taste, but I really wanted Kindra to help me decorate my room. I would have to mention Ikea to her to see about this ice cream and lamps.

"So, is she going to the concert?" Matt whispered to me. I had told him earlier about MC Spinner giving Kindra tickets to his show, but the lunch bell rang before we were able to talk about it.

"Of course, she's going; it's for OUR service dog. Why wouldn't she go?" I said.

"Well, a lot of people with PTSD don't like crowds, and a concert would be really crowded," he said. I thought about that. I didn't like being in really crowded places either. I wasn't in them often, so I didn't think about it much. I hoped the crowds didn't bother Kindra too badly. She just had to go to the concert. Matt's mom came flying back into the kitchen.

"You guys grab your stuff. We have to go," she said. "Go where?" Matt asked.

"Your father's car broke down, and we have to go pick him up. I told him days ago, when the check engine light came on, to take it to the shop, but no. Charli, honey, we are going to drop you off first. I don't know how long this is going to take," she said, trailing off as she left the room.

"I'm going to go get my cell phone off the charger; I will meet you at the car, Charli," Matt said, heading towards his room at the back of the house. Just that quick, I was sitting by myself in the kitchen. I stood up, put my jacket on, and threw my backpack over my shoulder. I'd started walking towards the front door when I stopped, turned around, and saw the two hot chocolate cups on the table. I ran back and got them, poured the remaining hot chocolate into the sink, and filled the cups with water. I didn't want Matt to get in trouble. Then I ran to the car.

Matt and I were pretty quiet on the ride to the house except for the occasional giggle when his Mom would yell on her cell phone at his Dad for not having taken the car to the shop like she'd told him to.

We pulled in front of the house and Jeremy was standing in the front yard smoking a cigarette. My whole body went tense. Matt grabbed my hand.

"You OK?" he whispered. He knew who Jeremy was. I nodded my head yes and pulled my hand away so I could grab my backpack. I wiped my palm on my jeans. It had become sweaty just that quickly.

"Mom, I'm going to walk Charli to the door," Matt said and jumped out of the car.

"OK, honey, but please hurry so we can get your father," she said. Matt stepped onto the walkway between where Jeremy stood, and I walked. I saw them lock eyes. Jeremy flicked his cigarette in Matt's direction, then turned and walked towards the shed.

"You OK?" Matt asked me again after Jeremy walked off. "Yeah, I'm fine," I said, giving Matt my best fake smile.

"OK, I gotta go keep my mom from killing my dad. I will see you tomorrow," he said, then turned and ran back towards his mom's car. I looked down towards the shed before I went into the house. I hoped Matt trying to protect me didn't get me picked tonight. I heard the music come on in the shed.

Kindra

"Six days until the concert. Are you ready?" Daniel asked me. We were on a midday Skype call. The new job had thrown a monkey wrench into my carefully planned life and schedule.

"Not the least bit," I said, straight-faced. The smile I had been wearing for days was beginning to crack.

"Sure you are," he said with his beautiful smile. I looked away from the camera, fighting back the tears.

"Hey, what's going on? Look at me," he said. I looked back at the camera just as the first tears started to fall. I heard him sigh.

"Babe, go pour yourself a cup of juice and come back and talk to me," he said. I did as I was told. We hadn't really spoken about fostering Charli because the MC Spinner concert had come up. Things seemed OK with us, but I was worried. I lived my life always waiting for the other shoe to drop. So now, besides being stressed about the concert and Charli, I was also stressed about my relationship with Daniel.

I sat back down at the table with my cup of juice. I saw he had gotten a bottle of Gatorade. I smiled.

"OK, so let's talk through this," he said. "OK," I said and took a sip of my juice.

"Let's start from the beginning because I want you to see something," he said. "OK," I said, feeling nervous but not sure why.

"You got accepted by this well-known service dog organization, who, after lots of paperwork, notes from doctors, and evaluations from therapists, decided you were deserving of a service dog. You fought that uphill battle knowing that very few survivors of rape get service dogs because very few people take their afflictions seriously because very few people take rape seriously. YOU did that," he said. I smiled a bit and nodded my head.

"OK," I said.

"Then they hit you with this $10,000 dollar price tag. You could have thrown your hands up and said *might as well be a million,* and given up, but did you?" he asked. I smiled a bit bigger.

"No," I said, shaking my head.

"And you almost have a thousand dollars raised from that big donor and donations here and there from friends. And I know a thousand doesn't seem like much compared to ten, but I remember when this first started how even a thousand seemed impossible," he said.

"True," I agreed, nodding my head again.

"And then things just started coming together like this is supposed to happen," he said and took a drink of his Gatorade. I took another sip of my juice. He had a point. Things over the last week had been coming together strangely for my benefit.

"First," he continued, "MC Spinner agrees to help you, and I know you never thought that would happen. Then he offers you tickets to a show that's only three hours away from you. This dude hardly performs anymore, but he just happens to be doing a show three hours away? Come on," he said.

"OK, OK," I responded.

"Then, of all the craziness, your mom just happens to be going too?" he said. This is where things had gotten really strange this past week. I hadn't much spoken to my mom about MC Spinner. I occasionally brought up the subject of my service dog, but she never really seemed interested, so I didn't push. However, one day last week, we were talking, and she was telling me how she and Fred (Fred is her boyfriend) were going to San Antonio in a couple of weeks for a work convention. Mom and Fred traveled for work all the time. They worked for different companies but always ended up at the same functions and traveled in the same circles. I'm pretty sure it's how they met. Anyway, she mentioned they were going to San Antonio about the same time I was. I felt like it was an opening. So I told my mom about MC Spinner and how he'd agreed to help me get a service dog and how he'd invited me to his show in San Antonio. Then Mom yelled for Fred and said, "Isn't MC Spinner performing after the convention in San Antonio?"

"Yeah, the companies like to put on a mix-and-mingle event for the young folks at these conventions when the work's all done, and they bring in some old-school celebrities sometimes. They can't afford the new cats," Fred remarked and laughed.

I was in utter disbelief. I had been invited to the same event my mom was already going to. What were the chances?

"Well, Candy got tickets to the show from MC Spinner himself," she said to him. Candy is a nickname my big sister gave me when I was born, and almost everyone in the family called me that.

"That's great; she can stay the night with you in your room since both of our companies are paying for our hotel rooms," he said.

"Whelp, there you go, Candygirl," my mom said to me. We spoke for a few more moments and said we would solidify plans for the concert as the date got closer, and then we got off the phone. I'd immediately messaged Daniel, who agreed it was too much of a coincidence.

"So your mom is going, and you can stay the night with her. I know you're nervous about the event and all the people, but that Eddie guy is going with you, right?" Daniel asked, bringing me back to our current conversation.

"Yeah," I said.

"Who is this Eddie again?" he asked me.

"He's like a son to Fred, so he's kinda family, I guess," I said. I didn't know much about Eddie. He showed up to events that my Mom and Fred put on at the house. He was a really good mechanic. Anytime my car had issues I was told to take the car to Eddie at his shop. He seemed very serious most of the time and came off a bit intimidating sometimes, but that was all I knew about him. Unfortunately, I hadn't really made many friends since I'd moved to Texas, my anxiety and all. So I had no one to go to the show with me, and I couldn't do this by myself. I'd thought about hiding behind my mom at the event, but I knew she wouldn't have that. Next thing I knew, I was being told that Fred had asked Eddie to come with me, and he'd said yes. I'm sure it was out of pity, but I didn't even care.

"I wish you were here to go with me," I said to Daniel.

"I wish I was too, but you got this. So, what are you going to wear?" he asked.

"What do you mean?" I said. I was not into clothes or fashion, especially after the rape. I tried to dress in a way so that I wouldn't stand out or be noticed. You don't want to rape a girl that's not sexy, right? So usually jeans and a T-shirt.

"What does what I wear have to do with anything?" I asked, partially nervous and partially offended.

"Nothing. But it's a special occasion, so it calls for you to dress up a bit," he said. I could tell he was choosing his words carefully.

"So someone could be attracted to me and grab me?" I snapped back at him. I don't know where the anger came from. I didn't mean to snap at him.

"No one is going to grab you. That's why Eddie is going, whether he knows it or not. So how about this? I will send you some money, and you go get a new outfit. Consider it a gift from me to give you confidence on your big day; sound good?" he asked. How could I say no to that?

"OK," I said reluctantly.

"And I will expect to see pictures of how beautiful you look before I send you out with this Eddie guy," he said, faking jealousy. It was cute.

"It will be a great night," he said. I hoped he was right.

Matt

The math teacher handed our tests back to us just as the bell rang for lunch. I looked at my test.

"Crap," I muttered under my breath as I stuffed it in my backpack. I picked up my things and walked out the door, heading to my lunch spot. My mom was going to be really upset about this test. I passed it, but just barely.

I sat down at the planter, pulled out Charli's lunch, and set it on her side where she always sat. I never started without her, and I usually always beat her to lunch, so I figured I had a few minutes. I pulled the test back out and started going over the problems I'd gotten wrong. It seemed like no matter how much I studied, I just was not getting this. I pulled out my math book too so I could look at how to do the problems correctly and try to figure out where I'd gone wrong.

I knew Charli was going to give me all the grief when she saw me going over this test.

She was so lucky that math came so easily to her.

I paused. I'd never really used "lucky" and "Charli" in the same sentence before. I went back to the test. I was about halfway through the problems when I looked up and noticed Charli hadn't shown up yet. The slightest bit of worry crept in.

"She's fine," I told myself.

I sat for another few moments, looking in the direction that she usually came from, but I didn't see her.

"She's just talking to one of her teachers," I said out loud, but deep inside, I knew something was wrong. I stuffed my things back into my backpack and walked to the nearest boys' bathroom. I went into one of the stalls and pulled out my cell phone to call her when I noticed I had one new text message.

"When did that come through?" I thought while unlocking my phone. That's when I noticed my phone was on silent and not vibrate. I opened the message and saw it was from Charli. It said one word: "Help."

I tore out of the bathroom at full speed, heading in the direction of the front of the school.

I had to get to her. I'd kill them if she was hurt.

"Young man, no running," I heard a teacher yell as I ran past him. I ran out the front of the school and toward Charli's house. I was frantic in my thinking. So I stopped for a second. She wouldn't have texted me from inside of the house, I don't think, for fear of getting her phone found out. I pulled out my phone and texted her back

Matt: Where are you? I'm trying to find you.

I waited for what felt like forever, but was probably only a few seconds. She didn't respond.

"SHIT!" I yelled.

"OK, if I were Charli and I was in trouble, what would I do? Where would I go?" I thought.

If she texted me, then she probably wouldn't text Kindra, so I wasn't going to either, but where would she go? The only places she really knew were the park, my house, and the school.

She wouldn't go to the park because Kindra was not there; she wouldn't go to my house because she knew I'd be at school. So she should have headed to school...but she didn't make it. I started power walking in the direction of her house and scanning everywhere around me, looking for her or some sign of her.

"Charli!" I yelled as I walked. No one was out in the neighborhoods; the kids were at school, and most of the parents were at work.

"Charli!" I yelled again. The neighborhood turned into an area that had more trees and was a bit more wooded between the houses. I was trying hard not to walk too fast so I didn't miss anything, but I needed to be fast so I could find her. I was scanning the area when my eye caught a patch of blue in the mostly brown wooded terrain. I stopped and looked in its direction. It was right off of the path, a few steps into the trees. I walked towards it and recognized the Bazooka Joe T-shirt. I ran towards it. She was laid out on the ground. Her jeans were covered with blood between her legs. So much blood. She looked so pale. I dropped to my knees beside her and shook her.

"Charli?" I said. She felt cold.

"No, No, No, Charli, please," I cried. I pulled out my cell phone and dialed 911. "911, what's your emergency?" a voice said.

"My friend, she needs help, please help her," I said, crying. "What's wrong with her?" the voice asked.

"She's been…" I paused in my tears. I couldn't say it. I'd promised her I wouldn't tell anybody. "She needs help; just send help, please!" I yelled into the phone.

"Sir, is your friend breathing?" the voice asked. I was afraid to look, but I did. Her chest wasn't moving.

"I don't think…" I was saying when I saw her chest rise just slightly. "SHE'S TRYING TO BREATHE, PLEASE HURRY!" I yelled into the phone.

"Sir, where are you?" the voice asked. I looked up at my

surroundings. “I’m on…Lexington Street near Haven Ridge, kind of in the trees,” I said.

“I’m sending help to you; just hang on,” the voice said. I grabbed Charli’s hand and held it. She felt so cold.

“Charli,” I said through my tears. “Charli, wake up. I got your lunch, but I left it at school. I put the brownie you like in it. Charli?” I was sobbing. I picked the leaves out of her hair. Then I looked down at all of the blood again. I took my shirt off and covered her down there. I didn’t want people to see her like that.

“Charli, please wake up,” I cried. Her chest didn’t look like it was moving at all anymore.

“NO, NO, NO,” I cried. “Charli, please! ”I yelled at her. I picked up my cell phone and dialed my mom.

“Matthew?” I heard her voice say.

“Mommy, please help, please,” I cried into the phone. Then I heard the sirens.

Kindra

I glanced at the clock again and yawned. It was almost time for Chipmunk's mom to get home, and I'd be off until my night shift started. I wanted to run to look for an outfit before giving up for the day. Shopping for an outfit for the concert was proving to be rather difficult. It didn't help that I didn't really have any friends to help me with this. It definitely seemed like something your girlfriends would help you with. I was kind of sad that I didn't have that, but not heartbroken. I got by.

I heard the keys in the door, letting me know that Chipmunk's mom was home from work. She came in and walked right up to Chipmunk, and kissed her on the forehead. Chipmunk held her music box out to her mother--inviting her to play.

"Not right now, sweetheart. Kindra, can you put her shoes on, please? And then you can go," she said. I grabbed Chipmunk's Velcro shoes and put them on her. Then I packed up my stuff.

"See you tomorrow," I said as I headed for the door. "Chipmunk, be good for your mom," I said and heard her mom laugh.

I got in the car and was heading towards my side of town and the clothing store Cato to look for an outfit when my cell phone alerted me to a text message. The phone was in my back pocket, so I waited until I got to a stoplight to grab it. It buzzed again as I was pulling it out.

"I'm coming, I'm coming," I said while unlocking the phone. The messages were from Matt.

Matt: Charli's in the hospital, please come quick.

Matt: We are at Methodist room 226.

"HOSPITAL?" I yelled, swerving across three lanes to make a U-turn. I hit the dial button to call Matt's phone. It rang and rang and then went to voicemail. I called Charli's phone. It went straight to voicemail. I called Matt's phone again, voicemail again. This time I left a frantic message.

"Matt, what is going on? Is Charli OK? Please call me back. I'm on my way." I said and hung up, then called his number again. It rang and went to voicemail.

"DAMN IT!" I yelled. I began to pray out loud. "Lord, please let her be OK. I'm going to get her and take care of her; just please let her be OK," I kept saying. My assumption was that she'd tried to hurt herself. Maybe she wasn't dealing with our time apart as well as I'd thought.

I was about 15 minutes away from the hospital when I left Chipmunk's house. I made it in 10. I parked, grabbed my things, and ran into the building. I went straight to the information desk.

"How can I help you?" an older woman with gray hair behind the desk asked me. "Room 226?" I rushed out the words.

"Take the elevators in the back to the second floor. When you get off of the elevator, go left," she said. I had started walking before she had finished talking. I just needed to get to my girl. I got on the elevator and pushed the button for floor two. The doors closed way too slowly. I silently prayed as the box moved up.

Ding. The doors opened, and I exited and went to the left. The room numbers were going up 220, 222, 224, 226. I stood at the door for a second. Scared to go in, scared of what I would find. I finished my silent prayer and walked in. I immediately saw Charli in the hospital bed.

There were tubes everywhere pushing all types of fluids into her. She wasn't awake, and she looked so small and pale. There was dirt in her hair and bruises on her arms. "Oh Bear," I said as tears slid down my cheeks. Matt was at her bedside holding her hand, and a woman I didn't recognize was sitting next to him, rubbing his back. They hadn't heard me come in, but when I said, "Oh Bear," they turned around.

Matt jumped up and ran to me. He threw his arms around my waist and began crying.

"I'm so sorry; I tried my best to protect her, I tried," he cried. Matt and I had never been this close before, so the hug caught me off guard. I put my arms around him in a hug just as the lady who had been rubbing his back stood up.

"You must be Kindra," she whispered. I nodded my head. "Matt, honey, go sit with Charli in case she wakes up. I'm going to talk to Kindra outside for a second," she said.

"Yes, ma'am," Matt said, pulling away from me and wiping his face on his shirt as he sat back down and took Charli's hand into his own. The lady put her arm in mine and led me to the door. "My name is Lindsey. I'm Matt's mom," she said. I nodded but kept looking over her shoulder into the room at Charli.

"What happened? What's going on?" I asked her.

"Matt called me this morning, frantic and crying about Charli. He'd found her on the ground covered in blood," she said.

"In blood?" I repeated.

"He won't tell me much. He wouldn't even speak for the first three hours we were here until they moved her from the emergency department to her own room," she said.

"Three hours? How long has she been here? "I asked. Lindsey looked at her watch. "About six hours now," she said.

"Six hours! Why didn't he call me sooner?" I asked in disbelief that he'd waited that long.

"I just got him to start talking about an hour ago. He won't tell me everything. I can tell he knows more than he's saying, but he told me about you and Charli and how you were pretty much her family. I asked him to call you, but he was scared you'd be mad at him, so he texted you," she said.

"Be mad? Why would I be mad at him? Lindsey, please tell me what is going on?" I begged. She grabbed both of my hands in hers.

"The nurses say she's been raped…" she started, and my legs gave out. Lindsey caught me and helped me to a chair. "They said, based on the extent of her injuries, this has been going on for quite some time," Lindsey continued. I felt blood rushing to my ears and tears rushing to my eyes. "She'd lost a lot of blood, and they gave her a blood transfusion when we came in, they said she is going to need surgery due to vaginal trauma," Lindsey said. Her words were coming in and out of range. I could hear what she was saying, but she sounded so very far away. How had I missed this. I thought back to the times I'd seen her with a limp. This is why she froze when I would ask about what happened because it was still happening, and I'd missed it. I'd always assumed, like me, she was raped once, but it was ongoing. With that realization, I shattered; the full awareness of what was happening hit me like a Mack truck. Lindsey put her arms around me and held me as my soul emptied in the form of tears for how I'd let Charli down. I cried till there was nothing left. One of the nurses bought us a box of tissues. I lifted my head from Lindsey's shoulder and wiped my eyes.

"The nurses have been really good; they said this is the worst case they have ever seen, and they have been hovering around Charli since we got here," she said. I was only half listening. Then it hit me again, and I got angry. I looked up at Lindsey.

"WHO?" I said in an all of a sudden very strong voice. Lindsey looked taken aback. She grabbed my hand.

"Kindra, we don't know," she said.

It had to be someone in that foster home. It just had to be.

"I believe Matt knows something, but he won't say. He just keeps saying she's safe here. I haven't been able to get him to leave her side since they put her in this room except when he got up to hug you when you walked in," she said.

I looked over into the room to Matt holding her hand. What a burden he must be carrying. I looked at Lindsey.

"You have an amazing son," I said to her. She looked surprised. "Thank you," she said.

"Why isn't she awake?" I asked her.

"The massive blood loss and major trauma. Her little body is tired. The nurses say she's OK, she just needs to rest and will wake when she is ready," Lindsey said. I stood up. I needed to be with my girl. I'd failed her. The whole world failed her. I walked back into the room. Matt looked up at me with worry in his eyes.

"Thank you for taking care of her, Matt," I said to him. I watched the tears stream down his cheeks as he turned his head away from me. I could see the feeling of guilt dripping off of him. He felt he'd failed her too. I pulled up a chair on the other side of the bed, pulled out my cell phone, and called in on my night job for the first time in two years.

A few hours later, Matt and his mother left. It was after midnight. I'd promised Matt numerous times that I wouldn't leave her and his mother promised they'd be back first thing in the morning. Matt reached over and squeezed Charli's hand and told her he'd be back in the morning and that I was there to protect her so she could wake up when she was ready. He turned as he and his mother were walking out of the door and said, "Charli, I will bring your lunch tomorrow."

After they left, I climbed in bed with Charli and just held her in my arms and cried.

"I'm so sorry, Bear, I'm so sorry. I'm going to fix this," I said through my tears. I fell asleep with her in my arms, wondering exactly *how* I was going to fix this.

Charli

I must be in Heaven. Something bad had happened, really bad. I couldn't quite remember what, but it was bad. I had flashes of memory--Matt crying, flashing red lights, and then just nothing. It was nothing like I thought Heaven would be...except it smelled like Kindra, like her lotion. I smiled on the inside. I was OK with Heaven smelling like Kindra. I inhaled deep to get a full whiff of the scent. Then the pain came.

It started slowly at my toes and worked its way straight up to my head. My whole body was hurting. Heaven wasn't supposed to hurt, was it? I tried to move to make myself more comfortable, and that's when I realized I wasn't in Heaven. I opened my eyes slowly and blinked a few times before the room came into focus. I heard a steady beeping. I looked in the direction of the noise. A weird machine with lines moving up and down was making soft beeping noises. Then I heard a slow, steady breathing that wasn't mine. I looked to my right, and there Kindra was, fast asleep with her arms around me. That's why I could smell her lotion. I kept looking around. I was in a hospital room. I got nervous. How much did everyone know? Kindra was going to be so mad at me, I thought to myself and tried to swallow the lump that was forming in my throat. I tried to shift again to a more comfortable position, and Kindra began to stir. I froze.

"Charli?" she said in a very sleepy voice as she opened her eyes. We locked eyes for a split second, but it felt like an eternity. Then I blurted out, "Sissy, I am so sorry. Please don't be mad at me," I cried out as tears ran down my cheeks. She squeezed me so tight.

"Oh, my precious girl. I'm not mad at you. I'm just glad you are OK," she said, and I saw the tears start to form in her eyes. "I thought I'd lost you," she said. I weakly smiled at her.

"Oh, I need to tell Matt you are awake," she said while reaching for her phone that was on the chair next to the bed. I wondered how much Matt had said.

"Hmmm, it's 4:10 am. He's probably asleep," she said, then she paused. "Maybe not, though. He's been really worried about you. I'm going to just send him a message telling him you are awake, so when he wakes up, he knows," she said, typing a message into her phone. She went to set the phone back down on the chair, but before she could it rang. She smiled as she accepted the call and put the phone to her ear.

"Hello, Matt," she said and paused. "Yes, she's awake." Pause. I guessed he was talking. She looked over at me. "Yes

she looks OK, and she is talking." Pause. "No, Matt, don't go wake your parents up; you don't need to come back right now." Pause. "Matt, no, let them sleep..." Pause. I could hear his voice arguing in the background. "Matt, I've got her," Kindra said. I leaned over and whispered to Kindra, "You have to say Matthew, or he won't listen." she nodded her head at me.

"Matthew, I have got her, let your parents sleep and you get some sleep and you can come when they get up, OK?" Kindra said and then paused. She smiled.

"Yes, Charli told me to use your full name," she said, and I laughed quietly because it hurt to laugh.

"OK, we will see you in a few hours. Try to get some sleep," she said and disconnected the call.

"Matt says he will be here as soon as his parents get up, and for you to stop telling people to call him by his full name," she said. I laughed harder this time and then abruptly stopped because of the pain.

"Sissy, can I have something to drink?" I asked her. She got up and went to a table next to the bed and poured me a cup of water from a pitcher.

"It's not cold," she said as she handed it to me. I drank the whole cup. She went and got the pitcher and refilled the cup. I drank that too. One more cup full before I was satisfied. Kindra set the pitcher back on the table and sat down in the chair next to the bed.

"Will you lay with me again?" I asked her.

"Of course, I will," she said and climbed back into the hospital bed with me. I snuggled in as close to her as I could get. I was scared of what would come in the morning and who would come, but I had her right now, and right now everything was OK. I closed my eyes, inhaled her scent, and went back to sleep.

Kindra

We'd been up for a couple of hours. Charli had eaten two breakfasts, which the nurses said was a good sign. They said her numbers were stable, and she was doing well considering. My girl was strong. Color had started to return to her skin, and she was looking a lot less pale. I had washed her hair in a small bin one of the nurses had given us with some shampoo another nurse had in her locker. I was brushing Charli's hair over the top edge of the hospital bed. Her eyes were closed, and she looked peaceful. I looked up just in time to see Matt, his mom, and who I guessed to be Matt's dad walk in the door. Matt had Charli's backpack thrown over his shoulder. His parents were holding hands.

For a moment, I ached for Daniel to hold my hand and have that support, but I quickly shook it off. Matt's mom had a brown paper bag in her free hand. Matt stood a few feet away from Charli's bed. No one moved. Matt looked unsure of what to say or do. So I nudged Charli and said, "Matt's here."

Her eyes shot open, and she sat up and then grimaced in pain from moving too fast. This morning, we discovered that most movements hurt her, and sudden movements hurt her badly. She and Matt just stared at each other. Again, no one moved. Then tears started trailing down Matt's cheeks, and he looked down at the floor.

"Matt," Charli said softly. He dropped her backpack, ran to her, and threw his arms around her. They were both sobbing. It was one of the most touching things I'd ever seen. I was crying. I looked and saw Lindsey crying, Matt's dad had tears running down his face, and a nurse was standing behind them.

I wasn't even sure when she'd walked in the room, but she was crying too.

"I can come back later," she said as she wiped her eyes and walked out of the room.

Matt and Charli let go of each other, and Matt sat on the edge of the bed. Neither of them said anything, but they kept looking at each other and then looking at the adults in the room. I could tell they were silently communicating with each other. Then Charli looked down at her lap, and Matt looked at his parents and me and said, "Can I talk to Charli for a moment, please?"

Was he asking us to leave the room? I thought about it for a second. As much as I needed to know what was going on, Charli needed Matt more, and Matt had earned this very adult request he'd just made. I reached over and squeezed Charli's hand.

"I'll be right outside, or I may run to the cafeteria, but I will be right back, OK?" I said to her. She nodded and smiled at me. I walked towards the door, put my arm in Lindsay's arm the way she had done for me less than 24 hours before, and led her out of the room. Matt's dad followed.

"Do you guys want to come with me to the cafeteria? Charli ate all of her breakfast and all of mine," I said.

"She can eat sometimes," Matt's dad said with a soft smile. Lindsey shot him a look.

"Shawn," she said to him. He held his hands up in defense.

"Kindra, this is my husband and Matt's dad. Shawn. Shawn, this is Kindra," she said, still giving him an evil look. I laughed. "Nice to meet you, Shawn," I said as we walked to the elevator.

Charli

The adults left, and Matt and I struggled to find words.

"I brought you lunch," Matt said, looking around, "but my mom took it with her. I just thought...hospital food isn't always great." He was fidgeting.

"Thank you," I said. "Not for lunch, well for that too, for everything."

"I was so scared, and when I found you... and all the blood, I thought..." Matt looked away.

"Matt, what did you tell them? About what happened?" I asked. The question almost felt selfish, but I needed to know what to be prepared for. Matt sighed loudly. I could tell he was frustrated. He stood up and began pacing at the foot of the bed. He ran his hands through his hair.

"I didn't tell anyone anything," he said, his voice just above a whisper.

"Matt?" I said. I'd barely heard what he said. He stopped walking and turned to face me. "I didn't tell anyone anything! I couldn't even open my mouth to talk because I knew it would come rushing out. So, I just stopped talking altogether. I didn't tell anyone anything, Charli," he said. He was very angry, and I didn't want him to be.

"But I think we should," he said, completely catching me off guard. "No," I said quietly.

"Charli, look around. We are in the hospital; look what they did to you. Everyone knows it's happening now. You just have to tell them who it was," he said.

“And then what?” I asked him. I felt tears starting to form behind my eyes. “What do you mean?” he asked.

“And then what? They take me away from you and Kindra and from family pizza night and picnics in the park, put me who knows where, with who knows who, and treat me just as bad. I can’t lose you guys.” I said, and the tears broke free.

“You can’t go back to that house,” Matt said. I knew I couldn’t, but what could I do? “We will figure something out. I promise,” Matt said. I looked out the window.

“Charli, we won’t tell...yet. Until we figure something out, OK? And you won’t lose us. We won’t let that happen.” Matt said. I nodded my head in agreement and wiped away my tears. I was scared for my future, but there wasn’t anything I could do about it right now, so I let it go.

“You found my backpack?” I asked, noticing it on the floor.

“Yeah, I went back and looked for it this morning. It wasn’t too far from where I found you.” Matt said, his voice getting low.

“I’m glad you texted me,” he said.

“I knew it was bad, worse than it had been. I thought I could make it to school, but then I knew I wouldn’t. You were the only person who would have known I was in trouble if I texted you,” I said.

Matt handed me my backpack. “I’m just glad I found you when I did,” he said. “ “Thanks, Matt,” I said.

Kindra

Chipmunk was lightly snoring; she'd finally fallen asleep. I sat on the floor in front of the couch to avoid disturbing her. I reached up and touched the knot on my forehead. It was still sore. Earlier in the day, I requested a packet of information on fostering a child in the state of Texas. I was filling out the required information online via my cell phone when Chipmunk's music box came whizzing through the air and hit me on the right side of my forehead. I guess she thought I wasn't paying enough attention to her. It had been such a difficult day. I really wanted to call out of work with Chipmunk so I could stay at the hospital with Charli, but I hadn't been on this job for 30 days yet, and calling out was a very bad look.

Lindsey promised they wouldn't leave until I got back. I don't think Matt wanted to leave at all. I'd finished filling out the requested info. I needed to speed up my timetable of being able to foster her. I then sent an email to the manager of my apartment complex asking what it would take to move into a two-bedroom from my one-bedroom.

I heard the keys in the door and thought, *finally*. The day had really dragged by. I let Chipmunk's mom know how her day was and was out the door and on my way back to the hospital.

When I walked into Charli's room, Lindsey was sitting in a chair, and Matt was showing Charli something on his cell phone. Lindsey jumped up when she saw me come in. She walked up to me and said, "They have Charli scheduled for surgery in four days."

"It's the same day as the concert," Matt and Charli said together.

Crap. With everything going on, I'd completely forgotten about the MC Spinner concert. "What concert?" Lindsey asked me.

"Well…" I paused. How in the world do I explain to this woman that I barely know that I am a survivor of rape that suffers from PTSD and is raising money to get a service dog with the help of an old-school rapper named MC Spinner?

"I'll tell you about it later, Mom," Matt said, rescuing me from that awkward conversation. No wonder people didn't want to donate to help me get my service dog. My story sounded crazy.

Lindsey began gathering her things. "I have to run some errands, Kindra. Is it OK if Matt stays?" she asked. Matt looked up at her with an expression that said he wasn't leaving anyway. I laughed.

"Of course it's OK," I said and went and sat in the chair on the other side of Charli's bed. Lindsey kissed Matt on the cheek and told him she'd be back in a few hours, then walked out the door.

"So about the concert?" Charli said as soon as Lindsey left.

"Oh, Bear, there is absolutely no way I'm going to that now," I said back to her without a second thought.

"I told you she wasn't going to go," Matt said to Charli.

"Kindra, you have to go," Charli said. I realized they'd had in-depth conversations about this without Lindsey knowing.

"How did you guys talk about this without Matt's mom knowing what you were talking about?" I asked them. Lindsey had no idea about the concert, even though the kids had discussed it at length. They both held up their cell phones in response to my question.

"You guys sat here and texted each other?" I said.

"Kindra, you have to go because WE need a service dog. Both of us," Charli said.

"Charli needs it now more than ever; her PTSD is bad," Matt said. I knew my PTSD was bad. I couldn't imagine what she was going through. I got up out of my chair and sat on the edge of her bed. I grabbed Charli's hand and locked her fingers in mine.

"Bear, how come you didn't tell me what was happening to you?" I asked her. Her face got really sad, and so did Matt's.

"They would have taken me away from you," she said.

"We don't know the foster care system like Charli does. She kept it a secret...I mean, we kept it a secret so she could stay," Matt said to me. They both just deserved to be kids; their innocence was gone, and it wasn't fair. I only partially understood their reasoning, but I had a feeling their logic might be sound.

"Bear, I need you to tell me who did this to you," I said to her. "No," she said quickly, and Matt looked away.

"Charli..." I started, but she cut me off. "NO," she said louder this time.

"Bear, listen, whoever hurt you needs to be punished. You deserve justice," I said.

"Did you get justice?" she asked me. Her question hit me like a sucker punch and knocked the wind out of me. She knew the answer to that question. We'd had that conversation on one of our park days. We were lying on a blanket, staring into the sky, and she asked me,

"What happened to the person who hurt you?" Her question caught me off guard, and my answer slipped out of my mouth before I had time to think about it.

"Nothing," I said.

"Nothing?" she repeated back to me as she turned on her side to face me. I sighed heavily and turned to face her as well.

"Nothing? she asked again. "No. Nothing," I said to her. "But why?" she asked.

"Because our justice system is broken, and not enough people care about people being raped to do anything about it," I said to her. Sitting in this hospital room looking at her, I wondered: if I had known then what was happening to her, would I have told her the same thing? I think I may have because the numbers don't lie. In America, statistically, 1 in 6 women will be sexually assaulted in their lifetime, and for every 1,000 rapes, only 25 rapists will see a day in jail.[1] How could I ask her to come forward, to possibly have to sit through a court process, possibly be questioned, be made to be the bad guy, have to relive what happened to her over and over to most likely not even get justice? Was it truly fair that I ask that of her? My mind flashed to conversations I'd had with women in groups who didn't report their rapes and the reasons they gave.

"The police didn't seem interested." "I was told it was my fault; I led him on/I'd had too much to drink." "I had no support and didn't want to do it alone." "The police talked me out of reporting." The list went on. Could I, in good conscience, knowing the full truth, do this to her? Was it the best thing for HER? I honestly didn't know, but what I did know was Matt was right; she needed the service dog. I had to go to the concert. That was the best thing I could do for her...for us.

"Let's make a deal," I said. They both looked up at me. "I

---

[1] https://www.rainn.org/statistics/criminal-justice-system

will go to the concert, but when I get back and Charli comes through her surgery, we will sit down and talk, and you guys will tell me everything and together we will figure out what the best plan of action will be. Deal?" I said.

"You *will* go to the concert?" Charli asked.

"I will go," I said. She looked at Matt, and he nodded. "OK, deal," she said.

I held out a pinky finger to each of them, and they looked confused.

"A pinky promise is the most important promise you can make with someone. We are all going to pinky promise to hold up to our end of the deal we just made, and we all lock our pinkies like this, and it seals the promise," I said, locking my pinky into Charli's pinky. They both smiled and locked all of our pinkies together.

"I promise," I said.

"I promise," they both said in unison, and we all smiled. I turned around and pulled a deck of Uno cards out of my purse. I grabbed them when I went home to change before going to work with Chipmunk today.

"Shall we play?" I asked, holding the deck up in front of them. "What's that?" Charli asked.

"It's OK, I'll teach you," Matt said, taking the deck from me and shuffling the cards. "And then I'll beat you." Charli rolled her eyes.

"Kindra, make sure he doesn't cheat," she said.

"I will make sure," I said. Matt began dealing the cards.

Charli

It was my third day at the hospital and two days until surgery and I had gotten really good at Uno. I had one Draw 4, one Wild, and 2 Draw Twos. Matt was about to go down.

Sometimes, Matt's mom played with us, but she wasn't playing right now. She was sitting in a chair reading a book, and Kindra was at work. So it was just me and Matt, and I was about to beat him good. I smiled a devilish grin as I put the first Draw Two down. Just as I was about to put the second one down, I saw a shadow from the corner of my eye enter the room. I thought it was one of my nurses. They were always coming and going, checking my vitals and bringing me meds.

"Hello, Charli," a voice said. I froze. It was a voice I vaguely recognized. I slowly looked up. It was my caseworker.

"Hello," I said quietly. Matt immediately turned around and stood up after he saw the look on my face.

"Who are you?" he asked my caseworker in a very stern voice.

"Matthew," his mom said, getting up and grabbing his arm to try to make him sit down.

He shrugged her off and stood between my caseworker and my bed. "Who are you?" he asked her again.

"My name is Rebecca; I'm Charli's caseworker. And you are?" she said in a too-cheery voice. She obviously couldn't read the room. Matt didn't answer her. He looked back at me and asked if she was OK with his eyes. I slowly nodded yes.

"Matthew, where are your manners?" his mom said. "I am so sorry. I am Lindsey, and this is my son Matt. He's Charli's friend from school," she said to Rebecca.

"Nice to meet you both," Rebecca said a little slowly. You could tell she was starting to get the hint she wasn't wanted there.

"Matt, honey, let's go get something to eat from the cafeteria and give Charli and Rebecca a chance to talk," Matt's mom said. Matt had not moved from his spot directly between the caseworker and me.

"I'm not hungry," he said to his mother, still staring straight at Rebecca.

"Matthew Evan Alexander," his mother said. I watched him sigh a frustrated breath. He turned and looked at me, asking if it was OK to leave with his eyes.

"I'm OK," I said out loud to him.

"I will be right outside your room, OK?" I'm not going to the cafeteria," he said to me while cutting his eyes at his mother.

"OK," I said. I could tell he was about to get an earful from his mom as they walked out the door. Rebecca came in and sat in the chair that Matt's mom had been sitting in.

"It's been a while since I've seen you," she said.

"Uh-huh," I responded. She pulled a pad of paper out of the bag she had with her. "I came as soon as I found out you were here," she said. I just nodded my head.

"Charli, can you tell me what happened to you?" she asked. I quickly turned my head away from her. I didn't answer her.

"Charli, can you at least tell me who hurt you?" she asked. A single tear made its way down my cheek.

"No," I said and began fidgeting with my hands.

"Charli, I can't help you if you don't talk to me," she said. I suddenly felt angry. I felt so angry that my head got hot.

"Help me?" I thought to myself. She wanted to help me? She had put me in one abusive home after the next, homes ranging from bad to worse. Most of the abuse I'd gone through in my life was because of the homes and the people she placed me with.

"NO!" I said again more forcefully.

"But Charli…" she started, but I cut her off.

"I DON'T NEED YOUR KIND OF HELP!" I yelled at her. She looked shocked. Matt came through the door, but just as he got one foot through the threshold, his mother grabbed him and dragged him back out. I laughed a little to myself on the inside. Rebecca could take a lesson from Matt on how to help people. I looked over at Rebecca; she was frantically writing notes on her pad. I didn't even care what they said about me.

"I can't make you talk to me, Charli. I know you are angry. I don't know what you have been through, but I am so sorry, Charli. I truly am. The police will come by to talk to you, and after you recover from your surgery, we are going to move you into a different house," she said. My head popped up.

"Because we don't know exactly what's going on or where the abuse is coming from, I think it will be in your best interest to put you in a new home," she said. All I heard was she was going to take me away from Matt and Kindra. How would I tell them? How had I let myself become so stupid as to become attached to them? I felt my heart breaking into a million pieces. Silent tears rolled down my cheeks. Rebecca saw the tears. She looked back at the door that Matt had gone out of, and then she looked at me.

"I promise I will try to keep you close. I will try to find a placement for you that's not far from here, OK Charli?" she said. I nodded my head yes; I hoped she could keep me close. She began to put her stuff back in her bag. A sign she was about to leave. I wiped my tears with my hospital gown, grabbed my cup of water off of the table, and drank from it. I didn't want Matt to know I'd been crying. I couldn't tell him they were moving me.

"I will be in touch, Charli; you be strong. I know going under the knife can be scary, but you will come through just fine. I will be praying for you," Rebecca said as she headed out the door.

"Going under the knife?" I whispered to myself. I hadn't really put any thought into what surgery would be like or what they would be doing until she said that. They were going to cut me open. Matt came back into the room and came straight up to my bed.

"Are you OK?" he asked me. I nodded my head yes. The social worker is talking to my mom, trying to find out what she knows, but it's OK because she doesn't know anything," he said.

"Are you sure you're OK?" he asked again. I shook off thoughts of being moved and thoughts of surgery and put on my brave face. I picked up my Uno cards and played the other Draw Two.

"You're in trouble now!" I said to him. He smiled big and picked up his cards to play.

We'd been playing for about an hour. I'd beaten him more times than I had lost, and I was pretty sure I was about to beat him again when I heard a male voice say, "Oh, Charli, I was so worried about you." I looked up, and Mack and Jeremy were standing just inside the entrance to my room. Jeremy locked eyes with Matt, then leaned over and whispered something in Mack's ear, and pointed at Matt. Mack nodded and took a step towards me.

"How you feeling?" he said. I couldn't breathe. There was usually a build-up to my panic attacks, but this one was instant. Matt jumped up into his spot between them and my bed. He looked so angry. I'd never seen him like this.

"What are you doing here?" he asked Mack and Jeremy.

"Checking on my daughter," Mack said and took a step closer. Matt took a step towards him.

"She's not your daughter! She's been here for three days, and you're just now checking on her? I think you should leave," he said.

"Matthew?" his mom said apprehensively. She was still sitting down. I think she was nervous about what was happening.

"Look, we're here to check on my sister." Jeremy said, then looked at me. I was starting to feel dizzy.

"You're probably the one that did this to her! I've seen you with her--

"MOVE!" Jeremy said and pushed Matt in his chest. As soon as Jeremy's hand touched Matt's chest, Matt swung and punched Jeremy in the face. Blood flew from his nose. Matt hit him again, and they both went down. Matt just kept hitting him. Mack jumped in and tried to pull Matt off but couldn't, so he punched Matt in the side of the face and his ribs. Matt's mom was up and screaming for help. A nurse ran in and then ran out. I heard security being paged to my room over the intercom, and then a bunch of nurses ran in and tried to break up the fight. Then, security ran in. They immediately grabbed Mack, who began yelling, "Call the police! This kid raped my daughter!"

One of the security guys grabbed Matt too, and began dragging him out of the room, but Matt was fighting against him.

Jeremy was struggling to get up from the floor.

"Take your hands off my son!" I heard Matt's mom yell. I pulled the blanket over my head. Everything was too much. Then I heard a voice yell, "Everyone OUT!"

I could still hear Matt struggling with security. Then I heard Matt's mom say, "Get your hands off me, we're leaving!"

A second later, the room was quiet except for the steady beeping of the machine. I was trying to control my breathing. I pulled the blanket off my head and looked around the room. It was a mess. There was blood on the floor where Jeremy had lain. A chair was flipped over.

Papers were scattered everywhere, and the blinds were all messed up. The destroyed room was making me panic more. One of my nurses came in and ran to me.

"Charli, are you OK? Try to calm down your breathing," she said. I couldn't. I tried to count five things I saw, but all I saw was destruction, making it worse. The nurse pushed a button on the remote next to my bed and said, "Shelby, we need you!"

A few seconds later another nurse came in. She came straight to my bedside. The first nurse grabbed my hand and held it.

"Charli, this is going to help you relax," the Shelby nurse said. Then she cleaned my arm with something cold. I felt a stick. Then, I felt myself start to float off to sleep.

"You're safe here. We're going to keep you safe." I heard the first nurse say as everything went black. I didn't fight it.

Kindra

I was just pulling into the hospital's parking lot after my shift with Chipmunk when my cell phone rang. It was Matt. I answered it and wedged the phone between my ear and my shoulder as I turned into a parking space. All I heard was Lindsey crying on the phone. I couldn't make out what she was saying--something about a fight.

"Lindsey, take a deep breath. Try to calm down so I can understand you," I said to her. I was already out of the car and sprinting towards the hospital. Lindsey seemed to be calming down. She started talking about Charli's caseworker coming to visit. I got in the elevator, pushed the button for the second floor, and prayed my service didn't drop. I was just stepping out of the elevator when Lindsey told me about the fight and how everyone had been kicked out of Charli's room. I walked up to Charli's room. The door was closed, and a security guard stood next to the door.

"I'm sorry, ma'am, no visitors in this room," he said. I was shocked. I went to the nurse's station and saw one of Charli's nurses that I recognized. Lindsey was still talking.

"Lindsey, hold on," I said into the phone.

"Jessica!" I called out to the nurse. She turned and once she realized it was me. She gave a pained expression.

"What is happening? Why can't I go in Charli's room?" I asked her. She walked off to the side where we would have a little more privacy.

"A fight broke out in Charli's room, and accusations were made as to who raped her, so until we know more, she can't have visitors for her safety," she said.

"But I would never, Jessica, you know me!" I pleaded with her.

"It's not up to me. We have to protect her until we know who hurt her. I'm sorry. Charli is asleep right now, but I will tell her you came by when she wakes up," she said and walked off.

"Came by?" I muttered.

"Lindsey, where are you?" I said back into the phone.

"We are downstairs in the ER. Matthew is getting checked out," she said.

"I will be right there," I said and hung up the phone. I was walking back to the elevator to get to the ER, but I stopped in front of Charli's room. I stared at the door, trying to send my energy and love through it. I just wanted her to know I was here. It was just a plain door, but it seemed like a mountain separating me from my girl.

"I'm here…" I whispered to the door. The security guard looked up at me. I gave him a weak smile and returned to the elevator to check on Matt and Lindsey.

Charli

It had been 24 hours since the fight in my room. I'd had no visitors, only the nurses and a police officer whom I refused to answer any questions for. I fought sleep because every time I closed my eyes, I dreamt Mack and Jeremy were coming into my room, and there was no one here to protect me. If I wasn't having nightmares about Mack and Jeremy, then I was having nightmares about the surgery--I was awake, and I could see and feel everything, and there was always a big knife over me. I cried off and on all day. Kindra called every few hours and texted often. Matt called and texted pretty often too. He was still in the hospital. He'd hurt his hand pretty badly when he hit Jeremy, and his ribs were hurt when Mack hit him. I was so lonely and scared. I remembered thinking that Heaven would be great if I could just float by myself in nothingness. I didn't think so anymore. I didn't want to be by myself.

A nurse had come in earlier with a late lunch. I'd already refused dinner last night, breakfast this morning, and lunch the first time they offered. I just wasn't hungry. I refused her second attempt at lunch.

"Charli, you need to eat something. You're having your surgery tomorrow and you need to eat to build your strength," she said. I just turned my head and looked out the window. I wondered what Kindra was doing. "I'm going to leave your food right here. You just try to eat when you're ready," she said, leaving the room.

I woke up with a start. I didn't remember falling asleep, but the nightmare about surgery woke me. The lunch tray was gone. I guess they'd taken it away. I sighed and rolled over on my side and let the tears flow. I heard my door open. It was probably one of the nurses to check my vitals.

"You can't stay too long, or we'll get in trouble," I heard a voice whisper. I rolled over just in time to see Nurse Jessica rolling Matt in a wheelchair to my bedside. I smiled with my whole face. Matt jumped up out of the wheelchair and ran to my bed. He gave me the biggest hug.

"Are you OK?" he asked. He pulled away, and we both had tears running down our faces.

Matt winced in pain and grabbed his ribs.

"Be careful, Matt. I'm going to set this on the table," my nurse said, setting two brown bags on my table.

"I will be back for you in a little while," she said. She smiled at us then walked out of the room. I looked down and saw Matt's arm was in a sling.

"What…?" I started, but he cut me off.

"You ever break your hand on someone's face?" he said, sounding macho. "Is it broken?" I asked, one eyebrow raised.

"No, but it sounds cool to say!" he said with pride.

"I heard you haven't been eating," Matt said, changing his tone. "I'm not hungry," I replied.

"You're always hungry," he said. I shrugged my shoulders.

"How did you know I wasn't eating?" I asked him.

"I come over here about every two hours to see if they will let me in to see you and make sure no one else has come by to bother you, and the nurses told me you won't eat," he said. All this time, he'd been right outside checking on me. I wasn't so alone. Matt got up and grabbed the two brown bags off the table with his good hand and came back and sat on my bed. He opened one bag, looked inside, and handed it to me. I was stunned.

"Is it...?" I couldn't finish.

"It's lunch. I asked Mom to go home and make us lunch. I wrote down all your favorites for her to put in there," he said with a smile. He started pulling the contents out of his bag, so I opened mine. A turkey sandwich with lettuce, tomato, and cheese. Two bags of Cheez-Itz, two bags of pineapple slices, two brownies, one Twinkie, and two Capri Suns, and a letter from Matt's mom that said, "Dear Charli, we tried to get your favorites. Please eat so you can get better. We love you. - Lindsey, Shawn, and Matt."

The tears started as I read the letter. I was loved by Matt's family. I looked up to see Matt smiling big at me.

"Eat," he said. All of a sudden, I was starving.

I'd eaten everything except the second bag of Cheez-Its. I was so pleasantly full. I just laid back in my bed while Matt cleaned up the trash.

"Matt..." I said just as he was finishing. He came and sat back down on the edge of my bed.

"I'm really scared about surgery tomorrow," I said. I'd only admitted that to Kindra.

"Oh!" he said and jumped up. He went back to the wheelchair he'd arrived in, grabbed something I couldn't see, and came back to my bed.

"Ta-da!" he said, holding up the brush Kindra and I used at the picnics. "What! Where did you get that?" I asked him in shock.

"Kindra gave it to me to give to you," he said with a smile.

"When did you see Kindra?" I asked him. I'd thought she'd gone home.

"Who do you think is wheeling me up here every couple of hours? Well…when she isn't at work. She's waiting to get the OK to see you too," he said.

"She is?" I asked.

"She's outside right now. They let me in because you weren't eating, and I'm a kid, and they don't believe I hurt you, but they couldn't let both of us in," he said. I felt so good knowing my Sissy was right on the other side of the door.

"I'm supposed to brush your hair," Matt said, holding up the brush with his left hand. He was right-handed.

"Um…" I said.

"Just let me try!" he said, and I laughed and turned around so he could brush my hair. He was very heavy-handed. It felt like he was trying to brush my scalp, and his motions were not smooth. They were jerky. Finally, I just turned away.

"OK!" I yelled, and we both laughed.

"Five minutes, Matt." The nurse's voice came through the bed. "No," I said.

"Give me your phone," Matt said. "What?" I asked him.

"Give me your phone, hurry up," he said. I got my phone off of the table and handed it to him. He began pushing buttons and swiping things, and then suddenly I heard a ringing like my phone was calling someone. Then I heard Sissy's voice say, "Hey Matt, how is she?"

Matt turned my phone around, and there was Kindra clear as day, video chatting with me.

"Hey there!" Kindra said. "Sissy!" I yelled.

"I made you a Skype account earlier today, and I just logged you into it so you can video chat with me and Kindra now," Matt said. He was quickly explaining how to make Skype calls when Kindra said, "Charli, what happened to your hair?"

I looked up at Matt.

"My whole arm is in a sling!" he said, laughing.

The nurse walked in and said, "OK, Matt." He gave me a hug.

"I will video call you as soon as I get back to my room," he said. Just as they got to the door, I heard the nurse say, "Make it quick," and Kindra came flying through the door. She ran to my bed and threw her arms around me.

"I've been here the whole time," she said. Then she leaned into my ear and whispered, "You are my Warrior Princess, and you can do this tomorrow. You got this, Charli Bear. I love you." I tried to inhale as much of her scent as I could before she pulled away.

"I love you too, Sissy," I said to her as she ran out the door.

Kindra

"NO, I CAN'T DO THIS!" I yelled at the screen. Tears streamed down my face. It was an ugly cry. My nose was completely stuffed up, and I could hardly breathe.

"Go get something to drink," Daniel said. It was the night before the concert and the night before Charli's surgery. They wouldn't let me in for a real visit besides the hug I'd stolen earlier. I'd spent so much time focused on Charli the last few days that I'd spent no time mentally preparing myself for the concert, for the number of people, for the concert setting, for going to a part of Texas that I really didn't know, with a person I didn't really know, for talking to MC Spinner about getting my service dog. It was all happening tomorrow, and not only was I not ready, I was freaking out. My PTSD was in overdrive. I was attempting to pour myself some juice, but my hands were shaking so badly I spilled it all over the counter.

"DAMN IT," I yelled.

"What happened?" I heard Daniel ask from the computer screen.

"My hands won't stop shaking, and I spilled the juice trying to pour it," I yelled in the direction of the computer on my dining room table.

"Just bring the whole jug over here and sit down," Daniel said. So I did. "Drink it straight from the jug," Daniel said. So I did. It calmed me down a bit.

"I wish I was there. Remember that night we had nothing to do, so we just drove around San Diego all night listening to music and stopping at a bunch of different gas stations trying to find Calypso Lemonade?" Daniel asked me.

"Yeah, that was a great night. Downtown San Diego is pretty at night," I said, remembering the sights.

"The weather was great; you had the windows down and your eyes closed while you vibed out to the music," he said. I hadn't realized he was watching me that closely.

"Close your eyes now and remember it," he said. I took another sip of the juice then made myself comfortable in my chair. I took a deep breath and closed my eyes. I took slow, steady breaths and focused on the memory of that night.

"What do you smell?" he asked me. I focus in and get the faintest smell of the beach.

San Diego is a beach town, so you get the slightest hint of beach water all over town. "It smells a little like salt water," I said.

"That sounds about right," he responded.

"What do you feel?" he asked. I focused on the memory again. I was sitting in the passenger seat of my Honda Civic. I felt my seat belt across my chest and waist, holding me firmly in place, and the wind rushing through my window.

"I feel the wind blowing on my face through the window," I said happily. "What do you hear?" he asked. I paused and listened.

"Girls All Pause," I yelled. It was one of my favorite songs at that time. The song started over, and I realized Daniel was actually playing the song on his computer, and I was hearing that. With this song actually playing, I didn't have to focus so hard on holding it in the memory.

Hearing the song made it easier to remember that night.

"What do you see?" he asked. I looked out the window.

We had just passed that 7-11 again. They didn't have any Calypso lemonades--we already checked. I looked over in the driver's seat, and there was Daniel, one hand on the steering wheel, the other holding my hand. He looked over at me and smiled. I felt calmer and safer in that moment than I'd felt in weeks.

"I see you," I said softly.

"Good-looking guy?" he asked. I laughed, trying so hard to hold on to this moment. "Now look in the back seat," he said.

"I don't see anything," I said, slightly confused.

"Your service dog is back there. You don't see him? He's got his head out the window!" Daniel said, laughing. I wanted to see it so bad. I wanted my dog to be there. I looked in the back seat again, and the most beautiful Golden Labrador was there. His head was out the window, and his tongue was flopping out of the side of his mouth.

"I see him!" A single happy tear rolled down my cheek. That was my service dog. "Open your eyes," Daniel said.

"I don't want to," I told him.

"Baby girl, open your eyes," he said. Slowly, reluctantly, I did. It was sad watching the memory fade away; my service dog faded away. I blinked Daniel back into focus. He was staring at me lovingly but very intense. He stopped the music and said, "Now go get your dog," and I was ready.

Charli

"No!" I yelled as I woke up. I was in my hospital room. I'd had another nightmare about the surgery. This time, it was Mack and Jeremy performing the surgery on me. I wiped the tears from my eyes and got up to use the restroom. I climbed back in bed and looked at my phone. It was 3:30 AM. I wondered if Kindra was up. She'd taken a few nights off her night job, but she still might be up. I opened my Skype app, found her name, and video-called her.

"Please be awake, please be awake," I whispered as it rang. Then she picked up. Relief washed over me, but as her screen became clear, I could tell she'd been sleeping.

"Bear, you OK?" She asked with sleep in her voice.

"I'm sorry I woke you, Sissy. Go back to sleep," I said with a sigh.

"No, hold on," Kindra said and set her phone down. I was now looking at her ceiling from where she had laid her phone down. I saw a light come on in her room and could hear her moving around. Then she popped back into the camera, and I was looking at her face.

"Hey, Warrior Princess! You OK?" she asked me.

"I'm no Warrior Princess," I said as the tears began to roll down my cheeks.

"Oh, Bear, yes, you are. To have gone through everything you have gone through and still be standing, you are a warrior. You didn't let all that stuff break you; you still find reasons to smile," she said. I felt like a fraud.

"But Sissy, I can't do this surgery, I just can't, I can't do it,"

I cried to her.

"I know you are scared; I'd be scared too, but I know you can do this," she said. "You'd be scared too, Sissy?" I asked, a bit in disbelief.

"Yeah," she responded.

"You wouldn't be scared--you're the bravest person I know," I told her, and I believed every word of it.

"I'm not always so brave either, Kiddo. I actually had a similar conversation with Daniel a few hours ago where I was crying to him because I'm scared about going to the concert," she said.

"Really?" I asked. There was no way that Kindra, who'd fought through suicide, helped counsel other girls, battled PTSD, had been raped herself, and got through all of that--mostly by herself, was scared.

"Charli, I am terrified to go to this concert. I'm scared when I'm in large crowds and I can't see everyone's hands and I don't know everyone's intentions that someone is going to grab me and hurt me. I'm scared when I go to new places that I'm not familiar with that I will get lost and won't be able to save myself if I come across some bad people. I'm scared that new people that I meet are just being nice so they can put me in a position to hurt me. I'm scared a lot too, Kiddo," she said. She really was scared, scared like me.

"How do you get over it?" I asked.

"Well…" Kindra said, then paused like she was thinking.

"Remember when we first met? You were scared of me, weren't you?" she asked me. "Yeah," I replied.

"But look at us now--you aren't scared of me anymore. How did you get over it?" she asked me.

"I… I…I don't know," I said.

"Little by little. We didn't build this relationship overnight. You trusted me a little bit more every day, even though you were scared. You decided that the good that could possibly happen was more important than the feeling of fear, and you pushed through. The more you learned about me, the less scared you were, right?" Kindra asked.

"Yeah," I said back. She was right. "But how do I learn about the surgery?" I asked her. "You ask," she said. I thought for a second.

"OK, are they going to cut…" I started, but she cut me off.

"Not me, silly bear. I don't know anything about it. You ask your doctors," she said. "Oh," was my response.

"There is a pen on the table next to your bed. Get it and a paper towel," Kindra said. I got up and did as I was told.

"Got it," I said as I climbed back into my bed.

"OK, let's write down your questions, and you can ask the doctor before surgery," she said.

"OK! I want to know if it will hurt. Matt says I won't feel it, but why won't I feel it?" I asked.

"Those are both good questions--write them down," she said. We came up with a list of questions, and I was feeling better when I saw Kindra grab a jug of juice from her nightstand and take a sip straight from the container.

"Kindra, you drink it straight from the jug?" I asked her. She looked at the jug and laughed.

"Daniel said I could," she said, and I laughed too. "Sissy, do you think Daniel will like me?" I asked her. "I think he will love you, Bear," she said with a smile.

"Are you sure, 'cause he doesn't want kids, right?" I asked.

“I didn't want kids either, but now I'm looking at different types of purple for your room and getting tips on lamps at Ikea,” she said.

“Oh right, Ikea! They have good ice cream for a dollar,” I said.

“Yes, I know. I've been there. I’ll take you once all this is over, I promise,” she said. Then I remembered I was moving.

“Sissy, I need to tell you something,” I said. “OK,” she responded.

“My caseworker is moving me away,” I said. I thought she'd cry, but she didn't. “I figured she would," she said calmly.

“You did?” I asked.

“Charli, they couldn't leave you in that house. Matt and I already talked about it, and we agreed that as long as you have your phone, there is nowhere they can move you that we can't find you. Plus, it's only temporary until I get you,” she said. She had already talked to Matt; everything was going to be OK. It felt like a weight lifted off of me, and I yawned. I was ready to go back to sleep, ready for my surgery.

“I'm ready to go back to sleep, Sissy,” I said.

“You are brave enough to get this surgery, and I'm brave enough to go to the concert. If you can do it, I can do it, right?” she asked.

“Right,” I said.

“OK, get some rest, and call me back if you need me through the night. Otherwise, call me before you go in for surgery, OK? I love you, Warrior Princess,” she said.

“I love you too, Warrior Princess,” I said back to her. “Goodnight,” she said, and the screen went black.

Kindra

The day started out fine. Charli called me before she went into surgery. She'd come up with 28 questions for the doctor. I laughed when she told me. That poor doctor. But she was ready. I thought I was ready for my day too. I'd been running around getting my last few things together. I made sure I had my paperwork from Little Angels service dogs to show MC Spinner, and that I'd packed my clothes in a way that they wouldn't get too wrinkled. I kept glancing at the clock. I didn't know how long Charli's surgery was going to take, but Matt was going to call me as soon as she came out. I was also waiting for Eddie to call to let me know what time he was picking me up so we could make the three-and-a-half-hour ride to San Antonio. Even though I knew next to nothing about Eddie, I started looking forward to having him there. He could act as a sort of buffer to everything else. I was sitting on the couch wondering if I should tell Eddie on the car ride why I was going to the concert. When exactly is a good time to tell someone you're just kind of getting to know that you were raped and suffer from PTSD?

I sighed, then heard my phone ring in the other room. It was either Matt or Eddie. I grabbed the phone off of my bed and looked at the caller ID; it said, "Mom." I was a little bummed.

"Hey, Mom," I greeted her.

"Hey honey, listen: Fred just told me Eddie got hurt at work, and he's not going to be able to come to the show tonight," she said. My whole world shifted beneath me. He wasn't going to go? How was I going to get there? Who was going to protect me?

"Kindra?" my mom's voice sliced through my thoughts and brought me back. "Did you hear me?" she asked.

"Um, yes, ma'am. Is he OK?" I asked her.

"Fred said he fell off something up high and hurt his arm or shoulder or something, so I think he's OK. Are you going to figure out how to get here for the show?" she asked.

"Yeah, and I'll call you back," I said as calmly as I could.

"OK, if I'm at the convention and don't answer, just leave a message," she said. "OK, love you," I said.

"Love you too," she said and hung up. I felt like I was going to explode into little pieces. I grabbed the comforter off of the bed and ran into my closet. I sat down on the floor and wrapped up in it. I was freezing all of a sudden. I sat rocking myself in the blanket, just trying to hold myself together but slowly losing my grip. The tears came, and I felt building deep within me one of those gut-wrenching cries that tear you to the core. I felt the panic coming and didn't even have the strength to fight it. My mind could not process one coping technique I had learned over the years to get myself through bad moments. I rolled over on my side and into the fetal position. I was struggling to catch my breath, and my head was pounding. I couldn't process what was happening. I couldn't fix it. I just lay stuck, and then I heard this sound. At first, I didn't know what it was. I couldn't even identify where it was coming from. I threw my hands over my ears, but it just got louder. That's when I realized the sound was coming from me. It was a deep guttural cry like something in pure agony, then quieted down to the whimpering of a wounded animal. I was exhausted from the panic attack I'd just had, wrapped in a blanket, shivering from cold and panic, moaning and gasping for breath with my hands covering my ears. I fell asleep. Things hadn't been this bad in a very long time.

I woke up slightly confused with a killer headache and began looking around. I was in the closet on the floor, tangled in a blanket. This must be bad. Then, it all came back in a wave. I mentally blocked the panic and fear that was trying to take a stronghold again. I got up and stumbled out of the closet. I felt like I had a hangover. I picked my phone up off the floor and looked at the time. I was out for about 30 minutes. No missed calls meant Charli was still in surgery. I began pacing. What was I going to do? I couldn't go to the concert by myself. I didn't even know how I'd get to San Antonio. I definitely couldn't drive myself. Then I thought of Charli, currently undergoing surgery she was scared to death of having because we agreed that if she could go through this scary surgery, I could go to this scary concert. She'd understand, wouldn't she? She'd understand why I couldn't go. No, of course, she wouldn't. I needed help. I pulled up Daniel's email but remembered that he was not reachable until later because he was doing some military training. I typed a message that said, "I need you," and sent it anyway. I looked back into my closet. I really wanted to go back in there and cry some more...but Charli. I needed help. I needed a plan.

I went into the kitchen to get something to drink. I stood in the kitchen drinking orange juice, then I smiled a bit, pulled out my phone, and dialed Kia. Kia was one of my best friends from my brief stint at Alcorn State University. We were roommates and best friends, and we were both extremely protective of each other. We had a very ugly falling out, and while we may not have talked regularly for a few years, if one of us needed something, the other would drop everything for them. In recent years, we'd reconnected a bit more. After finding out we had both been raped (one in six), we heavily leaned on each other. As we healed and got a bit more functional, we talked less, but we were always there if we needed each other. I needed her now.

The phone rang three times before she answered and said, “Hey Ace, you good?” It's how she always answered the phone. When we were in school, we called ourselves the ace of spades. We were sister aces, and it stuck over the years.

“No, I'm not OK,” I said.

“Hold on, let me go into my room so we can talk,” she said. I heard her three beautiful babies playing in the background. I loved her kids like they were my own nieces and nephews, and they called me Titi Kindra.

“What's going on?” she asked me. She knew bits and pieces 'cause we talked here and there. So I just ran through the gist of Eddie getting hurt and not being able to take me to the concert. I didn't have to explain the fear of going by myself or crowds. She suffered from PTSD due to rape as well. She shared my symptoms, so she already knew.

“Oh, Ace, I'm so sorry. Are you OK?” she asked. “Full breakdown,” I said.

“The closet?” she asked. “Yep,” I said. “Headache?” she asked.

“Pounding,” I responded. I was so glad to talk to someone who understood.

“Hey, hey, hey. We are going to figure this out,” she said. “Did you talk to Daniel?” “Unreachable, doing some military training,” I said.

“Ugh, stupid military,” she said. I smiled a bit. “Ace, you know you have to go,” she told me. “I can't,” I said.

“I know you can't, but you have to,” she said. That sentence may not make sense to a lot of people, but it made perfect sense to me. When she said, "I know you can't," she was validating all of my fears. She knew my PTSD mind would not allow me to do this, and she allowed space for that. Then, when she said, "but you have to" she was telling me we have to override my PTSD mind. And I did.

"How do I get to San Antonio, though?" I asked.

"How do you get here when you come to visit?" she asked. Kia lived in Dallas, which was a little over four hours away. I'd visited her a few times before, but I never drove.

"Megabus?" I responded. Megabus was this new bus line that did routes between major cities for really cheap, and the buses were clean and had Wi-Fi. They were giving Greyhound a run for their money. I'd gone to Dallas two or three times and never paid more than $10 for my ticket.

"Yes, Megabus, I'm looking right now, and they have a bus that leaves at 3:45 PM and puts you in San Antonio at 7:30 PM. You can make that one. The ticket is $7. I'm booking it now. Can you get to the bus station?" she asked.

"Yeah," I said.

"Good, and your mom can pick you up. OK, I'm booking your return ticket for 9 AM tomorrow, and it puts you back at 1:15 PM, OK? That ticket is $5," she said. I could hear keys clicking on her keyboard in the background.

"I will send you the money," I said.

"I know you will, Ace," she said with a smile in her voice. "But once I get there…" I started. "I can't do this by myself."

"You won't. Your mom will be there," Kia said. I sighed. "I know our moms don't get our turmoil and most times don't know how to react, but they won't let anything happen to us," she said. Our moms were similar in some ways.

"Kindra, she's going to be in the same building as you," she said. I'd kind of forgotten that.

"But I have VIP, and she doesn't," I said.

"Still in the same building. Your mom will be there to keep you safe, and Fred loves your mom, so he's going to keep you safe. If anything pops off, your mom is a phone call away," she said. She had a point.

"You have everything you need to uncomfortably do this, so get it done. You can get through the next 30 hours. Ace, I know you can do this," she said.

"OK, yes, I can," I said, still trying to convince myself.

"Get to it. I emailed you all of your bus info. Call me when you are on the bus," she said. "OK," I said.

"I love you, girl," she said.

"I love you too, and Ace...thank you," I said.

"You've done the same for me. Now go," she said and hung up. I called my mom and told her the new plan. She said OK, and she'd pick me up at the bus station. In a few hours, I'd be on the bus. I was nervous as hell, but I was going.

Charli

My body felt so heavy as I tried to pull myself out of sleep. Had something gone wrong? It seemed like they had just told me to count backward from 10, and now I was waking up. I blinked a few times, trying to bring things into focus. The world seemed bright with white light. Then, shapes started to form.

"Mom, she's waking up," I heard Matt say. I blinked more, and he slowly came into view, standing over my bed. I tried to talk, but my mouth was incredibly dry. Matt picked up a cup of water with a straw and put it into my mouth. I drank all of it.

"The nurse said your mouth would be dry and you'd be thirsty," he said. "They let me and Mom in your room because they said they didn't want you to wake up alone after the surgery," he whispered. So, I did have the surgery. I tried to sit up, but my body was still very heavy. I looked around the room. I saw Matt's mom smiling at me. No one else was in the room.

"Kindra?" I said in a hoarse whisper and then tried to clear my throat.

"She just got to San Antonio a little while ago, she should be going to the concert soon," he said.

Right, the concert. My brain was in such a fog. I felt myself wanting to go back to sleep. "Tell Kindra I'm a Warrior Princess," I said in a raspy whisper and began to doze back off.

"I will call her right now," is the last thing I heard Matt say before I drifted back to sleep.

Kindra

I was sitting in a corner in the VIP section, drinking water from a fancy glass. I had been there for about 45 minutes. My mom and Fred had gone a different direction than me once we came in because of my VIP wristband. I'm sure they were having a great time. I felt like I was going to vomit. Matt had called just as we were about to head into the concert. He told me that Charli had come through the surgery fine and that she had said she was a Warrior Princess. That was the last nudge I needed. If she could come through that surgery and claim Warrior Princess status, then I would too.

I was sitting in a corner with a file of papers pressed to my chest, my eyes were closed, and I was repeating, "I'm a Warrior Princess, I'm a Warrior Princess" over and over in my mind while trying to regulate my breathing. This place wasn't a regular concert venue. It was a club with two stories and a stage. The second story was VIP, and that's where I sat, doing my best to ward off a panic attack.

"Excuse me," a deep voice said, and a hand touched my shoulder. I almost jumped out of my skin. I opened my eyes to some random guy standing in front of me.

"Can I buy you a drink?" He asked, yelling over the loud noise of the club. My heart started racing, and my hands felt sweaty. I held up my glass of water and gave him a weak smile, hoping he would leave. He sat down next to me. My panic level jumped to 10. I began looking around, wondering how I could get away from him if I needed to. I scanned the room. How far away was the exit? Should I try to bring my papers, or should I just run? The clock in my mind was ticking, and each second brought me closer to danger. This would never have happened if Eddie was here. What if Eddie had been here and just in the bathroom or something? I looked over at the random guy. He had been talking the whole time. I hadn't heard a word he said.

"I'm here with someone," I said abruptly, cutting him off.

"Oh, my bad, Ma, no disrespect," he said and got up and walked away. I grabbed my things and ran to the bathroom. It was crowded but clean. I managed to find a free stall to go in and close the door. I was able to slow my breathing but not stop the tears that came. How did I end up here? At a concert of all places. This wasn't me, and this wasn't safe. I just wanted to go home. I thought about calling my mom, but she wouldn't understand this. I pulled out my phone and stared at it. There were no messages from Daniel; he was still working. No messages from Charli; she was still recovering, I'm sure. I felt so alone in the world, hiding in the bathroom in a club at an MC Spinner concert. What the hell was I doing here? The music stopped, and the DJ came over the speakers and introduced MC Spinner. The girls in the bathroom got excited and stormed out. I had the bathroom to myself. I came out of the stall and went over to the sink. I wiped the counter dry with some paper towels and set my folder down. I looked in the mirror. I was a mess, eyes puffy from crying and mascara running. This was a bad idea. I was done. I began wiping the makeup off my face and wondering how I could get back to the hotel without disturbing my mom when I remembered I was doing it for Charli too. I sighed, took some deep breaths, and splashed some water on my face. I reapplied my makeup and was just about to walk out of the bathroom when my phone alerted me to an email from Daniel. I stopped right at the doorway and read it.

"I love you. You doing OK? I'm here if you need me. Love, Daniel."

My heart squeezed. I wanted to run back into the stall, which looked as tempting as my closet, and spend the rest of the night messaging him. It was so loud outside and so quiet in here, so safe in here. But I slid my phone into my purse and walked out into the club.

The music was blaring. I thought about just hiding in the VIP section, but I couldn't see MC Spinner perform from there, and I wanted to be able to tell him he did a good job without lying. So I walked down the steps to the first floor. It was wall-to-wall people in front of the stage. Standing room only. Just the sight of all those people made me dizzy. I decided to stay on the steps. There were only a few other people there. I leaned up against the wall and watched the performance. MC Spinner obviously wasn't as young as he used to be, but he put on a good show with lots of energy. I was too nervous to really just enjoy it, so I just stood in a corner on the stairs, clutching my folder. When the performance was over, I ran back up to VIP and sat in my seat in the corner, away from everyone, but where I had a perfect view of the door he would enter through. The finish line was in sight. I was almost done. I got myself another glass of water and waited. I scanned every group of people that came out of that door so I would see him first. I held my papers tightly. I was ready.

Mom and Fred were buzzing with energy on the car ride back to the hotel. "Did you have fun, baby girl?" my mom asked me from the front seat.

"Absolutely!" I said with the biggest smile.

"Wonderful, this was good for you, getting out of the house," she said and turned back around. As soon as she was no longer looking, my smile fell. I stared out the window with one single tear running down my cheek. MC Spinner never showed up. He never came to the VIP. I sat and waited for more than two hours until they eventually started to shut things down, and my mom texted me and said they were ready to go. We got back to the hotel, and I peeled off my clothes, took a quick shower, and climbed into bed with my mom. I lay quietly as silent tears streamed down my cheeks and lulled me to sleep. The next morning, I put my smile back on and talked about what a great time I had at the show until my mom dropped me back off at the bus station. Then I cried all the way back to Houston.

Charli

"Well, what does a Warrior Princess bedroom look like?" I asked.

"It looks like whatever you want it to look like," Kindra said back to me. We were both lying in my hospital bed. It was the day after my surgery and the day after the concert. Kindra came straight to the hospital when she got back to town. The nurses let her in my room, and we didn't ask any questions. Kindra said the concert went well, but she didn't talk much about it. She had a smile on her face, but her eyes looked sad. I didn't push. I was just glad she was with me in the hospital. I kept falling in and out of sleep. The pain medicine made me tired. I fought sleep. I want to spend every waking moment I could with Kindra. I didn't know when they were going to take me away.

"Can I have swords in my room? A Warrior Princess needs swords," I said to her. "Sure, I think Nerf makes foam swords," she said, laughing.

"Aww, Sissy," I replied, half whining and half smiling. "Do you want to take fencing?" she asked me. "What's fencing?" I asked, wrinkling my face.

"It's sword fighting," she said. "Nah," I replied.

"So you want swords in your room, but you don't want to learn how to use them. What other nonsensical things would you like in your room, kiddo?" she asked me.

"Non…?" I said.

"Nonsensical, what other things do you want in your room that don't make sense?" she said.

"Oh," I said. Nurse Jessica walked in. "Hey Charli, you want to try using the restroom again?" she asked. I hadn't been able to go to the bathroom on my own since I came out of surgery. They told me it happens sometimes and that I just needed to relax and keep trying.

They said I couldn't be discharged until I peed on my own. I wasn't excited to be discharged because I didn't know where I was going next, but I wanted to pee because I didn't want there to be anything wrong with me. I didn't want another surgery.

"OK," I said, attempting to get up. Nurse Jessica came over and unhooked me from my IV.

"Turn the sink on in there," Kindra said as I walked into the bathroom. "Does that work?" I asked, turning on the sink and letting the water run.

"We'll see," she said. I sat on the toilet for about five minutes. The urge to go was there, but I just couldn't go. I got up frustrated, washed my hands, and went and climbed back in the bed with Kindra.

"No luck?" she asked me. I shook my head no.

"That's OK--it will happen," she said and hit the call light so a nurse could come hook my IV up again.

"Look at this," she said, holding her phone out to me. There were Nerf swords on the screen. I laughed.

"I figured we get two so we can fight each other," she said. I didn't know if she was serious or not, but I loved the idea of us sword-fighting in our home or maybe pillow-fighting. As long as I got to do it with her, I was happy.

Kindra

"Do we need to talk about it?" Daniel asked. "Nope," I responded quickly.

"I think we should talk about it," he said. "I can tell you are hurting."

This was my first time Skyping with him since the fiasco at the concert two days ago. "There is nothing to talk about. He didn't show. End of story," I snapped back at him.

Daniel took a deep breath. "OK," he said and paused before speaking again. I could tell he was thinking of how to talk to me without me exploding. He was navigating me like a live minefield.

"So what's next?" he asked.

Next?" I asked, trying to control my frustration and broken heart.

"With MC Spinner. Or are you done with him?" he asked. It was a good question. What was next? Did I even have the luxury of being done when I still needed help getting my service dog?

"No, I will wait a few days and reach out to him or Darla," I said. "That's good," Daniel said.

"I'm tired; I'm going to lie down," I told him. He looked a little hurt; I was cutting our convo a lot shorter than most days.

"OK, well, I will be around. Hit me up if you wanna talk. I love you," he said.

"I love you too," I said and exited the screen. He deserved better than that. I just was having a hard time holding everything together. I got up from the table, went into my bedroom, pulled the comforter off my bed, and dragged it into my closet. I wrapped up in it and let the tears I'd been holding back flow. I started to doze off. I had to be back at both jobs today, so I needed to sleep anyway. My phone started playing Charli's song. For once, the phone was right next to me. I unlocked it. There was a message from her that said

I peed!

I laughed to myself, but a small weight lifted. I had been a little worried about her not peeing on her own. They'd had to put a catheter in last night to empty her bladder before bed.

Kindra: Good Job Kiddo! I love you.

Charli: I love you too, Sissy.

I set the phone down, and a few more tears fell. Some of them were happy tears for my girl, who finally peed on her own. I fell asleep on the floor in my closet.

Charli

I sat bored in my hospital room. Matt's mom made him go back to school, and Kindra was back at work. I'd peed on my own four days ago, and things had been pretty boring since then. One of the nurses had played a game of Uno with me earlier, and now I just watched a bit of TV here and there and took naps. I heard voices outside my door and hoped it was the nurses bringing lunch. I was hungry. I smiled to myself, remembering how Matt says I'm always hungry.

"There she is," a familiar voice said. It was Rebecca, my caseworker. I froze as she walked into my room and over to my bed.

"You are cleared to get out of here, and I have a really nice place for you with a nice family, Charli," she said. My heart started to race. I didn't want to go with her. I needed to talk to Kindra and Matt. I had to get away. My phone was on the bed next to me. I pulled it under the covers. I didn't want Rebecca to know I had it.

"I've collected your things from your last home. They are in the car," she said.

"I need to use the restroom," I said to her. I needed to get away from her so I could think.

"Oh, of course. And here: I bought you some new clothes. You can change out of your hospital gown," she said, setting a Walmart bag on my bed. I grabbed the bag and hid the phone in it before walking into the bathroom. I closed the door, locked it, and quickly looked around. No windows. I pulled out my phone and called Kindra.

"Please answer, please answer," I whispered as the phone rang.

"Hey Bear!" she said.

"Sissy," I whispered into the phone.

"Hello? Bear? Why are you whispering, what's wrong?" she said.

"My caseworker is here; she's going to take me away. I have to run away. I am going to run away. Will you come get me?" I said into the phone.

"Charli, listen, I will always come get you, but not like this. I need you to go…" she was saying, but I cut her off--

"No, I can't. I don't want them to take me away from you. Please, Sissy." I started crying.

"Hey, hey, hey. No one can take you away from me. You are mine. We have to do this the right way, though, Kiddo," she said.

"But what if the family is bad? What if they hurt me?" I asked her.

"I will come get you. If this next family does anything to hurt you, I will come get you and take you away, but we have to try to do this the right way. OK?" she was pleading with me.

"You promise you will come and get me if it's bad?" I asked her. "I pinky promise," she said. Pinky promise was real.

"I'm scared, Sissy," I said into the phone.

"I know you are, but I need you to try, and if it's bad, I will come get you, and we will figure it out, but I know you can do this. You're a Warrior Princess, remember?" She said. There was a knock on the bathroom door.

"Charli, you OK in there?" Rebecca asked.

"Yes, just a minute," I said loudly. "I'm a Warrior Princess," I whispered into the phone. "And if anything goes wrong?" Kindra asked.

"You'll come get me," I said. "Are you OK?" Kindra asked. "Yes," I said a little shakily. "Are you ready?" she asked. "Yes," I said.

"Call or text me when you get settled in, OK? I will be right by my phone waiting on you," she said.

"Will you tell Matt? I have to hide my phone," I said. "I will tell him," she replied.

"OK" I said.

"You ready?" she asked me again.

"Yes," I said, more sure of myself this time. "Bear?" she said.

"Yes, Sissy?" I responded. "I love you, Kiddo," she said.

"I love you too. OK, I gotta go," I said to her. "OK, call me soon," she said.

"I will," I said and hung up. I quickly dressed in the new clothes. They were too big. I put my phone on silent and put it in my pocket. I opened the bathroom door and walked back into the room.

"You look great. Are you ready?" Rebecca asked in a chipper voice. I couldn't even force a fake smile.

"I'm a Warrior Princess," I told myself.

"Yes, I'm ready," I said out loud to Rebecca. Nurse Jessica had entered the room. She ran over to me and gave me a big hug. She had tears in her eyes.

"You take care of yourself, OK?" She said and stuffed something into my hand, then turned and ran out of the room before I could respond. I just put it in my pocket. I would look at whatever it was later. I didn't want Rebecca to see. I picked up my deck of Uno cards and followed Rebecca out of the room.

"We can stop and get a nice lunch on the way, OK?" Rebecca said. "I'm not hungry," I said as we got on the elevator.

SECTION 3:
WAKING UP

Kindra

I pulled my car over to the side of the 45 freeway to calm myself. I had just hung up with Charli. They were moving her, and there was nothing I could do about it. I'd done my best to stay calm with her on the phone. She'd needed me to be the strong one, so I was, but now…I couldn't breathe. They were taking my girl away. At least at the hospital, I knew she was safe, but now? A new family? I'd yet to have my conversation with Charli and Matt, but I'd put the pieces together that her abuse had come from inside that house. So what about this new house? How did they vet these people? Would she be safe with them?

Charli had wanted to run away. She wanted me to come and get her, and I told her no. Had I made the right decision? Had I just sent her into more danger? If I *had* taken her, would that have been a kidnapping? So many questions ran through my mind, and so little air ran through my lungs. I was starting to get dizzy. I needed to calm down. I forced myself to slow my breathing. I began naming things I could see. I felt the panic reside, and the calm started to take over. I focused on the air coming in and out of my lungs.

I closed my eyes and prayed out loud,

God, please protect her. Keep her safe and put her with a family that will take care of her and do right by her until she can be with me. Lord, please move the obstacles so I can get custody of her. I know she is scared, Lord, and I'm scared too. Please give us both peace in this situation, and Lord, please give me the wisdom to make the best decisions on her behalf. Help me to be the love that she needs. Please, Lord, keep her safe. In Jesus' name, Amen.

I opened my eyes and wiped the tears. I felt calmer. I felt at peace. I pulled out my cell phone and scrolled to Matt's number. I was just about to hit dial when I thought better of it. He should be at school, most likely at lunch. I didn't want him to get in trouble for having his phone out. Also, I didn't need him leaving school and going to try and rescue Charli. He was that loyal. Everyone should have a friend like Matt.

I paused to think if I had one, and my best friend Stitch's face popped into my mind. He'd been there with me through hell and high water, marriage, divorce, rape, heck, starving in college--he always looked out for me. If he were in Matt's shoes, he'd be on his way to help me run away without a second thought. Stitch was my Matt. I needed to call him later and tell him how much I appreciated him.

I closed out Matt's name and scrolled up to Lindsey (Matt's Mom) on my phone. I would tell her but ask that she not tell Matt until he got home from school. I hit send on my phone and pulled back out onto the highway as the phone began ringing in my headset.

Charli

The new house wasn't too bad, but it wasn't where I wanted to be. The mom and dad were Cassie and Randy, and there were five other kids in four bedrooms and three bathrooms. I shared a room with a girl named Kylie, a couple of years older than me. I hadn't had a chance to really sneak away to call Matt or Kindra, but I'd texted them both before I went to bed last night. I told them that I was OK and I loved them. Then I fell into a really deep sleep. I hadn't realized how tired I was.

This morning, I found out we are homeschooled. Cassie left the house early, and Randy was in charge. I got nervous knowing I was in the house with just him there as the only adult, so I kept my distance. I sat quietly and just observed how things were run in this house. We ate a family meal together around a table every day for dinner, with real home-cooked food.

We pretty much fended for ourselves for breakfast and lunch, but there was plenty of food in the cabinets, and we had free reign of it all. Kylie was showing me the ropes of the house. I studied her to see if I could tell if they were abusing her. I asked leading questions about Randy, but she showed no signs of abuse and had nothing bad to say about Randy. I still didn't trust him. They always played nice at first.

It was after dinner, and all of us kids had to help clean up. Cassie and Randy were nowhere to be found, but the house ran like a well-oiled machine. Each kid knew their job and promptly started once Cassie and Randy announced dinner was done and left the room. Kylie was washing dishes and handing them to me to dry, and another kid would put them away.

"Kylie, do you mind if I go lay down? My head is hurting," I said.

"Everyone has to help with chores, Charli," she said without looking up. I sighed and continued to dry the dishes. I wiped the sweat from my forehead and looked around. It wasn't hot in here to anyone else?

"Here," Kylie said, handing me a bottle of water and taking the dish I was drying. "I can finish this up by myself. You can go.

"Thanks," I said and left the kitchen.

I went to my room and sat on the edge of my bed. I opened the bottle of water and drank almost the whole thing. The water was cold and felt good going down my throat. I felt a little better, but my head was still hurting. I was probably just stressed. I figured I had a little while before Kylie came in, so I pulled out my cell phone. I hadn't really had a chance to look at it all day. I pulled my feet out of my shoes and laid back in my bed. *Seven new messages*, my phone said. I unlocked it.

Matt: Good morning.

Matt: Are you doing OK?

Matt: Having lunch without you sucks.

Matt: Respond when you can.

Matt: Haven't heard from you all day.

Matt: Charli, are you there?

Kindra: Hey, Kiddo, just checking in. Hope your day is going well. I love you.

A tear ran down my cheek. I missed them so much. I responded to Matt first.

Charli: Hey Matt.

He responded instantly. He must have been sitting on top of his phone.

Matt: Hey, are you OK?

Charli: Yeah, sorry I didn't text you all day. I didn't really have any time alone.

Matt: OK, I was just worried. Are they…ok?

Charli: I hate it here.

Matt: Are they hurting you? Where are you? I'll come and get you right now.

He was so sweet, and I honestly believe he would ride his bike from Clear Lake to Baytown to come get me.

Charli: No, they aren't hurting me. They actually seem pretty nice. I just hate being away from you and Kindra. I'm in Baytown.

Matt: But you are OK?

Charli: I'm OK.

Matt: I miss you too, Charli.

Tears streamed down my cheeks.

Matt: Mom says Baytown isn't that far. It's only like 30 minutes, so hopefully we can visit soon. She said to tell you Hi, and she loves you.

More tears.

Charli: Hi, Mrs. Lindsey. I love you too. Matt, I still need to message Kindra. Talk to you tomorrow, OK?

Matt: OK, glad you are OK. Goodnight.

OK? I guess I'm OK, I thought, wiping the tears from my eyes. No one was hurting me. I went to Kindra's message.

Charli: Sissy…

She didn't immediately respond. I look at the time. It was almost 8 PM. She was probably asleep before her night job. I sighed heavily when the phone lit up in my hand with a text message coming through.

Kindra: There's my Bear, how are you?

I smiled.

Charli: I'm ok. It's not bad here, but I miss you.

Kindra: I'm glad you are OK, and I miss you to pieces.

Charli: Were you sleeping?

Kindra: Yep, gotta be at work in a few hours.

Charli: Go back to sleep. Talk tomorrow. I love you.

Kindra: Are you sure, Bear? We can chat a little longer.

She needed her rest, and as much as I would have loved to stay up all night talking with her, I knew Kylie would be coming into the room soon. I missed Kindra so much.

"I'm a Warrior Princess," I whispered and then responded to Kindra's text.

Charli: Go to sleep, Sissy. I'm OK. I love you.

Kindra: OK, but if you change your mind or want to talk later, I'm here. I love you little girl.

I let the tears flow freely down my face. I sat up and put my shoes back on (the ones Kindra gave me), then I got back in bed and climbed under the covers. My headache was worse, but I figured it was because of the crying. Tears wet my pillow till I fell asleep. I hoped I would dream of a picnic with Kindra.

Kindra

Charli had been in her new home for a few days, and she seemed OK enough. Our conversations were limited to mostly text since she was homeschooled, but no major red flags were going off, so that alleviated some pressure and worry.

"Hey Darla, I didn't get a chance to tell you how much I enjoyed the show. MC Spinner was great. Thank you guys again for the tickets."

I stared at the message. I had been going back and forth on what to say after the concert. I didn't want to seem ungrateful. I didn't want to complain; I still needed their help. I finally decided this Twitter message was as good as it was going to get and clicked send. I needed to get the communication going again. I didn't want them to forget about me. I hadn't gone to that concert for nothing.

With the message sent, I felt a little lighter. I had just gotten home from my shift with Chipmunk and had to be at my night job in a few hours. I was going to lie down for a nap soon, but I wanted to get some things done online first. I closed out my Twitter account and opened my email. There was an email from my apartment complex. The email said the only thing needed to move into a 2-bedroom was to pay a transfer fee of $300 and to give 30 days' notice that I wanted to move. The email ended with them saying they had a 2-bedroom coming available in 60 days and to please let them know if I was interested in moving to the bigger unit. I was smiling so hard my cheeks hurt. Getting a bigger place was a major step in getting Charli, and it sounded like I could really make this happen. I could be moving into a place big enough for Charli in two months. I was going to get my girl. I closed down the laptop and went and lay on the couch to get a few ZZZ' s before work.

I hadn't been lying down longer than 15 minutes when my cell phone began ringing. It was Charli.

"Hey there, how are…" I started, but she cut me off.

"You have to come get me now," she said, sounding like she was running and out of breath. I sat up straight on the couch.

"Charli, what is going on?" I asked, my voice thick with panic. She didn't respond. I just heard her heavy breathing through the phone, like she was running. Finally, she stopped and began crying into the phone while catching her breath.

"Sissy, please come get me. I'm scared," she said, and my heart shattered into pieces. I was up and looking for my shoes. If someone was hurting my girl, then I was going to go get her. I didn't care if it was kidnapping.

"Charli, calm down and tell me what happened," I said, locking my apartment door on the way to my car to get her. She was still breathing heavily.

"Charli, did someone hurt you?" I asked, putting the key in the ignition and turning the car on. I was just putting the car in reverse when I heard her say "No," through her tears.

"No?" I asked her back while shifting the car back into park. "No, but he was going to," she said.

"OK, Kiddo, tell me what happened," I said to her. "Calm down and tell me what is going on. Where are you?" I asked her. I could tell she'd run somewhere.

"I'm at the neighbor's house in the side yard hiding in the bushes," she said.

"OK, tell me what happened," I said to her. "It was after dinner, and we all had chores. I was drying dishes, but I asked Kylie if she'd dry for me because I wasn't feeling well, and she said, "You said that the last two days," so she went and got Randy, the foster dad and told him I wasn't doing my chores. When he came up to me, I could tell he was angry, and he put his hand out to grab me, and it was like it wasn't him anymore; it was Mack…I mean the last one that hurt me. He would grab me too. So I just ran," she said. She seemed a little bit calmer. Lord, she needed this service dog more than I did.

"Bear," I said.

"Yes, Sissy?" she responded.

"I don't think Randy was trying to hurt you. I think he just wanted you to do your chores, but because of what's happened to you in the past, your brain went into protect-you mode and told you to run. It was the PTSD," I said, hoping she understood.

"You think so?" she asked me.

"Yes, I do, but if he really does try anything, I'm on my way. You know that, right?" I asked her. It was important to me that she knew that.

"Yes, I know," she said. "Sissy, Cassie, the foster mom, is outside looking for me. I think I have to go," she said.

"OK, I'm here if you need me. I love you so much," I said. "I love you too," she said. Then the line went dead.

Crap. I forgot to tell her about the bigger apartment.

Charli

I slowly walked out from the bushes towards Cassie. When she saw me, she ran to me. “Oh, Charli honey, I'm so so sorry he scared you after what you've been through. We just didn't think of how it would affect you,” she said and threw her arms around me. I stood completely still. I didn’t hug her back. She didn’t smell like Kindra. Eventually, she let go and told me I could go take my shower and lay down if I wanted too. I said, “Thank you,” and headed back into the house. I had washed up and been laying in my bed for hours now. I could hear Kylie breathing evenly on the other side of the room, letting me know she was asleep. I pulled out my cell phone and texted Matt.

Charli: How was school today?

I waited for a response, but none came. It was after 11 PM, and he was probably asleep. My head was still hurting, so I got up to get some water out of the kitchen. I was quietly walking down the hallway towards the kitchen when I heard Cassie and Randy arguing. I stood right outside their closed bedroom door and listened.

“She’s been through a lot, Randy; give her a break,” I heard Cassie say.

“She still needs to adjust to the rules of this house, and her getting out of chores and running when someone tries to discipline her is not adjusting,” Randy said.

“You probably scared her! You heard what Rebecca said: she’s been abused, most likely by older males. She is probably terrified of you, and all you want to do is discipline her,” Cassie said.

"We have rules," Randy snapped back.

"Look, just leave her alone for a few days. Give her a chance to trust us. Don't pressure her about school or chores; just let her be for a while," Cassie said.

"Fine, I won't bother her, but you are creating a problem by letting her run around like she owns the place. She needs to move on from what happened to her," Randy said. I sighed and walked the rest of the way to the kitchen. At least I knew I'd be left alone for a while. My head was still hurting badly. I'd even gotten a little dizzy in the shower and felt like I was going to throw up. I wondered if it was the PTSD. I would have to ask Kindra.

Kindra

I was off work tonight and was glad of it. I was tired. Working two jobs was definitely taking its toll, but it was worth it. I was hoping to talk to Charli in depth tonight. She'd been at this new home a little over a week, and while things seemed OK, something also seemed off. I could tell when I talked to her, she wasn't feeling well. I couldn't tell if she was struggling to adjust or if it was something else. She told me about the argument she overheard and how she mostly just stayed in bed all day and hardly ate, and no one really bothered her. I worried she was becoming depressed. So tonight, after everyone in the house was asleep, I hoped to have a real conversation with her--even if it was via text.

It was still early evening, though, so in the meantime, I stalked MC Spinner's Twitter page. I'd had a few communications with Darla since the concert. She'd said she and Spinner were glad I'd enjoyed the show and that I was very welcome. Not much else going on conversation-wise, though. So tonight, I looked for an in. I came across a Tweet that said MC Spinner was going to be on an internet radio station tonight, and they were encouraging fans to call in. I immediately wrote down the number, then opened another tab to go to the radio station. The interview didn't sound like it had been going on long when I tuned in. The radio personality discussed Spinner's career and his attempt to stay relevant in changing times. Then they opened the phone lines up for calls. I sat there listening. Should I even try to call? I'm sure I wouldn't get through. What would I even say? I sat for a few more minutes listening. Then I just picked up the phone and dialed before I could talk myself out of it. The phone rang twice, then someone answered.

“Hey, you're on the radio,” a voice said. For a split second, I froze. I didn’t think they’d actually answer. Then MC Spinner said, “Hey, who are we talking with?”

“MC Spinner, this is Kindra!” I said, shocked that words were coming out of my mouth. “Kindra, how you doing tonight?” Spinner asked.

“I’m great, hey, I saw you perform a couple of weeks ago in San Antonio--you sent me VIP passes. The show was great, and you were awesome. Thank you for having me!” I said. Who was this, speaking with all of this confidence? I didn’t recognize myself right then.

“Oh, Kindra! Man, so glad you got to come out, and you had a good time,” MC Spinner said. “Kindra, be honest, how did he do?” the radio host asked me. I laughed.

“He did really well, high energy; these young performers could learn a thing or two from him,” I replied. Still shocked, I was conversing with MC Spinner and a radio host, and I was holding my own. The conversation went on for another minute or so, and before we got off, MC Spinner said he would be in touch regarding that project I was working on. I was floating on air. He hadn’t forgotten. I shut the computer down and went to watch Netflix while waiting to hear from Charli.

About an hour later, my phone rang from a number I didn't recognize. I looked at the number for a moment and then answered. A woman’s voice said, “May I speak to Kindra, please?” I sat up.

“Speaking,” I responded.

“Ma’am, my name is Joyce. I'm a nurse at Houston Methodist Baytown Hospital. We have Charlotte here, and she asked me to call you. She said you are her family,” Joyce said.

I was up and getting dressed. *Not again*, I thought to myself.

"Is she OK?" I asked while looking for my shoes.

"I can't speak to her condition over the phone. I will tell you she's awake and asking for you," she said.

"I'm on my way," I said into the phone as I grabbed my keys.

"We are moving her to the ICU on the fifth floor. Just come to the fifth floor when you arrive," she said. I stopped in my tracks.

"ICU?" I said into the phone.

"Ma'am, please just get here so she's not alone," the nurse said.

"Alone? Where are her foster parents?" I asked. The nurse sighed heavily into the phone. "They came in with her, then they left and came back with her belongings. They said she was more than they could handle, and they were so sorry. The mother even cried. They said they had contacted her case worker and informed her they were returning her, and they left," she said. I could hear the disdain in her voice.

"They left her?" I repeated back into the phone.

"Please just get here," she said.

"I'm on my way," I said and hung up. I punched Houston Methodist Baytown Hospital into my GPS and began driving. I plugged my headset into my phone as I pulled onto the freeway and called Matt's mom.

Charli

I woke up so confused. Where was I? What had happened? I looked around. I was in a hospital room...again. My eyes landed on a black trash bag in the corner. All my stuff, everything I owned. The new fosters bailed on me. I started to remember bits and pieces. I was at the house, but I started to feel funny, so I went to look for help. I woke up in an ambulance, then I was in a hospital room, and Cassie was crying, but she wouldn't look at me.

They put my stuff in the corner and left. I knew they were getting rid of me, but I didn't know what was wrong with me.

Kindra

I haphazardly turned into the parking lot. I wasn't familiar with this hospital, so I drove around trying to find the correct entrance. I finally parked and headed inside. I bypassed the information desk since I knew I was going to the fifth floor. Lindsey and Matt were on their way. Initially, Lindsay was going to wait until I got there and could find out what was going on before she talked to Matt and brought him over, but once she heard Charli was in ICU, she said they were on their way.

I got off the elevator on the fifth floor and walked to the nurses' station. This floor was so quiet and seemed so much more serious than the last place Charli was. It scared me. I spoke to the first nurse I saw at the station.

"I'm Kindra. I received a call that my little sister Charlotte Lauren was here," I said.

Another nurse turned around.

"Kindra, I'm Joyce; I called you," she said as I walked around the nurse's station to where she was. She got up and motioned for me to follow her, so I did. We walked a few paces and stopped in front of what I assumed to be Charli's room. Joyce turned and looked at me. She had a very serious expression on her face. I was worried. Joyce opened her mouth to say something, then closed it again.

"Let's go take a seat over here and talk before you go in," she said and walked in the direction of some chairs. I looked at Charli's door and then obediently followed Joyce. We both sat down. I waited for her to speak.

"Charli had a seizure today, and that's what brought her to

us," She said.

"A seizure? What caused it? Is she epileptic?" I asked. At this moment, I again realized how little I knew about her. I couldn't even tell them if she was allergic to something because I didn't know.

"She does not have epilepsy," Joyce said.

"Then what?" I asked, becoming frustrated. What was going on with my girl?

"Charli developed an infection from her surgery, and the infection led to the seizure," Joyce was saying.

"An infection? But wouldn't there have been signs, fever, or something?" I asked. Joyce took another deep breath before she spoke.

"Charli said she's had very bad headaches the last week or so. She's had dizzy spells, and she's been very tired," Joyce said.

"I missed it again," I said as the tears came. How had I missed it again? "I thought she was depressed," I said.

"She doesn't live with you, correct?" Joyce asked me.

"No, her new foster family," I said in tears. Joyce grabbed my hands in hers.

"You didn't miss it. They missed it,"' she said. How could they have missed this, though? Then I thought back to the argument Charli had overheard Cassie and Randy having and them agreeing to leave her alone and give her space, plus having five other kids in the house.

"Damn it!" I yelled. Why was life so cruel to this little girl? I tried to calm myself. I looked back at Joyce.

"OK, so what do we do? How do we treat her?" I asked. "Kindra, at this point, Charli has sepsis," she said. "Sepsis?

What's that?" I asked.

"When Charli's body attempted to fight the infection, it released chemicals that caused inflammation of her organs. Basically, her body has turned on itself," she said.

"But there *is* something you can do. There has to be something you can do, right?" I asked.

"We have her on broad-spectrum antibiotics to fight the infection, but Kindra, the infection has had a while to spread through her body; the antibiotics may not work. If that is the case, her organs will begin to shut down…" she said.

"NO…NO…the medicine will work," I said defiantly.

"Yes, that is our hope. The next 24 hours will tell us more," Joyce said. "Does she know?" I asked the nurse.

"No, we were waiting for her family," she said. "What do I tell her?" I asked.

"Be with her, Kindra. Tell her we are treating her for an infection, and in 24 hours, you will know what else you need to tell her," Joyce said. I saw the tears start to form in the nurse's eyes. She thought my Charli was going to die. Well, she was wrong. Charli was just a child--and she's my Warrior Princess.

Charli

I woke up to someone coming into my room. I didn't realize I was holding my breath until I saw it was Kindra walking through the door, and I exhaled.

"Sissy!" I yelled and held my arms out to her. She dropped her purse on the floor and ran to me. She wrapped me up in the biggest hug.

"Oh, baby girl," she said. She'd never called me that before. She held me in that hug for a while, stroking my hair. I loved every second of the hug, but she was acting funny. I finally pulled away, and she let go. I looked at her face, expecting to see tears, but I didn't. Her eyes just looked…sad, so very sad, but she smiled.

"Kiddo, you gave me a scare," she said.

"I don't even know what happened," I said. "What do you remember?" she asked.

"I was laying down in my bed, and I started feeling weird. I can't explain the weird feeling. I just knew something was wrong. I knew something bad was going to happen, so I got up to go find Randy or Cassie. I don't remember what happened next, but then I woke up in an ambulance, and then I woke up here." I shrugged my shoulders.

"OK," Kindra said.

"What happened to me, Sissy?" I asked.

"You had a seizure, Bear. You developed an infection from the surgery, that's why you haven't been feeling well," she said.

"The headaches," I said. "Yeah," she responded.

"Oh," was all I could think to say. Kindra squeezed my hand.

"My head doesn't hurt anymore, Sissy. First time in days it hasn't hurt," I said, realizing that the pain was actually gone. Kindra smiled--a real smile that went all the way to her eyes and knocked out the sadness.

"They have you on some pretty strong medicine," she said, pointing to the IV pole.

"Does it make you sleepy? Cause it's been hard to stay awake," I said and yawned. Her eyes got sad again.

"Maybe," she said. Before I could say anything else, the door opened, and Matt and his mom walked in. Matt stumbled over Kindra's purse that was still on the floor, and she jumped up to pick it up.

"Sorry, Matt," she said.

"It's OK," he said as he walked up to my bed. "You OK?" he asked slowly.

"Yeah," I said, and then he came in for a hug.

"Charli, Matt, I'm going to step outside and talk to Lindsey for a sec," Kindra said. "OK," we both said. Once they left the room, I confided in Matt.

"I think it's bad," I said to him. "What's bad?" he asked back.

"Whatever is wrong with me. Kindra is acting weird," I said. "What's wrong with you?" he asked.

"I had a seizure because I have an infection from the surgery," I said. Matt got quiet for a moment. He looked up at my IV pole.

"But they are giving you medicine, right? That's going to make you better?" "Yeah, I'm already starting to feel better!" I said enthusiastically.

“OK,” Matt said. Then things got awkwardly quiet. Matt was looking around the room. I saw his eyes stop on the trash bag in the corner. He looked up at me with questions in his eyes. I looked away from him in shame.

“They didn’t want me,” I said. He grabbed my hands.

“We want you, they must have been stupid…” he was saying just as the door opened and Kindra and Lindsey came back in. Lindsey's eyes were red and puffy, like she’d been crying and trying to clean her face. I looked at Matt, saying, “See?” with my eyes. He sighed.

“Matthew, I will be right back. I need to go call your father,” Lindsey said and walked out of the door. The room was silent. It was like no one knew what to do or say. Then Matt said, “She called me by my full name.”

Kindra

It had been about 24 hours since Charli was admitted to ICU. I kept a close eye on her. She didn't seem to be getting any worse. She actually seemed better, but she was still sleeping more than I'd like and complained of being cold off and on. I was sitting in the chair next to Charli's bed, texting my boss at my night job. I had taken a bit of time off when Charli was in the hospital last, so they weren't being as understanding this time. I was given the night off but needed to be back at work tomorrow. Chipmunk's mom was a bit more understanding. Lindsey left to get food, and Matt was sitting on the edge of Charli's bed, telling her about all the cool things he'd seen in the hospital's gift shop downstairs, when nurse Joyce walked in and asked me to step outside of the room. I told the kids I'd be right back.

I closed the door behind me as I stepped out and was surprised to see Charli's doctor standing outside her room. We'd met him yesterday. The look on his face said the news wasn't good. He shook his head at me, and I broke down.

"No, no, no, please," I cried. Joyce grabbed my arm to hold me steady.

"Kindra, I'm so sorry. The infection is too much, the antibiotics aren't working," the doctor said.

"Please, can we try something else? There has to be something else," I begged through tears.

"At this point, we will do our best to make her comfortable. Her organs are going to start shutting down," the doctor said. I did my best to pull myself together.

"How long?" I asked the doctor.

"48 hours, maybe," he said. Forty-eight hours, that was all I had left. How had we gotten here? How did all this happen? Just as quickly as she came into my life, she was being taken away.

"Kindra," Joyce said, interrupting my thoughts. "Do you want us to help you tell her?" she asked.

"Um, no. I need to make a phone call, and then I will," I said while wiping my tears. "If you need anything, please let us know," the doctor said.

"Thank you," I responded and walked away from Charli's room and towards the elevator. I needed to call Lindsey; I needed her to come back to the hospital immediately. We would need to tell the kids together. I needed to talk to Daniel. I needed some air. I ran out of the building when the elevator doors opened, and as soon as I hit the fresh air, I fell to my knees and cried. I didn't care if people were staring at me. I was losing my child.

Charli

Kindra walked back into the room with Matt's mom. She'd been gone for a while, and I didn't even know Matt's mom was back at the hospital. They came in with solemn faces. Kindra sat on my bed with me, and Matt's mom told him to come sit next to her on the chairs.

Something was going on. They were scaring me.

"Sissy?" I said, and tears ran down Kindra's cheeks. She reached into her purse and pulled out the brush. Tears ran down my cheeks as well. She sat the brush in my lap and took both of my hands in hers.

"Bear, the medicine they gave you, it's not working, they can't stop the infection," she said.

"Will I have to have surgery again?" I asked. She squeezed my hands.

"No, baby, the doctors…they can't fix you," she said. Matt started sobbing. I looked over at him. His mom was rocking him in her arms, and tears were running down her cheeks. Kindra was fighting to hold back the tears. What was she saying? That I was going to…die? That's what she was saying. That's why they were crying.

"But Sissy, my head doesn't hurt anymore. I'm starting to feel better," I said. I couldn't be dying.

"I know, Kiddo," she said and picked up the brush to brush my hair.

"NO!" I yelled and snatched the brush from her and threw it across the room. It hit the wall with a loud "SMACK." Everyone in the room jumped, and the brush landed on the floor, broken into three pieces. Joyce, the nurse, came running into the room. She must have heard the brush hit the wall. Kindra held her hand up in a stop motion to her.

"We're OK," Kindra said firmly, and Joyce left.

"Sissy, I'm sorry," I said between gasps. I couldn't catch my breath, and it wasn't a panic attack. I couldn't catch my breath; it was like I just ran up and down a flight of stairs, and I was sweating. Just from throwing a brush?

It was true. I was dying.

"I need my shoes, Matt, I need my shoes," I said, still trying to catch my breath. Matt wiped his tears on his shirt sleeve, ran over to the trash bag in the corner, and started pulling out clothes until he found the black New Balance sneakers Kindra bought me. He ran over to the bed. Kindra jumped up and moved out of the way with a confused look on her face. I moved the blanket off me and started trying to put the shoes on, but I was too winded. Tears streamed down my cheeks as I tried to catch my breath and put my shoes on.

"Charli Bear, what are you...? "Kindra started to ask, but Matt cut her off.

"She puts her shoes on when she's lonely or scared; she even sleeps with them on sometimes," he said as he stepped up, took the shoes from me, and sat at the foot of the bed, putting them on me. His back was to me, and I could see his shoulders rising and falling as he cried while he tied my laces. The room grew quiet. All you could hear was Mrs. Lindsey crying, my machine with the slow and steady beeping, and me attempting to catch my breath. I was finally able to slow my breathing and sit with the realization that I was going to die. I looked up at Kindra, who was still standing to the side of my bed. No one said anything. I guess no one knew what to say.

"When?" I finally asked Kindra.

"A couple of days," she said, and her voice broke. The tears gushed down her face. "Oh," was my response. The room went still again. A sob escaped my throat as I asked,

"Sissy, is it going to hurt?" Lindsey broke down again, and Kindra ran to the side of my bed and put her arms around me.

"They are going to do everything they can to make sure it doesn't, OK?" she said.

"OK," I said. I looked over at Matt. His back was still to me. I couldn't see his face, but his hands were in fists. He was angry.

"Sissy, will you come lay with me?" I asked.

"Of course, I will," she said. She came to the other side of the bed and climbed in with me. Matt got up and left the room. He never looked at me.

Kindra

I lay in the hospital bed with my arms wrapped around my dying girl. It had been about two hours since I told her what the doctor said. She had taken it better than I expected. She took it better than me. Lindsey had found me on the ground outside of the hospital, sobbing. She'd help me pull myself together so we could tell the kids. Matt had left the room after I broke the news to them, and she'd gone after him. They'd been gone for two hours. I imagined he was crying, and she was holding him.

Charli was asleep. She'd cried for a while when I told her and then fallen asleep. She'd been in and out of sleep, and I could hear it becoming more difficult for her to breathe. I was lost in my thoughts, reminiscing on our time together, our picnics at the park, her smile the first time she'd tried pineapple soda, and how she'd squeal when I tickled her when her small, tired voice brought me back.

Sissy? What's Heaven like?"

I gave her a squeeze. "Well, I think you do cartwheels in the clouds," I said.

"But I can't do cartwheels, so I'll just land on my butt," she said and smiled. I never thought I'd see that smile again, and there she was, giving it to me. How lucky was I?

"Bear, when I was just a bit older than you, my favorite youth pastor, Doug, told me that Heaven was better than anything we could imagine. He said we should spend some time imagining things because then we could be sure that it was better than that. So should we give it a try?" I asked her.

"Yes!" she responded, and she sounded excited.

"I imagine there's always really good food," I said, remembering that she had hardly eaten anything since she'd been here.

"And you can have pineapple soda and broccoli whenever you want, and it's the best tasting ever," she said with a smile.

"And there are beaches with soft sand that doesn't hurt your feet, and the water is warm and not cold," she continued.

"You like the beach?" I asked her, realizing it was another thing I'd never be able to do with her. A sob attempted to rise in my throat, but I pushed it down. She was happy and smiling right now, and I wasn't going to take that from her.

"I love the beach! I've been twice, except I didn't like how cold the water was or that there were a lot of rocks in the sand that sometimes hurt my feet," she said and paused like she was deep in thought. I sat quietly. I didn't want to interrupt her.

"I went to the beach with Mama Inissa," she said.

"Who?" I asked. She'd never mentioned this person before.

"Mama Inissa, she was the best foster mom… Well, mom, I ever had. She introduced me to pineapples and always cooked me broccoli. She called me her strange child because I was the only one of the kids who liked broccoli, and she'd sing all the time, and her voice was so beautiful. I lived with her and Papa Joel the longest of anywhere I've been, but then Mama Inissa got sick; she got cancer and died, and Papa couldn't take care of us anymore, so we got sent to new foster homes." She paused, and we sat quietly for a moment. I had no idea what to say.

Then she continued: "I think Mama Inissa and my parents will be in Heaven, and they will want me and…" She paused again and looked over at me.

"Better than I imagined, right?" she asked with uncertainty

in her voice. I nodded my head yes.

"And I will never be alone," she said.

"Your parents?" I asked. She'd never mentioned them before, either. I never knew how she'd ended up in the foster care system, and I'd always been too nervous to ask.

"They died in a car accident when I was three," she said, "but they wanted me." She was quick to add that. "And I imagine they will be there," she said, smiling, and for the first time, she seemed like she was at peace with all of this. Life had been so cruel to my precious girl. How had we gone so quickly from planning what her room was going to look like to planning what Heaven was going to be like? And now she seemed at peace with it all while I was fighting to understand. This world had been so mean to her in her 12 short years. Perhaps she was ready to go, but I wasn't ready for her to go. I'd wanted to show her that the world wasn't all bad and that I loved her and wanted her...but now I'd never get my chance. It was too much. I didn't think I could hold myself together much longer when, thankfully, Matt and his mom walked in. Both of their eyes were red like they'd been crying, but Matt didn't seem so angry. He walked up to Charli's side of the bed and said, "Hey."

She said "Hey" back to him. This was my moment to escape. I got up from the bed and announced to the room that I needed to run home and get some clothes. I also needed to get something from the house for Charli, but I didn't mention that part out loud. I hadn't left the hospital in over 24 hours. I'd found someone to take my shift at work tonight. They said I couldn't be approved for time off but that I could get people to cover my shifts for me. So far, I had tonight covered.

"You'll come right back?" Charli asked. I could hear the panic in her voice.

"I promise I am coming right back," I said to her. She stared at me for a second, trying to make sure I wasn't lying.

Charli

Matt's mom was walking Kindra to the car, so it was just me and him for the moment. It was our first time alone together since we found out I was dying. Matt came and sat down on the edge of my bed and held my hand.

"You were angry," I said to him. "Yeah," he said without looking at me.

"And you aren't anymore?" I asked him.

"Mom told me to put it away," he said. I raised my eyebrows in confusion. He looked up at me and explained.

"Mom says I don't have much time left with you and that I shouldn't waste it being angry, that I will regret it later. She said I should figure out a way to be helpful," he said.

"Helpful?" I asked.

"Yeah, I didn't know either, so Mom and I Googled 'how to help someone preparing to die?'" he said.

"Oh," was my response.

"I know, right? But there were all of these articles and tips, and one said you can help them go through their belongings and decide who gets what so that the family doesn't have to do it later," he said. I looked over at my trash bag in the corner. Everything I owned was in one bag.

"OK," I said. He looked up at me and kind of smiled a bit. "Yeah?" he asked.

"Sure," I said. He hopped off the bed, got the trash bag, brought it back, and sat it between us. I opened the bag and began pulling out clothes.

"Trash," I said and threw a pair of worn shorts on the floor.

"Wait," Matt said and jumped up. "We have to check the pockets. I leave all kinds of things in my pockets, and when Mom cleans my laundry, she keeps it all," he said, shaking his head. He dug through the pockets of the shorts, but there was nothing in them, so he threw them back on the floor. Most of the clothes were hand-me-downs, so I didn't feel bad trashing them. I came across the Bazooka Joe T-shirt. This shirt was how Matt had found me on more than one occasion. I handed it to him.

"I want you to have it," I said. He took the shirt and looked at it. A tear ran down his cheek. He gently folded it and set it in his chair. I was getting tired, so I stopped for a few minutes, and Matt would just pull things out of the bag. We had two piles: one for trash and one that had nicer clothes I hoped would be given to other foster kids.

Matt held up some jeans and a shirt. They were new. It was the clothes the social worker had bought me when I left the hospital last time. I'd never worn them again because they were too big.

"The donate pile," I said. Matt checked the pockets like he did all the other clothes.

"Whoa, Charli," I heard him say as he pulled some folded-up money and a letter out of the pockets.

"See? That's why mom says check the pockets," he said, handing the money and letter to me. I only took the letter out of his hands, opened it, and scanned the bottom. It was signed "Jessica and the nurses of Methodist 2nd floor." My mind flashed back to Nurse Jessica running into my room and hugging me, then sticking something in my hand. I'd put it in my pocket and had completely forgotten about it. I read the letter out loud.

"Dear Charli,

It's been a joy and an honor nursing you back to health. You've kind of become our own child on this floor, and we all love you. I can't imagine all the things you have gone through, and it broke our hearts knowing what was done to you. We all wanted to get you a parting gift to remember us by, but we couldn't agree on what to get you. We just didn't know what you needed as a foster child, so we decided to give you the money and let you get what you wanted most as a gift from us. Hope you get something great. Take care of yourself.

Love,

Jessica and the nurses of Methodist 2nd floor."

I looked up at Matt with tears running down my cheeks. They loved me and cared about me. Other people loved me.

"It's $126!" he said in awe.

"What?" I was shocked at the amount. "What do you want to do with it?" he asked.

"I have no idea. Can you just hold on to it for me until I think of something?" I asked.

"OK," he said and put the letter and money in his pocket. We went back to sorting my stuff. Matt's mom came back a little while later. She saw us sorting through my things, and she smiled. Wiping tears from her eyes, she came over and kissed Matt on his cheek. Then she sat down next to the chair that had the Bazooka Joe T-shirt on it. She washed that shirt at Matt's request when I was brought to the hospital last time. She gently patted the shirt with her hand, dabbed more tears from her eyes with a tissue and watched her son help his friend sort her things.

Kindra

I was just pulling into the hospital parking lot. I had taken a hot shower, packed clothes, grabbed something for Charli, and had a quick conversation with Daniel. We hadn't really talked much since she went back to the hospital. Although it wasn't for lack of him trying. As much as I loved him, I couldn't share what I was going through, knowing he wasn't 100% behind fostering her. I wasn't mad at him or anything, but I couldn't share losing her with him when I had never been 100% sure of keeping her with him. Our conversation had been quick; he was telling me that I'd have to go back to work tomorrow if I couldn't find someone to cover my shift, which I was having trouble doing. He reminded me that although I loved her with all of my heart, I would still have to take care of myself after she was gone, and losing my job was not going to help that. He said going back to work was something I needed to be prepared for. I loved him for having the hard conversations with me. I had been gone for a little over an hour and a half. I wished the hospital was closer to home.

I raced back upstairs, not wanting to miss another moment of her. I entered the room to find Charli asleep in her bed, Matt on his phone, and Lindsey reading a book. There were two piles of clothes on the floor, and the black trash bag that once held Charli's belongings balled up on the floor as well. Lindsey explained the piles and what Matt and Charli had done. I gave Matt a big hug. He smiled and fought back tears.

Then I heard a little tired voice say, "Sissy, you're back!" I turned to face her. I had a duffel bag on my shoulder with clothes in it, my purse, and another bag in my hand. Charli locked eyes with a bag in my hand. She recognized the black and white stripes with the red letters across, spelling out "FOOTLOCKER."

"Sissy, you didn't!" she cried in disbelief.

"I never took them back!" I said while pulling the box of the original shoes I'd bought her--the ones she told me she couldn't have, out of the bag. I placed the box on her lap. She opened the box and gave the brightest smile I'd ever seen on her. Tears running down her cheeks.

"No one can tell you that you can't have them now. They are yours, Kiddo," I said through tears of my own. She tried to throw her blanket off of her, but she was too weak.

"Matt, help me, help me put them on!" she squealed. Matt was up and at her side in a split second. His mouth was hanging open, looking at the shoes.

"I told you they were the brightest you'd ever seen!" she said, gloating. All I could do was laugh. Matt pulled the blanket back to show she was still wearing the New Balances I'd gotten her. My heart squeezed at the reason she wore shoes to bed, but that's why I knew I had to bring her these. They were HER shoes. Matt took the New Balances off and put the Nikes on. They did seem abnormally bright.

"Don't put the covers back on, Matt. I want to show Nurse Joyce," Charli said. Matt tucked the blanket down behind her feet. Then he held the New Balances in the air.

"Donate!" Charli said.

Charli

"Kindra, can you take Matt to the cafeteria to get some dinner?" Matt's mom asked. Matt looked strangely at her. Kindra stood up, no questions asked, and said, "Come on, Matt, let's go see if their cheeseburgers are as good as the other hospital's," as she walked towards the door. Matt slowly followed but kept glancing back like he was unsure.

Once they were gone, Matt's mom scooted her chair right next to my bed. She reached up and moved a strand of hair out of my face.

"How ya feeling?" she asked me.

"Tired, and my body *gasp* feels heavy," I said.

"Charli, I am so sorry about…all of this. I wish we would have known you sooner so we could have made you a part of our family and loved you longer," she said.

"You guys…gave me one of the best *gasp* family experiences I ever had," I said. It was becoming really difficult to complete sentences without having to take breaths.

"Do you think Matt will be OK, *gasp* after I'm gone?" I asked. It was something I'd been thinking about. How was this going to affect Matt and Kindra? Matt's mom sighed, "He blames himself" she said.

"What? No! Why?" I said quickly, losing my breath.

"He thinks he should have protected you better, that he should have done more. I worry about him," she said.

"He did everything I asked. He protected *gasp*me better than anyone," I said. My heart broke that he blamed himself when, to me, he was my hero. He kept my secret so I could have what I hadn't had in such a long time--a friend and family.

“Maybe you could tell him that,” she said.

“I will. I love you, Mrs. Matt’s Mom *gasp*” I smiled at her, remembering calling her that the first time we’d met. She smiled too.

I continued, “Thank you for showing me *gasp* hot chocolate with almond milk *gasp* and family pizza night,” I said.

“Thank you for trusting us to love you; I know you have been through so much,” she said.

“Mrs. Lindsey, do you think you could *gasp* help me with something? It's for Kindra,” I asked and reached for my cell phone.

“Absolutely, I would love to help you with whatever it is,” she said with a smile.

Kindra

I looked at the time on my cell phone. It was almost 8:00 PM. I would have to leave for work soon, and I didn't know if I could do it. We had just hit the 48-hour mark not too long ago. I'd spent the day with her. I'd brushed her hair and washed her face. I hugged her, held her, and told her how important she was to me and how much I loved her. I did most of the talking because she was so tired. She knew I had to go to work tonight. I'd told her early in the day that I was having trouble finding someone to cover for me. She wasn't mad; she understood and squeezed my hand and said, "It's OK, Sissy," but it wasn't OK.

If she would have asked, if she would have just said, "Please, Sissy, don't leave me!" I would have lost that job in a heartbeat. Anything for her, and I think she knew that I would stay if she asked. And I think that's why she didn't. I felt her shift in the bed next to me. I looked down at her. She was staring at me, her eyes wide and full of wonder.

"Sissy?" she said. Her voice was stronger than I'd heard it in over 24 hours. "When I get to Heaven, the first thing I'm going to do is talk to God about getting OUR service dog," she said and smiled. The initial thing that stunned me about her statement was that she didn't gasp for air or have to stop and take any breaths when she said it. She sounded as strong and confident as she did when she'd told me she made a good grade on a test. The next thing that stunned me was that she was worried about this. That service dog was my issue now. I didn't want her worrying about anything.

"Hey, you don't have to worry about that," I said as my

tears started. "When you get to Heaven, you go find your parents and Mama Inissa. You don't worry about me, OK," I said to her, crying. She didn't say anything back. She just snuggled in closer to me and squeezed my hand. The clock seemed like it was moving way too fast. I would have given anything to make it slow down. I knew it was closing in on my time to leave, and I wanted to beg and plead with her to fight and hang on until I could make it back in the morning. I just wanted to be holding her hand when she left this world, but when I looked over at her and saw how tired she was, I thought about how she had been fighting all of her life. I realized how selfish it was of me to ask that of her. She deserved her rest.

I started to get up from where I lay next to her in her hospital bed. It was time for me to go.

"Sissy?" her tired voice said.

"Yes, my Warrior Princess," I responded. She smiled.

"I know you don't have an all the time *gasp* favorite song. Mrs. Lindsey helped me pick one out *gasp* for you. Will you listen to it later?" she asked.

I often doubted my place in people's lives. I went hard for them so not only would they never feel rejected the way I felt but also so they'd see my worth and want me in their life.

Charli had just shown me that she chose me, that I was worth her fighting to show me I was loved. It was clear that I belonged to her as much as she belonged to me. I climbed back into the bed with her. I could be a little bit late to work tonight.

"I promise I will listen to it later," I said, wrapping my arms around her. She laid her head on me, and I began to sing her favorite song to her.

Charli

It had been a couple of hours since Kindra left. I knew it was our last goodbye. I was tired. I felt like I almost had everything wrapped up with her, and I knew she'd be OK. Now, I had to make sure Matt would be OK too. I needed all of my strength for this.

"Matt," I said barely above a whisper. His head popped up from the position he was sitting in. He got up and walked over to me.

"Do you need some water?" he asked, reaching for my cup.

"No...Sit by me," I said. He sat down. I held out my hand, and he took it.

"Matt *gasp* this wasn't your fault," I said. Tears sprang from his eyes, and he put his head down.

"I should have told. I should have protected you," he said between his tears.

"You kept my secret. You gave me time *gasp* to have a family; you gave me Kindra when you *gasp* sent me to that meeting. If you would have told, they would have taken me away, and I wouldn't *gasp* be here with you, with my family," I said.

"You wouldn't be dying," he said.

"I'd be dying by myself *gasp* just slower," I said.

"Please, Charli, just forgive me?" he begged. The tears were coming quickly now.

"I won't forgive you for saving me *gasp* you're my best friend and my hero," I said. Matt dropped his head in my lap and balled so hard his whole body shook. I looked over to his mom sitting in her chair, and she mouthed the words "thank you" to me. I smiled back at her. Once Matt had calmed down a bit, I asked, "Can we send Kindra the message and song now?

gasp"

Matt looked confused. "What message and song?" he asked.

"I helped Charli pick a song for Kindra and write a message for her, but she wanted to wait till just the right time to send it," Mrs. Lindsey said.

"Can you read it *gasp* out loud?" I asked.

"Sure, and as I read it, Matt, can you type the message into Charli's phone to send to Kindra?" Mrs. Lindsay asked.

"OK," he said, reaching over to grab my phone. Mrs. Lindsey pulled a pad of paper out of her purse and began to slowly read.

"Kindra, I'm not good at goodbyes because I usually don't get to say them. So here is my attempt. When we first met, there was just something about you that made me feel like I could trust you. I don't trust many people, so I knew you must be special. I didn't want to love you though. I was afraid I would switch families again, and I would lose you. But I failed because I love you so much. Failing was one of the best things that ever happened to me. Even though we haven't known each other for a long time, we've shared so much. You changed my life. You gave me hope. Thank you for wanting me and being my Sissy. I've learned that life is really hard for you sometimes too, but promise me that you will never change who you are. You are the most beautiful person I know. I don't want you to be sad, Sissy, and I won't be either because I got to have family with you. I love you.

Matt finished typing the message, wiped the tears from his eyes, and said, "Now what

song?"

Kindra

This felt like the longest shift I'd ever worked. I received a message from her in the middle of the night that Lindsey helped her write. I heard Charli's voice as I read the most beautiful letter I'd ever received. The message included a song I hadn't listened to yet. I’d made a difference in her life, and now all I wanted to do was get back to her. I went back to work, getting everything set up for my residents to go about their day. My cell phone chirped, alerting me that a text message had just come through. I glanced at the clock on the desk. It was 6:05 AM. I set the phone aside. It would have to wait. I had to make sure the last of my residents had their clothes put away and were ready to head to the workshop. I got up out of my rolling chair and headed to the other side of the room, where a few pieces of laundry were still hanging on the door frame, waiting to be claimed by their owners. I glanced at the tags on a pair of overly starched jeans and yelled for Clay to please come get his clothes. Clay looked up from the X-Men comic book he was reading. The pages were so worn and creased it was a miracle the binding still held, but you never saw Clay without his X-Men comic book. He got up and shuffled towards me to retrieve his clothes. I heard my phone alert again. I paused and stared at the phone on the desk. It seemed very far away.

At this point, I believe I knew. I think perhaps I knew when the first alert came through. I just wanted to give myself more time to be living in a world where she still lived too. I picked up the jeans and handed them to Clay as I passed him on my way back to my desk. I sat down in my chair, noticing for the first time how worn the cushion was that I sat on and how the chair rolled back and to the left when I sat in it because one of the wheels was cracked. I looked at the papers scattered around the desk: the meal prep menu for the week, the resident's upcoming appointments, and my personal notes for how the night had gone. I needed to straighten up the desk before my relief came. Then I looked at the phone. Heavy-hearted, I picked it up and punched in my code to unlock the screen. The two messages were from Matt. I took one last deep breath, filling my lungs with air in preparation. I opened the first message.

Matt: She died.

Then I opened the second message:

Matt: I don't know what to do. The nurses won't tell me what I'm supposed to do.

I set the phone down and exhaled the air in my lungs that was left over from a time when I thought, when I hoped, when I prayed she was still here. I organized the papers on the desk. I didn't respond to Matt because I knew his mother had to be nearby. I sat at the desk, unmoving, numb. The residents moved around me. They made noise, sang songs, and dropped things on the floor. Monica asked me to tie her shoes. I never moved. Eventually, my relief showed up. I still didn't move.

"Kindra, are you OK?" my relief asked, and I snapped out of it.

"Yeah. I have to go, and Monica needs you to tie her shoes," I said while gathering my things. I didn't even clock out. I walked straight to my car and sat in the front seat. I didn't know what to do. Should I drive to the hospital knowing she wasn't there? I picked up my phone and opened her last text message, the beautiful letter she'd written me. I read it over again and looked at the link at the bottom of the message to the song she chose to be my favorite song.

The song she had asked me to listen to later. It was later. I plugged my phone into the auxiliary port and clicked the link. Soft music poured into the car. I laid my head back on the headrest and closed my eyes just as Lee Ann Womack started to sing "I Hope You Dance." I let the tears flow as the words my kiddo picked for me filled the car.

Tears trailed down my cheeks. I reminisced on our time together. The tears flowed harder. I paused the song and wiped my tears. I couldn't take much more right then. I turned the car on and began my drive to the hospital.

SECTION 4:
NEW REALITY

Kindra

It had been three days since Charli passed. I was attempting to get back to my normal before she came into my life. It was so hard and so sad and so boring. With her, I always had something to look forward to. I had something I was working towards that mattered. Nothing much seemed to matter now. I quit my job with Chipmunk. I didn't need the extra money for a bigger place, plus I could barely manage to pull myself out of bed during the day. Matt's family and I had planned to have a memorial service for Charli in two days at the park where we'd had picnics. It was the best we could do. When I'd gotten to the hospital, they had already taken Charli's body. Matt and his mom sat in her empty room. Matt wasn't ready to leave yet. Charli was a ward of the state, and as such, the state would handle her burial. Matt's mom and I spent days making phone calls, trying to find out if a service was going to be had for her. Could we pay for a proper funeral for her? What was going to happen to her? Where would she be laid to rest? We got the runaround. We got, "We will have someone call you back," and we got, "That's privileged information." Defeated, we decided to have our own ceremony for her. Planning her memorial was about the only thing I was able to pull myself out of bed for besides work. All the plans had been made, so today, I lay in my bed staring at the ceiling. Remembering. I heard her voice in my mind saying, "OUR service dog!" I needed to work on that. I felt like I needed "OUR service dog" now. I sat up in the bed, grabbed my laptop off of the nightstand, and put it in my lap. I opened my Twitter account and scrolled through some recent tweets by people I was following. It had been a minute since I'd been on here. I saw that MC Spinner was currently tweeting, so I reached out.

@MC Spinner- Hey, how are things going?

I wasn't really expecting him to respond directly to me. I tweeted to him all the time, and he rarely responded. So you can imagine my surprise when a notification popped up saying he'd responded.

@Kindra- Things are great, and I haven't forgotten you. I'm waiting on a number for someone I want you to talk to because I think you want the wrong thing.

I froze, and my heart started racing. This could not be happening. Not today, not with him. "someone I want you to talk to" was code for 'I think you are crazy and need to talk to a shrink or be admitted.' I tried to stay as calm as possible when I responded to him.

@MC Spinner- I've seen numerous doctors, been a part of group therapies, and have personal therapists and psychiatrists.

He quickly responded:

@Kindra, with all due respect, you also went clubbing. So, it may be all psychological. If you want to talk to this person. I'll make it happen.

Clubbing? Clubbing? Is that what he thought? I thought back to that horrific night. I remembered hiding in the corner and crying in the bathroom, and he never even showed. I couldn't let him back out now. He said he was going to help. I needed his help. I couldn't get this service dog without him. He couldn't do this to me, to Charli, not now. I had to make him understand. I Tweeted in desperation:

@MC Spinner- No disrespect, I didn't go "clubbing," I came to the show you invited me to. I was petrified the whole time.

He responded

@Kindra- I don't believe a pet is going to help you.

I responded, my heart was racing out of my chest.

@MC Spinner- I'm not asking for a service dog because I want a pet. A service dog will help me make my life better.

@Kindra- So, you wanna talk to this person or not?

It was a slap in the face. I literally felt it. He had just slammed the door on me. I would never get "OUR service dog" now. I had let her down again. Why had I ever thought...? Why had I believed? No one wanted to help me. My own family didn't care about helping me get a service dog. Why would anyone else? I was a failure.

I couldn't breathe. I pushed my laptop off my lap, and it fell on the floor. I didn't care.

My heart was still racing. I ran into the closet, but it didn't help. I tried all of my grounding techniques, and nothing worked. I dug my nails into my hands; I threw cold water on my face, but nothing stopped the panic. Nothing stopped the pain. I'd lost her, I'd lost OUR service dog, I'd lost everything that mattered. I ran to the kitchen, grabbed a box of matches, and took them back into the closet. I set them on the floor in front of me. This was my bad coping skill. Self-harm. Before I'd learned my healthy coping skills, when I would have bad panic attacks or nightmares, I'd put matches out on my skin. The pain from the match always stopped the panic in its tracks, and I could breathe. I hadn't done that in over eight months. I'd learned new techniques, healthy techniques, but none of them were working right now. I stared at the matches, feeling like such a failure, but I just wanted it to stop. I wanted everything to stop.

I quickly picked up the matchbox, took one out, lit it, and put it on my right forearm. It sizzled as the skin burned. I felt the familiar pain, but the panic didn't stop. It only dulled a bit. That had never happened before. The matches always worked. I lit another and put it out on me, then another and another. Six matches later, I was still in a panic. My head was hurting, my chest was aching, I was sweating and dizzy, and it didn't feel like it would ever stop. The pain would never stop. I knew how to make it stop, I knew. I went into my bathroom, got all of my pill bottles, and brought them back into the closet. I dropped them next to the pile of burnt matches. I would just take all of them and end it. No panic, no failure, no racing heart, no people who didn't believe you, no people who lied about helping you, no pain. I picked up a bottle. It said Trazodone. I poured the contents on the floor. I scooped up a handful of pills then I heard her little voice in my head say, "Sissy, will you stay alive with me for 10 seconds?"

I had no one to stay alive with me for 10 seconds. I'd lost her. I didn't want to stay alive for 10 seconds. I just wanted the pain to stop. I thought about Daniel--he'd be heartbroken. He wouldn't understand, but he would at the same time, and then he'd find someone normal to love. My phone alerted me to a text message outside of the closet.

"NO!" I yelled out the closet door. I shoved all the pills in my mouth. I heard her voice again.

"Sissy, will you stay alive with me for five seconds?"

My phone alerted me to another message. I spit all the pills onto the floor. My heart was still racing. I got up to go find the phone on my bed. The messages were from Lindsey.

Lindsey- Hey, Matt suggested we have pizza with pineapple at Charli's memorial. We will bring it if that's OK with you. He's been really having a hard time. I hope you are ok over there. Haven't heard from you.

Lindsey- I hope you dance.

I fell to my knees with my phone in my hand. I lay on the floor and pulled up the song through blurry eyes on YouTube. As soon as the music started, the panic began to slow until it completely stopped. I could breathe. My heart wasn't racing. I was calmer. I fell asleep on the floor while the song she picked for me played.

Kindra

I'd gotten to the park for the memorial a little early. I wanted to spend some time in our space alone. I was still reeling from the MC Spinner incident. I wasn't sure what I was going to do, but when I woke up on the floor with burn marks on my arms, the taste of pills in my mouth, and "I Hope You Dance" playing, I knew above anything else I wanted to give my girl a proper sendoff. All of the other stuff I'd worry about later. I dragged my hand across our picnic table and remembered the excitement on her face when she tried on her sneakers, how intense her face would get when she was telling me about her schoolwork, and how the smallest things would make her light up, like a bag of peanut M&M's. I sat down at the table and looked over at the area where we had our picnics. I could hear her laugh in the wind from the times I'd tickled her. I looked down the sidewalk that led to the table and remembered the times she'd come running and yell, "Sissy!" before she'd fall into my arms for a hug. I was lucky to have had her in my life for even a short time.

"Thank you, Kiddo, for letting me love you," I said out loud. Then I got up and began to unload stuff from my car to start setting up. Matt and his family would be arriving soon.

A minivan pulled into the parking spot next to my car just as I was setting up a picture of Charli smiling and showing off her shoes at this exact table not too many months ago. I waved as Matt and his family piled out of the vehicle. Shawn, Matt's dad, had his arms full with two pizza boxes, Lindsay had a grocery bag full of things, and Matt also had a grocery bag and a bouquet of sunflowers and lilacs. We were all dressed nicely, business casual, but Matt had on a full suit and tie. He looked so handsome. He always went all out for Charli. I loved that about him.

Lindsey set her bag on the table, came around, and gave me a big hug. “How are you doing?” she asked.

“I don't even know. Some days are better than others,” I said. She grabbed my hand. The guys were setting up glasses and plates on the table.

“How's Matt doing?” I asked her. She sighed heavily.

“I'm not sure. He still won't tell us everything fully, like he's still protecting her. He had a nightmare last night and woke up crying. I'm going to set him up with a therapist. I think he needs help processing all of this,” she said. It made sense. This was a lot to process for an adult, let alone a child. I felt glad that Lindsey was going to get him some help. I glanced down at the burn marks on my arm. Maybe it was time for me to reach back out to Paige.

“I think we're ready,” Shawn said, bringing me back to the moment. The table was beautifully decorated with candles, soft lights, and flowers. There were fancy plates set out, cloth napkins, and wine glasses. In the middle of the table were two boxes of pizza, a two-liter bottle of pineapple soda, and a pan of brownies Matt had baked. At the head of the table was the picture of Charli I’d brought. The setup was perfect. Shawn came over and gave me a hug, and Matt motioned for me to come sit by him. Before I sat down, I spoke.

“I just want to thank you guys for coming and celebrating the life of Charli. I couldn't imagine trying to do this alone. Thank you for loving her and making a meaningful impact on her life.” I sat down.

Lindsay opened the pizza boxes and started putting a slice on everyone’s plate. “If Charli were here, she’d ask for two slices,” Matt said with a smile.

“Or she’d just take a slice off of your plate when you weren't looking,” Lindsey said to Matt, and we all laughed. We ate in silence for a few minutes. Then Matt stood up, opened the pineapple soda, and filled everyone’s wine glass.

“Can I make my toast now, Mom?” Matt asked Lindsey. She nodded her head yes. I looked at Matt as he held up his glass in his suit. He seemed a lot older suddenly.

“Charli was my best friend. She was smart and stubborn; she was funny and loving, and she was always hungry. And she taught me about loyalty and how to be a good friend even in the worst situations. Charli said that I was her hero…” Matt began to tear up as he talked, but he kept going. “But she was my hero because she lived in hell almost every day and still showed up with a smile. She was hurting, but she still listened to me talk; she made me do my homework, and she always told me to be nicer to my mom. I think I will always be a better person because I knew her,” he finished, and we all took a sip. Lindsey stood up.

“I don't know if I will ever know all of Charli's story, but I know one day she showed up in our lives with her beautiful smile and made us all better people. I hope I gave as much to her as she gave to my family,” Lindsey said, reaching across the table to squeeze Matt's hand. She took a sip from her glass, and we all followed suit. Shawn stood up.

“I spent the least amount of time with Charli, but in that short time, I grew to love her as well. I love what she brought to my family with her smile, laugh, and willingness to finish whatever was on your plate. For brief moments, I felt what it was like to have a daughter.

When she smiled, I smiled. She made my house seem warmer. I will miss her,” he said, and we all drank.

It was my turn. I stood up.

"The world can be a mean and cruel and ugly place. I have seen it firsthand. But Charli reminded me that there was still beauty in it--she was beauty in it. She gave me something to hope for when I hadn't realized I'd lost most of my hope. And if I could find that hope before that she reminded me of, I believe in time, I can find it again. I know she would want me to. Thank you, Warrior Princess," I said and sipped from my glass.

Matt cut the brownies and put one on everyone's plate while I pulled a package from the bag under the table.

"I ordered this sky lantern. It says, "I love you" in 100 different languages. I was hoping we could all write a message to Charli on it before we released it into the sky," I said, holding out pens for everyone. They all grabbed one and took turns writing messages to our girl. Then Matt helped me assemble it. We were just about ready to send it into the sky when my cell phone rang. I quickly silenced it.

"Are we ready?" Matt asked.

"Almost," I said. I was pulling up a song on YouTube to play as we released it. I found the song "Missing You" by Brandy. Matt put the lantern in my hands and said, "You do it." The words of the song filled the air.

I couldn't let go of the lantern. It felt like I was letting her go, and I just wasn't ready. I wasn't ready to say goodbye. My shoulders rose and fell as the tears poured from my body. Lindsay came up and put her arm around my waist. Then Matt put his hand on my hand, and Shawn came and put his hand on my back. I drew from their collective strength and their collective pain, and I let go. With tears in our eyes, we watched the Sky Lantern float to the heavens.

Kindra

Charli's memorial was two days ago, and yet I still checked my phone for messages from her. I sat on my couch, contemplating taking a nap. What was next? I rechecked the phone, then got frustrated with myself for looking for messages from her when I knew she was gone. Something on the phone caught my attention, though. The voicemail icon was showing, and now that I thought about it, it had been showing for a while. I tried to think back. When had I gotten a voicemail? And then I remembered my phone had rung, and I'd silenced it during Charli's service. I listened to the message.

"Hey, Kindra, it's Crystal. Call me back when you get a chance. I wanted to talk to you about a service dog."

The message ended, and I sat staring at the phone. Crystal was an old coworker from when I lived in Florida, was married, and worked at Disney World as a photographer. That seemed like a lifetime ago now.

Why would she want to talk to me about a service dog? Crystal was fairly active on my Facebook page, and I shared my struggles and victories in my quest for my service dog, but she and I never really spoke on the phone. I still had not nearly recovered from the MC Spinner letdown, and with the death of Charli, I didn't feel like I had space to basically mourn what I felt was the loss of my service dog too. I didn't want to get my hopes up regarding a service dog anymore. I didn't know if I had any hope left. I sighed and set the phone on the couch next to me, turned my TV on, went to Netflix, and clicked on *House*. Then, I stretched out on the couch to take a nap.

Moments passed, and I kept glancing at the phone.

"What could she have wanted?" I said out loud. I quickly picked up the phone and hit dial on her number before I lost my nerve. The phone rang and rang, and then voicemail clicked on. I felt foolish.

"Hey Crystal, it's Kindra calling you back," I said and hung up. The phone had beeped while I was leaving a message, alerting me that a text message was coming through. I opened the message; it was from Matt.

Matt: Hey Kindra can you meet me at Charli's table after school today?

That's a strange message, I thought. I hadn't talked to Matt or his family since the memorial. Charli was our connecting factor, and she was gone. We had nothing in common besides her, and I wasn't ready to just have open conversations about her. Right now, I could only keep her tucked away safely and quietly in my heart. So, I hadn't reached out to them. Actually, I hadn't reached out to anyone. After my rape, I'd learned to grieve alone. I was barely sharing what I was going through with Daniel. I knew he was extremely worried about me. I began to pull away from him a little bit, not because I loved him less, but because he couldn't give me what I needed right now. He was on the other side of the world.

Matt needed me for something, and I wasn't going to let him down. I looked at the time on my cell phone. He would be out of school in about an hour. I texted back and got up to get a shower and brush my teeth.

Kindra: Sure

I got to the park, to our table, and was overcome with a wave of emotions I hadn't expected. I'd stopped and gotten two pineapple sodas on the way. It was a habit I wasn't comfortable breaking yet. I saw Matt walking down the sidewalk towards the table, and in my mind, I could see her walking with him. Like the first day I'd met Matt, and he walked down this very sidewalk with her. It seemed like it happened just weeks ago and so long ago at the same time.

I snapped out of my thoughts just as he reached the table. I stood up, and both of us just stood there, kind of unsure of what to do. So I held out my arms and said, “Hug?” He immediately dropped his backpack and stepped into my arms for a hug. I hadn't really had much human contact before Charli. I won't lie. I needed this hug, and I could tell that he did too, when he didn't immediately let go. So I just held him till he was ready and just enjoyed sharing my pain with him in the form of this hug. Eventually, he pulled away. He wiped his eyes on the sleeve of his shirt. I didn't realize he'd been crying. He took a seat on one side of the table, so I sat on the other.

“How have you been?” I asked him and handed him a pineapple soda. He smiled. “I'm doing OK, I guess,” he said. I nodded.

“I eat lunch by myself now. It's lonely and boring, but I'm not ready to eat lunch with someone else yet. I used to eat lunch with Charli, and I don't want her to think I forgot about her,” he said as a single tear slid down his cheek. He didn't move to wipe it away. I knew the pain he was suffering, and I hated it for him. I'd have gladly taken it on me if it meant he wouldn't hurt.

“Life is pretty boring without her, huh?” I said, and he nodded. I continued, “I think Charli knows you won't forget her, and I don't think she would want you eating lunch by yourself unless you wanted to. So you eat lunch with others when you are ready, OK?” I finished. He smiled and said, “OK.”

We sat for a moment, and then he reached into his backpack, pulled out an envelope, slid it across the table, and said, “I forgot to give this to you.”

I picked the envelope up apprehensively and slowly opened it. Inside were two sheets of paper and quite a bit of cash. I looked up at Matt.

"Read it," he said. I unfolded the first sheet of paper and read it. It said

For OUR service dog Love,

Charli Bear

I quickly unfolded the other sheet and read a letter in handwriting I didn't recognize. It was from the nurses at the first hospital.

I finished the letter and looked up at Matt with tears in my eyes.

"It's what she wanted most," he said, and the dam inside me broke. I'd thought I had no more tears left. I thought I'd cried all I could, but it seemed a new well had been tapped, and with that new wave came new determination. I had to figure out how to get our service dog.

Kindra

At home, I put the envelope with the money in a drawer in the kitchen, but I took out Charli's note. I found a pushpin and pinned it to the wall in my bedroom so I could see it. It would be my motivation. I sat down on my bed and thought about how to raise money. Nothing came. I lay back on the bed in frustration, and as soon as my head hit the pillow, my cell phone rang from the other room.

"UGH," I said as I pulled myself back up and ran to the kitchen for the phone. It was Crystal calling. I took a deep breath and answered.

"Hello?" I said.

"Hey, Kindra! It's Crystal," she said. "Hey!" I said with feigned excitement.

"Do you have a minute to talk?" she asked. "Sure," I said.

"Great, so I know you've been working on getting a service dog. I see the company you are going through, and they look great, but I did a little research, and I found an organization right in Houston where you live that trains service dogs for a lot less money. I hope you don't mind, but I reached out to the owner on your behalf and shared a bit of your story. His name is Donald, the organization is called Jerry's Paws, and he's waiting to hear from you," she said.

I sat in stunned silence. "Hello?" she said.

"Uh…Yes…Holy crap, Crystal, you did that for me?" I said, fighting back tears.

"Well, yeah, you used to post all the time about getting your service dog, and your Facebook page kinda got quiet, and

I got worried. I know how much getting a service dog means to you, so I just did some research and made some calls." She said like it was no big deal. When I started my hunt for a service dog and looked at organizations in Texas, I could never find one that would take on someone with PTSD due to rape. It was all military vets with PTSD.

"So give them a call, they are waiting to hear from you, OK?" she said. "OK," I said, still in disbelief.

"I'm texting you the info now! Let me know how it goes," she said.

"I will!" I responded. We said our goodbyes and hung up. Then, sure enough, a text message came through with the info. I walked back to my room, sat on my bed, and attempted to wrap my head around what had just happened. I thought about it and decided I wasn't going to get my hopes up. I emotionally couldn't afford to. I set the phone on my nightstand and laid back in bed again, deep in thought. The timing of this just seemed really strange. I glanced over at the piece of paper I'd just pinned to the wall.

"For OUR service dog, Love Charli Bear." Was this her?

"Charli, is this you?" I asked out loud. Then I felt silly. I rolled over to take my nap, but quickly peeked back at the paper one more time.

Kindra

"But what do you have to lose?" Daniel said.

"You said that about MC Spinner," I replied and rolled my eyes. It had been two days since Crystal texted me the info, and I had yet to call. I was currently on Skype with Daniel (things were starting to get back to normal between us).

"She would want you to try," he said. I quickly shot him a glance and said, "Don't."

He threw his hands up in defense. I didn't want him talking about her. I didn't want anybody talking about her that didn't know her. I remember how people talked about me after my rape. I wouldn't let them do that to her.

"I'm sorry," he said. I nodded.

"I want you to try," he said, and that stirred something in me. I had kind of put a wall up lately, and his words cracked my armor.

"I know you have needed me the last few weeks, and I haven't been able to be there in a more beneficial way, but I'm here right now, I'm with you. Make the call while I'm on Skype with you," he said. I thought about it. It would be easier with him right there on the screen. If it didn't go well, he'd already be right there. I couldn't run from this forever. The "what if" of it all tickled the back of my mind.

"OK," I said hesitantly and smiled. I picked up my phone and went to Crystal's text message. I retrieved the number, dialed it, and put the phone to my ear.

"Put it on speaker," Daniel said.

"Right," I said and put the phone on speaker and set it on the table in front of the laptop. It rang three times, and I was just about to hang up when a male voice answered and said, "Hey, this is Don."

I froze. Daniel waved his hands, signaling me to say something.

"Hello, this is Kindra. I was given your number by my friend Crystal and told to contact you," I said.

"Oh, Kindra, yes. I've been waiting for your call," Don said. "Really?" I asked.

"Yes, Crystal told me about your situation, and I truly think we can help you. I actually think we may have a dog for you already," he said.

"I...I don't have much money, but I can try to raise it," I said. I felt like money was the elephant in the room. If this was going to cost as much as the other organization, I would just stay where I was at.

"Crystal told me how much you are trying to raise. $10,000 is a lot. To get a service dog with us would be $3,000," Don said.

I could do $3000. I already had $1,000 raised.

"Can I tell you a bit about our organization?" Don asked me. "Sure," I responded.

"I started Jerry's Paws nonprofit because my father is a retired vet with PTSD. We were trying to get him a service dog, and the prices were astronomical. People who typically suffer from illnesses that require them to need a service dog oftentimes have trouble holding down jobs due to said illnesses. Asking them to come up with all that money causes more depression because it seems impossible. I felt like there had to be a better way. So, I began my research. A lot of the money for these dogs has to go towards the breeding, fostering, and then training the dogs before they even get to you. What we do is train dogs you already have, and if you don't have one, we help you find a rescue that has the right temperament to be a service dog. That knocks out a large chunk of money right there. Then, we don't just train the dog. We train you on how to train your dog. Our trainers come to you two to three times a week and work on techniques with you and your dog and give you homework on what to work with your dog on between your sessions. So, in essence, you are training your dog, and you guys are learning together. That's how we can keep our costs so low."

Daniel was nodding his head. It made sense.

"Now, don't get me wrong, it's a lot of work, and a lot of the success rides on how hard you are willing to work and making sure you are working with your dog. Also, we do help with fundraising. I hate for money to be the reason people can't live fuller lives due to these illnesses. So do you think you want to give us a try?" he asked. Daniel was feverishly nodding his head yes and smiling at me.

"Yes! I said.

"OK, great. I will email you the application. You should have all the necessary paperwork we need from your doctors because you would have had to submit it to the other organization. So just fill out the application and get it back to me with the paperwork from your doctor," he said.

"OK, I will text you my email right now," I said.

"OK, that will be great, and we can get the ball rolling," he said.

"Hey, Don, what's the name of the dog you are thinking of pairing me with?" I asked him.

I'm not sure why I asked that. Maybe having a name would make it more real.

"Her name is Vicky. She just came to us not too long ago. We will know pretty quickly here if she is fit for service dog work. She has a story of her own, which is why I think you guys might be great together. But let's not get ahead of ourselves. Let's get your paperwork in and finish testing her temperament. If she's not fit, we will help you find a dog that is. So get that paperwork done and get it back to me, and we should be able to move forward in just a couple of days. Sound good?" he asked.

"Yes, it sounds great. I'm sending you my email now!" I said, smiling from ear to ear.

Daniel was smiling too.

"OK, great, you have a good day, Kindra. We will speak soon," he said. "OK, thank you, Don," I said.

"Bye-bye," he said and hung up. I set the phone down and stared at Daniel with my mouth hanging open.

"You didn't even need me," he said with a smile. "Yes, I did," I said back.

"You really don't see how strong you are," he said. I shrugged my shoulders. I didn't feel strong. I felt like I was just getting by most of the time.

"I think you have some paperwork to fill out, correct?" he asked. I smiled to my eyes. I hadn't smiled that hard in a while.

"Yeah," I said.

"Well, go do that and email me later, OK?" he said.

"OK," I said.

"I love you," he said.

"I love you too," I said and disconnected the Skype call. I went straight to my email on my computer, and there was a new email titled "Application" from Don. I clicked on it and blinked back happy tears. This was happening. Just as I began to fill out the application, I paused. Vicky. What a strange name for a dog.

Kindra

I sat in my car, wringing my hands. Three days had rushed by between work and regular conversation with Don regarding my paperwork, my story, what tasks I wanted my service dog to help me with, events coming up for fundraisers, my official approval and acceptance, Vicky passing all the tests, and being deemed fit to be a service dog, and a good conversation with Matt that yielded a new GoFundMe page he put together and told me how to share on my Facebook page. It was already up to almost $300 from my friends, and now I was sitting in my car in front of Don's house, preparing to meet Vicky for the first time in his backyard.

Once Vicky had been deemed fit for service dog work, Don sent me a couple of pictures of her. She was a Brindle-colored pit mix and she had wounds on her face and body. They weren't the best pictures, and compared to the beautiful golden Labs I had been looking at for months with the other organization, I was a little disappointed when I saw Vicky.

“What happened to her?” I asked Don just after he'd sent the pictures of her. “Remember I told you she had a story?” he asked.

“Yeah,” I responded.

“Well, the vet says, based on her wounds, she was a bait dog before she found us,” he said.

“What's that?”

“Whoever had her fought dogs, and you can see from her pictures she's a bit smaller than a full-blooded pit, so she wouldn't make a good dog for fighting. So they’d tie her up and let the other dogs attack her to get them geared up to fight. They used her as bait," he said solemnly.

"Oh my God, that's terrible," I said.

"Yeah, that's why we had to test her temperament. But after everything she went through, she's not aggressive, and she's not scared--she's actually very loving. That's why I felt like you guys would be a good fit together. You both have been let down and hurt by humans and maybe you guys can help each other heal," he said.

After he told me her story, I felt a lot of compassion for her. She'd been hurt, too. Later that same day, Matt texted asking if I had gotten any pictures of the dog that he could put on the GoFundMe page. I warned him that they were not great pictures, and I sent them. He immediately asked, "What had happened to her?" and I explained the way Don had explained to me about her being a bait dog. Then Matt responded with a message that completely knocked the wind out of me. He said

Matt: Yeah, that's exactly the kind of dog Charli would send you.

I paused and reread the text over and over. Then, I cautiously responded.

Kindra: Why do you say that?

Matt: Because this dog has a story and needs to receive love as much as it needs to give it. Charli used to think no one would adopt her because she wasn't pretty enough, and the kids that got adopted were beautiful.

Kindra: But Charli was beautiful.

Matt: We both knew that, but I don't think Charli ever did. So, of course, she sends you a dog that has been through some stuff and isn't the prettiest like those other dogs you were looking at. She sent you a dog that she thought no one else

would want 'cause she knew you would love it like you did her. It was totally Charli.

I couldn't say whether what Matt was saying was true, but I immediately felt ashamed of how I first viewed Vicky. If she was to be the dog for me, I would love her with everything I had.

I sat in the car full of anxiety about meeting this dog, Vicky, with the story. I reread Matt's messages and heard Charli's voice say, "Sissy, when I get to Heaven, the first thing I'm going to do is talk to God about getting our service dog." I looked up at the house and thought about how everything had transpired with this new organization and this dog so quickly. Then I looked up at the sky. Could it be possible?

"Thank you, Charli Bear," I said out loud, just in case it was her. Then I took a deep breath, said, "I'm a Warrior Princess," got out of the car, and went to meet OUR potential service dog.

Kindra

I sat in Don's backyard, waiting for him to bring Vicky out of the house. I looked around while I waited. The yard was big, with lots of space and room to run around. There were dog toys all over the yard. I thought the dogs that lived here must have been happy. I heard the sliding door open and looked up to see Don walking out with Vicky on her leash. She looked much better than her pictures, but I thought maybe that was partly because I had changed the way I was looking at her. Most of her wounds looked healed or in the final stages of healing. Don took her off her leash and she slowly began walking the yard. She'd occasionally glance back at me but came nowhere close to me.

"How did you find her?" I asked Don as Vicky continued to move around the yard.

"It's more like she found us. Let's see: it was a Tuesday, December 3rd. I remember because my father had a very important appointment at the VA that we had all been looking forward to. One of our trainers called me just as we were coming out of the appointment and said this stray dog had walked up to him and was now following him. He said he knew there was a guy in the neighborhood who fought dogs, and this dog seemed to be in bad shape. He said she had on a collar that had "Vicky" written on it in marker. I told him to go ahead and take the dog to our vet and have her checked out and see if she had a chip so we could find out if anyone was looking for her. He told me she hopped up in his car and laid down in the passenger seat. She had no chip, so we put some flyers out but got no calls on her," he said.

I just watched her. She didn't seem scared but maybe a bit

apprehensive. I wasn't sure what to do, so I looked at Don for help.

"Do you mind sitting on the ground?" he asked me. I shook my head no, got down on the ground, and sat Indian style. I looked over at Vicky. She had stopped what she was doing and was now watching me.

"She's more comfortable with you down on her level. Here, put these a few feet in front of you," he said, handing me some dog treats out of a fanny pack he was wearing. I set the treats in front of me and waited.

Vicky slowly walked over, and in that moment, I was transported back to sitting on a curb in front of the women's center with a Sprite next to me, hoping Charli would sit down. Vicky ate the treats and walked right up to me. Don handed me some more treats, and Vicky ate them out of my hand. She came face to face with me. I put my forehead against her head. I put one hand on her jaw and my other behind her ears. I looked her deep in her eyes and whispered, "I'll take care of you if you take care of me."

She licked my face, her tail wagged, and I knew I found our service dog.

I started thinking about what Don had just said. December 3rd was the day Vicky came to them, and December 3rd at 6:03 AM was the day Charli died.

Too many coincidences.

"Isn't Vicky a strange name for a dog?" I asked him. He chuckled.

"Yeah, I've never met a dog named Vicky, but hey, she answers to it," he said.

"Could I change it if I wanted to?" I asked him. I wanted her to have a name that would remind me of Charli somehow.

"Sure, when you get her, she will be yours. Just make sure if you change her name, it has at least two syllables. It's easier for dogs to learn names with two or more syllables than just one," he said.

Vicky had laid down next to me. I stroked her coat and wondered what I could change her name to.

Kindra

The past 48 hours were incredible. Yesterday, my GoFundMe hit $846, plus the $126 dollars from Charli, putting my total at $1,972 with only $1,028 more left to raise. I couldn't believe how my friends from all walks of life were donating to help me get this service dog. I'd never felt more supported. Then Matt texted me and told me he'd eaten lunch with some friends of his on the baseball team. It was such a big deal. It was the first time he'd eaten lunch with someone since Charli passed. I was so proud of him! Today, I spoke at a Behavioral Health Center on the importance of service dogs. It was something Don set up for the organization. I had the chance to speak to a room of doctors and therapists and tell my story and tell how rape affected me. I felt so empowered. I was telling my story for every girl or boy who was ever raped and not believed; I was telling my story for every time I was told or a survivor was told to just get over it or we should be over it by now. I was telling my story for every rape kit that was never tested, for every time someone asked, *what were you wearing? How much did you have to drink?* And *why didn't you report it or report it sooner?* I told my story for me, I told my story for Charli, for the women in the group, and I told my story so these doctors and therapists could understand what life was like after rape and how survivors could greatly benefit from service dogs. I told my story. I was an advocate, and it was amazing.

Don told me what a great job I'd done. The doctors and therapists seemed impressed, and I was still floating on cloud nine, even though the presentation was over two hours ago.

I sat on my couch in my living room, not knowing what to do with myself. I was so proud of myself. For the first time ever,

I actually felt like a Warrior Princess. I grabbed my remote and pulled up YouTube on my television. I typed in "I Hope You Dance" by Lee Ann Womack and pushed play. I slowly danced around my living room with the biggest smile on my face. The song was about halfway through when my cell phone started ringing. I paused the video and picked up the phone off the couch. The caller ID said it was Don calling.

"Hello."

"Hey, Kindra!" he said. "Hey," I responded.

"Listen, I know I told you earlier, but you were amazing today," he said. I was glad he couldn't see me blushing.

"Thank you," I said.

"Hey, remind me: what were those two things you said you were going to do once you were able to bring Vicky home?" he asked.

"Buy her a purple leash and change her name," I said, wondering where this was going.

"Well, you better get to PetSmart!" he said. I was confused--we still had $ 1,000 or so to raise before I could bring Vicky home.

"Huh?" I said.

"You did such a good job and impressed those doctors so much that after you left, they asked how much more money you needed to raise before you could bring your service dog home. I told them a little over $1000, and they said they would like to donate the money. They wrote a check for you for $1000!" he said.

The tears were rolling down my cheeks before I fully comprehended what Don was saying.

"Are you serious?" I asked him.

"I would never joke with you about something like that. We are going to present Vicky to you on Saturday at the Pupalooza event in Bay City," he said. "You better start thinking of new names and go get your dog a purple leash. You'll need it for Saturday," he said.

After we hung up, I ran into my bedroom, threw myself on the bed, and screamed into a pillow. I couldn't believe we were here. I was bringing our service dog home.

"We did it, Kiddo," I whispered. Then, I stood up with excitement. I really did need to go to PetSmart and get a leash. I ran into my closet to find some different clothes to put on. I pulled on some jeans and a T-shirt. Then I went into the bathroom. I stared at myself in the mirror. I was not the same girl I'd been just a few months ago. Life had changed me; Charli changed me. Life had given and then taken away, and now life had given again. Life gave me Vicky. Vicky--what a strange name for a dog. I had to come up with something else.

"OK, I want her name to have something to do with Charli," I said out loud.

"Bear!" I said. Her color was brindle; she kind of looked like a bear. Then I remembered Don saying dogs needed to have at least two syllables in their names, so that was a no for bear. I couldn't just name her Charli; that would just be weird. I thought and thought.

"Charli Lauren, Charli Lauren, Charli Victoria Lauren," I said and laughed, remembering how Charli would frown at the mention of her middle name, even though I thought it was beautiful.

"Victoria. I guess that could be a name for a dog," I said, my mind moving ever so slowly.

"And for short, I could call her…" I froze. It was like time stood still. The air in the bathroom stood still.

"I could call her Vicky!" I yelled out loud, and I heard her laugh. I heard Charli's laugh in that bathroom as clear as day. I turned around, almost expecting to see her sitting on the side of the tub. One single happy tear made its way down my cheek.

"Our service dog," I said.

Epilogue

When I started writing this book, it had a completely different title. The original title came from a place of great emotion, anger, and pain. I loudly wanted my story to be told, but the hurt and anger dissipated through edits, rewrites, and rereading. What was left was this book's true purpose—healing. Healing for me and healing for you.

After writing the book, one of the number one questions I received was, "Were the fosters ever brought to justice?" Sadly, as far as I know, they were not. There was never any follow-up with the caseworker or the police. None of us were ever questioned at the hospital or at a later time. I learned later that this is almost commonplace for abuse in foster homes. I've known for years that this is how things are handled for adult survivors of sexual assault. You'd think...you'd hope it will be different for children.

As far as I can tell, it's not. It seems they just move these children to a different home. It broke my heart to think of how many foster children have suffered in such a way. If you truly want insight into how sexual assault cases are viewed and handled in America, I strongly encourage you to watch the painfully insightful documentary "I am Evidence" with Mariska Hargitay from Law and Order SVU.

I felt like the only justice Charli and I ever received was the love we shared. Through our horrific situations, we were simply collateral damage in a system that proved it couldn't be bothered with these types of crimes. Regardless of the horrific injustice we suffered, love led the way and offered gifts we wouldn't have otherwise known.

As for the other characters in the book, I stayed in touch with Matt for a few months after Charli passed, but one day, I received a phone call from his mother, and we had a long conversation. She told me in the most loving way possible that she and Matthew's therapist thought it best if he and I didn't speak anymore, and I completely understood why. The only connection Matt and I had was Charli. So, our relationship was a constant reminder of what he'd lost and how he lost it. Continued contact would have made it very challenging for him to move forward in a healthy way. I absolutely agreed as long as she let me know how he was doing every now and then. I can happily say Matt graduated from college about a year or so ago, and he is doing well. I hope one day we can reconnect, but if not, that is OK too.

Not too long after Charli's passing and my adoption of Vicky, I decided I wanted to do something with my life; I wanted to become a nurse. I've always remembered that horrific night of my attack and how the nurse, a S.A.N.E. (Sexual Assault Nurse Examiner), got me through. I wanted to be that person for others who'd suffered like me. So, with much opposition from my doctors and some family members who didn't think I was strong enough to handle the stress of nursing school, I packed Vicky and myself up, and we moved to Mississippi, where I was accepted into a nursing program. Nursing school was tough, so incredibly hard, but with Vicky by my side and my instructors, Ms. Barbara Olander, Mrs. Joice McGowan, Mrs. Karen Stringer, and Mrs. Brenda Wilson, pushing me and telling me I could do it, I made it. Not only did I graduate, but I graduated valedictorian with a newfound confidence in myself.

I moved back to Texas, and while being a S.A.N.E. nurse was in my heart, my mental health just couldn't handle it. So, I became the next best thing, a pediatric nurse working with children, and it has been so incredibly fulfilling.

It wasn't long after I settled into nursing that I started writing this book. I don't think I really planned to write it; the words just began to pour out of me one day. The book itself took five years to write and two years to edit. In that time, with Vicky's help, immense healing took place. I no longer count the number of men in the rooms I walk into. (I still immediately identify all of the exits in a room. Some habits die hard). I go places and do things. Vicky and I have traveled, we've ventured, we've danced, we've lived! She's retired now. I can live on my own. I even went to a concert by myself by my favorite artist, Tobe Nwigwe, last year and had a great time!

Vicky has slowed down quite a bit, and her fur has started to turn grey. Now, she lives the life of a spoiled retired service dog. And I continue to live. I recently went skydiving. Yes, I jumped out of a perfectly good plane. I did it simply because I was tired of being scared. Now, when I come across things that scare me, I say to myself, "You jumped out of a plane. This should be a breeze compared to that," and it usually is.

I've started doing motivational speaking. I have something to say: a message of love and hope in a world that is sometimes greatly lacking in those areas. I did my first international speech last year at a wellness retreat in Mexico. I think Charli would have been so proud of me.

Another question I get asked after people have finished the book is about my relationship with Daniel. Sadly, we are no longer together, but we are still good friends, and he is one of my biggest cheerleaders. My heart is still holding out for love. I think if there is one main thing I want you to take away from all of this, it's that I'm OK, and you can be OK, too. Am I healed? Sometimes, but sometimes I still have bad days and nightmares, and sometimes I give motivational speeches and go to the beach with my dog! You don't get perfect, you get better, and then you get better than that. The goal is to keep living, keep putting one foot in front of the other, and, as a little girl told me, to always dance.

Shocking Statistics

Children in foster care are removed for many different types of abuse and neglect. Sexual abuse is, unfortunately, very common to see.

The following statistics are staggering in the general population, but the rate of sexual abuse is even higher in foster care, as noted below.[2]

- 1 in 4 girls will be sexually abused before their 18th Birthday.
- 1 in 6 boys will be sexually abused before their 18th Birthday.

OUT OF EVERY 1,000 SEXUAL ASSAULTS, 975 PERPETRATORS WILL WALK FREE

310 are reported to police[i]

50 reports lead to arrest[ii]

28 cases will lead to a felony conviction[iii]

25 perpetrators will be incarcerated[iii]

RAINN

National Sexual Assault Hotline | 800.656.HOPE | online.rainn.org

Please visit rainn.org/statistics/scope-problem for full citation.[1]

---

[2] https://www.d2l.org/child-sexual-abuse/prevalence/

Get Support

Contact The National Sexual Assault Online Hotline

Call: 800-656-HOPE

Scan to chat online with a trained staff member who can provide confidential crisis support.

Scan me

Healing

Made in the USA
Columbia, SC
13 October 2024